The American Family on Television

The American Family on Television

A Chronology of 121 Shows, 1948–2004

MARLA BROOKS

McFarland & Company, Inc., Publishers
Jefferson, North Carolina, and London

FRONTISPIECE: From the left: Jean Stapleton, Carroll O'Connor, Rob Reiner and Sally Struthers on the set of *All in the Family*.

LIBRARY OF CONGRESS CATALOGUING-IN-PUBLICATION DATA

Brooks, Marla.
The American family on television : a chronology of 121 shows, 1948–2004 / Marla Brooks.
p. cm.
Includes bibliographical references and index.

ISBN 0-7864-2074-X (softcover : 50# alkaline paper) ♾

1. Family on television. I. Title.
PN1992.8.F33B76 2005
791.45'6552 — dc22 2005003508

British Library cataloguing data are available

On the cover: Background ©2005 PhotoSpin; Foreground *Leave It to Beaver* (courtesy The Program Exchange/Photofest)

Manufactured in the United States of America

McFarland & Company, Inc., Publishers
Box 611, Jefferson, North Carolina 28640
www.mcfarlandpub.com

To June Cleaver, Sheriff Andy Taylor, Samantha Stephens, Charles Ingalls, Rhoda Morganstern and all the others who kept me on course and piqued my imagination.

Table of Contents

Introduction

Television families have been around even longer than television itself.

To some, this implausible statement may have just lessened my credibility. But if you bear with me and continue reading, you'll see that in a convoluted sort of way, my statement makes perfect sense.

Let's start out by admitting that it's in our very nature to be curious about how other people live their lives. Sticking one's nose into someone else's business has been in our nature since the dawn of time.

While slaving over an open fire, painstakingly preparing the "kill of the day, " Mrs. Ogg would often be heard complaining to Mr. Ogg about how overburdened she was with cavework and their large brood of kids, how the Urg family next door had a bigger, nicer cave with a granite fire pit, how Mr. Urg was a better hunter, and how Mrs. Urg always had a new skin to parade around in while she, Mrs. Ogg, was pitifully wearing last year's warthog. Nag, nag, nag.

Seeing as how privacy was at a minimum and discussions between cave dwellers were never held behind closed doors (mainly because doors weren't invented yet), everyone knew everyone else's business. The Haves and Have Nots were always at odds, and jealousy abounded. This led to gossip, and every cave dweller in Pangaea was trying to keep up with the Urgs.

This nagging curiosity about how people live their lives has continued throughout the centuries. Initially, word of mouth was the only manner in which this information was passed on. Then came hieroglyphics, smoke signals, and papyrus, which eventually lead to ink and quill. The advent of mail delivery was helpful in spreading the word over long distances, as was Morse code. But it wasn't until Guglielmo Marconi, an Italian physicist, invented a successful system of radio telegraphy in 1896 that the intrusion of people into the lives of perfect strangers became possible.

Several decades later, radio not only was used as a form of communication, it also became a source of entertainment. Individual broadcasting stations were formed, and before long, nearly every household owned its own radio. Programmers were now forced to develop programs that would appeal to the masses, involving situations that most people could relate to.

News programs, sports, quiz shows and musical programs were a good start, but each of these formats usually had specific audiences. Women didn't necessarily listen to sports, and kids weren't all that interested in the news. So in searching for common ground, and given the fact that nearly everyone lived in a family unit of some kind, programs were written about the everyday lives of fictional families. This was a subject to which all listeners could relate. Many of our favorite television programs, including *The Life of Riley, Ozzie and Harriet* and even *I Love Lucy* started out on radio, which validates my opening statement: Television families *have* been around even longer than television itself.

Family shows made the transition from the little box to the small screen in January 1949 with the introduction of *The Goldbergs.* And with each ensuing decade, television's fictional families have reflected the changing values within our society.

In the early 1950s, television families depicted the ethnic working-class, usually first generation, European immigrants. Black, Hispanic or Asian family life was almost never dealt with. *The Goldbergs* and the Hansen family of *Mama* were two prime examples of hardworking immigrant families, struggling hard to make their way and a better life for their children, in the land of opportunity. It was an era when men went to work and women stayed home and raised the children. The television executives were afraid of what would happen to the ratings if they portrayed women as breadwinners. It was Mary Tyler Moore in the 1970s who brought about the acceptable notion that a single woman could survive on her own without a man. That sensibility did not, however, deter the writers from making these women the focal characters. While husbands and fathers were certainly included in the scripts, their characters were often depicted as ineffectual or bumbling. They were often as responsible for family foibles as their (usually teenage) offspring. It was the wise, patient and loving mother who ultimately stepped in to sort the situation out.

In attempting to emulate their real-life counterparts, many television families of the 1950s packed up the apartment, called the movers and joined the throngs of Americans who, aided by a strong postwar economy, were leaving the crowded, noisy inner city for the relative calm of the new mass-produced housing developments springing up in the suburbs. Once settled into their new abodes, story lines always depicted husbands rushing off to the station each morning to catch the train into the city for work. Because it was a long haul into the city, they usually left early and came back late. This led to sentimental portrayals of wives bonding with other wives in the same situation, thus creating extended families. The husbands did the same by passing time with their new neighbors on the long ride to work on the train, usually discussing their lawns, or planning the weekend barbecue. Although one doesn't perceive ethnic minorities as midcentury suburbanites, in keeping with this urban exodus, even the not-so-white-bread Goldbergs moved from their cramped city apartment.

Maybe the Goldbergs in the suburbs was too much of a stretch to be credible, because by the early 1960s, ethnic domestic comedies had all but disappeared and were replaced by the suburban domestic comedy. Programs such as *Leave It to Beaver* and *Father Knows Best* portrayed idealized versions of the suburban, white middle-class experience. Children were, for the most part, portrayed as loving and obedient, and their parents offered moral guidance through love and respect and based on clear cut rules. The portrayal of fathers changed from bumbling and ineffectual to patient, caring and wise. In general, mothers lost quite a bit of their clout and began deferring to their husbands in all matters related to family, including finance, running the home and child rearing. The man was not just the breadwinner. He was king of his castle, and his regally attired queen was always well-coiffed and dressed to the nines with high heels and the requisite pearls, even while attempting the most rigorous of household chores.

While these idealized families continued on television, family dynamics were changing in the real world. Eventually, writers had to come up with new TV families that reflected the current culture, because if Lucy and Ricky were to split up, the ensuing backlash from viewers would have been ruinous to the network.

Coinciding with rising divorce rates of the 1960s, *My Three Sons* and *The Andy Griffith Show* featured families with an unmarried father at the helm, while others like *Julia* and *The Big Valley* featured single mothers. It must be noted that even though there was a cultural necessity to represent single-parent families on television, compromises had to be made. Censorship codes of the day demanded that the parent not be divorced. Instead, the missing parent was always explained away as having met a tragic, early demise.

By 1967, most of the classic domestic comedies that featured intact nuclear families were canceled, while the aforementioned broken families thrived. They alone could not sustain the perfect family image for very long, and accordingly, two trends in television families emerged.

First came the animated family. Viewers were taken back to prehistoric times with *The Flintstones*, then flung far into the future with *The Jetsons*. It's interesting to note that both these programs, millenniums apart in time and culture, depicted the wholesome family values of the 1950s. Were viewers already waxing nostalgic for the "good old days?"

The second new trend brought about in the 1960s was the introduction of improbable family units such as *The Addams Family* and *The Munsters*. The notion that such fantastical families could possibly exist brought this new wave of programming to the forefront. Yet even though the characters might have been "otherworldly," the current perception of classic family values remained intact. Farfetched or not, audiences were shown that even a Frankenstein monster married to a vampire could produce a lovable werewolf baby. Who knew?

The sweeping change on television was only a small measure of what was going on in the world. The swinging '60s was a decade of cultural upheaval. We were a youth-oriented society where hippies, flower children, sex, drugs and rock 'n' roll were commonplace. Propelled by millions of baby boomers, the material and social changes of this decade transformed American society. Towards the end of the decade, television families had to join the bandwagon to keep current. While never sticking their necks out quite enough to be on the cutting edge, new programs introduced viewers to mothers like Shirley Partridge and Carol Brady, who were the closest thing we had to counterculture moms.

By the 1970s, a significant change in the family unit and in programming came about. Shows focused on demographics to break down the viewing audience by age, sex, income and other variables for advertisers. Shows were grouped by the type of viewing audience and their spending habits.

The portrayal of family life became more diverse, as did our collective sensibilities. Vietnam, Kent State and revolutionaries were on everyone's mind. Women were steadfastly clinging to their miniskirts and equal rights and were no longer depicted as dependent housewives. Television fathers seemed to get the short shrift and were relegated to the background once again. With the possible exception of Tom Bradford in *Eight Is Enough*, writers were forced to turn back time with shows like *Happy Days, The Waltons* and *Little House on the Prairie* to find decent, hardworking, self-respecting dads.

Although the introduction of the African American experience on television began in the 1970s, writers weren't exactly sure how to portray it. *The Jeffersons* were an upwardly mobile family who finally found a piece of the pie. But the Evans clan of *Good Times* fame remained in the ghetto. There was even the bold move to interracial families, as in the case of *Webster* and *Diff'rent Strokes*, where African American children were being reared by Caucasians, although the opposite has never been attempted.

Television in the 1980s was transformed by the advent of cable, the videocassette and home video games. The '80s also became the golden age of prime-time soap operas. Programs such as *Dallas, Dynasty, Falcon Crest* and *Knots Landing* presented a world of high fashion, high finance, and low moral fiber. The Ewings and the Carringtons were not typical of how most families went about their lives. Like their daytime counterparts, these nighttime soaps dealt with marital infidelity, incest, rape, alcoholism and a range of other issues that pictured the family as decidedly dysfunctional. Perhaps because these families were extremely wealthy and most of the viewers weren't, viewers could compartmentalize their problems as a symptom of upper-crust decadence rather then a more general failure in American family life.

Maternal perfection was back in vogue, as evidenced by *The Cosby Show's* Clair Huxtable, who was not only a loving wife like June Cleaver, but also a successful lawyer and all-around supermom. Other moms, like Maggie Seaver in *Growing Pains* and *Family Ties'* Elyse Keaton, also fit a very conventional pattern. The television mom who ultimately broke this perfect mold was Roseanne. She was unconventional in a strangely conventional sort of way. A working mom out of necessity, not by choice, Roseanne was pushy, loud, and overbearing, and the household revolved around her. Her laid back parenting skills were often brought into question, especially when her young son, complaining about being bored, was told by Roseanne to "go play in traffic." In spite of all the yelling, bickering, and wisecracking in the Connor household, when audiences peeled back the layers of this seemingly dysfunctional family, they saw a strong, loving family unit. Roseanne's family just had a weird way of showing it.

Some pretty strange things happened to the portrayal of television dads in the '80s. It's frightening to think that regular, ordinary guys like Cliff Huxtable and *Roseanne's* Dan Conner seemed larger-than-life just because they enjoyed spending quality time with their children, but Al Bundy, of *Married ... with Children* broke the mold. Homer Simpson, an animated contender for the Worst Father of the Year award, followed shortly thereafter.

As with prior decades, writers in the 1980s again turned to nostalgia to create sentimental versions of family togetherness with family dramas. Shows such as *The Wonder Years* and *Brooklyn Bridge* offered up even more sentimental memories to the millions of aging baby boomers wishing that they could turn back time.

Cable television took viewers looking for a little excitement in the 1990s to new heights ... and lows. Brilliantly done original syndicated series, like *The Sopranos,* depicted a grittier family dynamic than we'd been used to watching, but nobody could deny that such families existed. At times, it is almost scary. But violence aside, the show is replete with family values, both good and bad, depending on which of Tony Soprano's "families" are being depicted. MTV's cartoon series *Beavis and Butt-head,* on the other hand, just plain scared the hell out of any parent looking for good role models for their kids.

All in all, there was more programming to choose from and new territory to discover in the '90s. It was all about personal choice, and wherever a viewer's sensibilities lay, there was plenty to choose from. The Family Channel and TNN were two stations that catered to wholesome family values, and Nick at Night brought back reruns of the family shows we grew up with. Whether it was a warm, loving family like the Taylor clan of *Home Improvement,* a single-parent family as in *Grace Under Fire,* or family units born out of necessity, such as *Full House* or *The Golden Girls,* practically any television viewer, no matter what their race or family circumstances might be, was able to find a family they could relate to. Gone was the notion of a typical American family, and ethnicity was not just limited to the black and white experience. In the mid–1990s, ABC's *American Girl* was the first sitcom to feature the generational conflicts in a Korean family.

The question of morality came to the forefront in the '90s as well. For example, the acceptance of unwed mothers on TV shows, something that wouldn't have gotten past the censors in earlier decades, demonstrated just how much times had changed. In 1992, then–Vice President Dan Quayle admonished Murphy Brown for giving birth out of wedlock, claiming that she was "mocking the importance of fathers by bearing a child alone and calling it just another lifestyle choice." Meanwhile, on *The Golden Girls,* Blanche DuBois was spreading the word that even senior citizens were not above having illicit, one-night stands. The brouhaha over unwed mothers and family values ensued.

Most fathers seemed to have been reduced to background players in this decade, and either they were not around much, or if they were a regular part of the story lines or even one of the show's central figures, they were not interacting with their children often. Although African American fathers came on strong, like Dr. Huxtable in the 1980s, black fathers on shows like *The Parent 'Hood* and *The Hughleys* were taking an equal role in child rearing. TV moms were often busy working outside the house, balancing work, home and family.

With the new millennium came a new reality in television families. Literally. Reality shows were all the rage, many depicting a kind of family life that was even stranger than fiction. But unknown to some, this had been done before. On January 11, 1973, the first broadcast of *An American Family* changed television history forever. A 12-hour documentary series on PBS, *An American Family* chronicled seven months in the day-to-day lives of the William C. Loud family of Santa Barbara, California. An audience of ten million viewers watched in fascination the unfolding real-life drama of Bill and Pat Loud and their five children, Lance, Kevin, Grant, Delilah and Michele. The series challenged conventional views of middle class American family life with its depiction of marital tensions that led to divorce, an elder son's gay lifestyle and the changing values of American families.

As groundbreaking as that show was, nothing could have prepared television audiences for *The Osbournes*, which debuted in 2002. The next generation of family-oriented sitcom, the show was labeled a "reality-based comedy" and followed the day-to-day lives of Black Sabbath rocker Ozzy Osbourne, his manager and wife, Sharon, and two of their children. The show quickly became MTV's highest-rated show ever and delivered an interesting dynamic. Wife Sharon rules the roost and husband Ozzy, for the most part, is just an older version of his kids. Ozzy feels it's his parental duty to warn his children about the dangers of drugs and alcohol, but actions speak louder than words, and Ozzy is usually shown in an altered state of consciousness. Talk about setting a good example for your kids. Both son Jack and daughter Kelly have done a stint or two in rehabilitation facilities. Ah, yes, the times they are a-changin'.

Most television mothers now work outside the house, and that has done a lot to shake up TV family dynamics. Career women are not presented as they were in the '70s, as superwomen, but as women who have to try to balance work, home and family. The latest batch of television mothers runs the gamut from the passive to the dominating. The father figure seems to have made a resurgence as well. Even shows that are centered around the children have expanded Dad's role, regularly involving him in the story conflict as well as in the decision-making and discipline.

In order to maintain high ratings, television families continually strive to conform to the changing times, and for the most part, TV writers and program executives have made a decent attempt to keep current. In recent years, they've made allowances. Divorced couples who remarried and joined their families started with The Bradys, and in 1991, ABC's *Step By*

Step followed suit. The homosexual barrier was broken with *Will and Grace* and *It's All Relative*, in which Liz, a bright young woman who attends Harvard, has been raised since infancy and is still living with a gay couple, art gallery owner Philip and his life partner, Simon, a school teacher.

Censorship laws on television have come a long way, baby, and because of the monumental changes, television families can involve themselves in a wide variety of questionable situations. Each decade has found itself getting bolder and bolder.

The first incident of censorship on network television is considered to be a broadcast of a performance by Eddie Cantor on May 25, 1944, on NBC. During this time there was a great deal of controversy around the censorship of radio broadcasts involving both Fred Allen and Eddie Cantor. Many people felt that some of Cantor's songs, "Making Whoopee" and "If You Knew Susie," for example, were risqué.

The famous Production Code, published by Will Hays' Motion Picture Producers and Distributors of America in 1930, governed television's depiction of family life and male-female relationships well into the 1960s. It was because of this "moral" code that Lucy and Ricky, and Rob and Laura, slept in separate twin beds and kept one foot on the floor at all times when kissing.

When the Rolling Stones appeared on the Ed Sullivan variety program in the 1960s, they were set to sing their hit song "Let's Spend the Night Together." Sullivan found the chorus of the song "objectionable." The Rolling Stones agreed to change the lyrics and sang "Let's Spend Some Time Together" instead. It was fairly common at this time and well into the '70s for rock bands to censor the words of their songs for TV and radio broadcast. In 1971 the *Smothers Brothers Show* was canceled because it had become too controversial.

The landmark Supreme Court case FCC v Pacifica Foundation (438 U.S. 726 1978), decided on July 3, 1978, led the way to changes in censorship on television. While the Court upheld the right of the FCC to censor "offensive, indecent or obscene" language, it made a point of the fact that it was broadcast during a time of day when children could be expected to be among the audience.

This distinction lead to the debate over "family viewing hours" and eventually the loosening of restrictions over broadcasting during late-night programming. By the 1990s shows such as *NYPD Blue* on ABC were broadcasting partial nudity, and words such as "asshole," "son of a bitch," "turd," "dickhead," and "bastard" have become commonplace.

Whether we're better off having our sensibilities jostled by the current jargon on television is anybody's guess. Because television families throughout the decades have endeavored to accurately portray the period in which they were set, one could conclude that these sometimes harsh words or phrases merely reflect a sign of the times.

Expletives notwithstanding, it is safe to conclude that the influence of television on our lives is significant. It has become one of the most influential socializing agents of our time. For better or for worse, the characters portrayed on the small screen become our teachers and role models. *All in the Family* was not merely one of the most successful sitcoms in history, it, along with other series such as *Maude* and *Will and Grace,* have ushered in new eras in American television characterized by programs that did not shy away from addressing controversial or socially relevant subject matter.

We have all been drawn to and influenced by the television families we grew up watching. Whether it was because we longingly dreamed of being a member of a particular TV family, copied their manner of dress or speech, or garnered a greater appreciation of our own family unit after getting a glimpse of how the "other half" lived, there is no doubt that this particular genre of television programming has shaped the way we see and react to our world.

Hundreds of television families have been paraded before us throughout the ages. So how does one decide which families merit inclusion in a single volume such as this? Flip a coin, consult an oracle, or just try to reason it out?

The word *family* is classically defined as a group of individuals descended from a common ancestry. Because families come in many shapes and sizes, they better fit the definition of a *family circle*— the close group relationship of a household. In both definitions, the word *group* comes into play, so while shows like *The Honeymooners* or *Newhart* indeed depict a family unit of sorts (a husband and wife), it was often the non-familial players that the story lines favored. For that reason, I have chosen to omit shows of that genre and concentrate on those "family circle" shows whose storylines revolve around a household and members of the immediate family.

Another fact to consider was the popularity and longevity of a particular series. There were a number of shows that did fit the "family circle" criteria but did not have the staying power to last more than one season. In several instances, they were yanked off the air after just a few airings. Many were pitted against strong contenders and just didn't stand a chance, while others were truly dreadful and deserved their swift extinction. But as the distinction of what comprises a good or bad program is subjective to the individual viewer, I've given some of these long-forgot-ten short-lived series a nod, and they have been catalogued in the Honorable Mentions section at the end of this book.

Please accept my profound apologies if I have inadvertently omitted any of your favorite families within these pages. Space limitation was one necessary factor to consider, and subjectivity another. If you're not content with that brief explanation, take heed. With multitudes of thanks to J.K. Rowling and the Addams Family for their inspiration, I live by the following creed: "*Draco dormiens nunquam titillandus, quod sic gorgiamus allos subjectatos nunc.*" Which means, "*Never tickle a sleeping dragon, because we gladly feast on those who would subdue us.*"

1

The 1940s

On March 19, 1939, *The New York Times* expressed its doubts about the viability of television in an article that stated: "The problem with television is that the people must sit and keep their eyes glued on a screen; the average American family hasn't time for it. Therefore, the showmen are convinced that for this reason, if for no other, television will never be a serious competitor of broadcasting." Untruer words were never spoken.

While many radio "families" were making the transition to television, in 1948 the FCC instituted a "freeze" which held television on the verge of a major expansion. Despite the delays, TV viewers were privy to a wide variety of televised events. The DuMont Network premiered television's first soap opera, *Faraway Hill*, on October 2, 1946. On January 3, 1947, the telecast of the opening session of Congress marked the first pictorial broadcast of any congressional event. By July of the following year, party campaign organizers arranged an 18-station broadcast of both national political conventions. President Truman appeared in a white suit, a color he was told would look good on the small screen. On January 25, 1949, the National Academy of Television Arts and Sciences presented the first Emmy Awards for outstanding programs, performers and productions in television broadcasting. The Emmy for Most Popular Television Program was awarded to *Pantomime Quiz Time* and the Most Outstanding Television Personality award went to Shirley Dinsdale and her puppet, Judy Splinters. On January 31, 1949, an audience of ten million witnessed the first televised presidential inauguration. That number exceeded the total number of Americans viewing all other inaugurations since George Washington. In April of that year, Milton Berle hosted the first telethon, a 14 hour program that raised $1.1 million for cancer research. The Western

Gertrude Berg starred as Molly Goldberg on *The Goldbergs*. Berg's character, a middle-class Jewish mother, was one of several immigrant women portrayed on television in the late 1940s.

made a smooth transition from radio to television in 1949 when General Mills bankrolled $1 million for 52 filmed episodes of *The Lone Ranger* starring Clayton Moore.

DuMont expanded programming into the daytime hours in November 1949 with fashion and cooking shows to please the housewives. Ten years earlier, *New York Times* writer Jack Gould wryly commented, "The idea of a nation of housewives sitting mute before the video machine when they should be tidying up the premises or preparing the formula is not something to be grasped hurriedly. Obviously, it is a matter fraught with peril of the darkest sort." It's a good thing nobody took him seriously.

A decade later, despite Mr. Gould's doom and gloom, TV sales skyrocketed with an estimated 250,000 sets installed every month. With advertising opportunities opening up, sponsor costs doubled from $1000 to $2000 for an evening. By the end of 1949, there were one million television receivers in use throughout the United States.

Mama

First Broadcast; July 1, 1949
Last Broadcast: July 27, 1956

Like many other television families of the era, the Hansen clan were immigrants to the United States, a Norwegian-American family living in turn-of-the-century San Francisco. The weekly family comedy-drama was based on Kathryn Forbes's book, *Mama's Bank Account*, as well as the play and film adaptation, *I Remember Mama*. Unlike earlier incarnations of the Forbes material, which had focused on the relationship between Mama and eldest daughter Katrin, the television series centered episodes on all of the characters. Each episode dramatized the working-class family's adventures, as seen through the eyes of Katrin, an aspiring writer who records their daily activities in her diary and whose off screen voice is heard at the start of each episode.

Mama was loving, wise and hardworking, but never blind to the emotional needs of her family. She kept the house, set the standards, and was in charge of the family's meager bank account. Papa was soft-spoken unassuming, and a carpenter by trade. Mama and Papa had three children, Nels, Dagmar and Katrin. Each episode opened with Rosemary Rice as the family's oldest child, Katrin, looking at the family photo album and thinking back over her childhood and the people she had known so well. "I remember the big white house on Elm Street and my little sister, Dagmar and my big brother Nels, and of course, Papa. But most of all, I remember Mama." Or alternately, "This old album makes me remember so many things in the past. San Francisco and the house on Stiner Street where I was born. It brings back memories of my cousins, aunts, and uncles; all the boys and girls I grew up with. And I remember my family as we were then. My brother Nels, my little sister Dagmar, and of course, Papa. But most of all when I look back to those days so long ago, most of all I remember Mama."

The stories revolved around the experiences of normal, everyday life, such as Dagmar's getting braces, Nels starting a business, or the children buying presents for Mama's birthday. Mama's eccentric sisters and her bombastic Uncle Chris were semi-regular characters. Each episode ended with the family sitting at a table, sharing the lessons learned with a steaming pot of the sponsor's Maxwell House coffee.

When the show was canceled in 1956, faithful viewers were outraged. Public demand prompted CBS to bring the series back. In the second version, which lasted only 13 weeks, daughter Katrin had become a secretary, son Nels was in medical school and a new actress, Toni Campbell, took over the role of Dagmar.

Broadcast History

CBS

July 1949–July 1956	Friday 8:00–8:30
December 1956–March 1957	Friday 8:00–8:30

Cast

"Mama" Marta Hansen	Peggy Wood
"Papa" Lars Hansen	Judson Laire
Nels	Dick Van Patten
Katrin	Rosemary Rich
Dagmar (1949)	Iris Mann
Dagmar (1950–1956)	Robin Morgan
Dagmar (1957)	Toni Campbell
Aunt Jenny	Ruth Gates
T.R. Ryan (1952–1956)	Kevin Coughlin
Uncle Chris (1949–1951)	Malcolm Keen
Uncle Chris (1951–1952)	Roland Winters
Uncle Gunnar Gunnerson	Carl Frank
Aunt Trina Gunnerson	Alice Frost
Ingeborg (1953–1956)	Patty McCormack

One Man's Family

First Broadcast: November 4, 1949
Last Broadcast: June 21, 1952

Anyone who listened to radio between 1932 and 1959 will no doubt remember *One Man's Family*. The show started out on a 13 week trial basis on local west coast stations and quickly moved coast to coast. The show was so popular it eventually ran for a staggering 27 years. But early on, it didn't look as though it would be successful at all. At the program's inception, both the program manager and production director referred to the show as "pure tripe!" Their theory was that everybody lived a family life, day in, day out, so who would want to turn on the radio and listen to more family life? As it turned out, millions of Americans remained faithful followers of this weekly nighttime drama until it left the air in 1959.

The saga of the Barbour family of San Francisco was written by Carlton E. Morse, a former journalist from San Francisco. His aim in writing the serial was to reflect his belief that the family unit was a primary source of moral and spiritual strength. Inspired by John Galsworthy's novel *The Forsythe Saga*, Morse opted to divide his show's stories into "books," with each episode a "chapter." After 27 years, 136 books with 3,256 chapters had been written, and the show became the longest-running noninterrupted serial in the history of American radio.

With a long-running hit under his belt, Carlton E. Morse went to New York in 1949 to put together the TV version, but there were some rocky beginnings there as well. In an early interview, Morse recalled that he went to New York in 1950 to do a television version of his popular series and found they couldn't satisfy viewers who had been loyal radio listeners. "For all those years, people had pictured the Barbour family in their own minds, and nobody in our television production fit those pictures," he said of his show. Not one to be deterred by minor details, he kept plugging away. Finally, the original scripts were dusted off and a new cast assembled. The show began with chapter one, book one. Two separate versions were attempted on NBC TV: a prime-time version from 1949 to 1952 and a daytime offering from 1954 to 1955.

Most of the drama centered around mundane family matters and the conflict between the generations. The upper class Barbour family lived in Sea Cliff, a suburb of San Francisco that overlooked the Golden Gate Bridge. During the show's run, the Barbours, Father Henry, Mother Fanny, and children Paul, Hazel, Claudia, Clifford and Jack, grew up, got married, went to war, and watched their children and grandchildren grow up, all the while pondering the decisions made by their "bewildering offspring."

Father Henry Barbour, a stockbroker, was old-fashioned, conservative, bullheaded, and overbearing. He firmly believed that the foundation of the nation was the family and the bigger the better. Opposed to anything revolutionary, he had a deep concern for the future of the world. When things went wrong he sulked. But somehow, he still came off as a lovable, warm character. His expression "yes, yes," in a deep sigh became the show's catch phrase. Mother Fanny Barbour epitomized traditional virtues. A housewife, very loyal to her husband and fiercely protective of her children, she was tolerant, loving, understanding and the family peacemaker.

The series' plots were rather dark in nature and revolved around stormy marriages, assorted illnesses, family feuds and lots of intrigue. With the exception of Jack, all the Barbour children were famous for having spouses die off early.

BROADCAST HISTORY

NBC

November 1949–January 1950	Friday 8:00–8:30
January 1950–May 1950	Thursday 8:30–9:00
July 1950–June 1952	Saturday 7:30–8:00

CAST

Henry Barbour	Bert Lytell
Fanny Barbour	Marjorie Gateson
Paul Barbour	Russell Thorson
Hazel Barbour	Lillian Schaff
Claudia Barbour (1949–1950)	Nancy Franklin
Claudia Barbour (1950–1952)	Eva Marie Saint
Cliff Barbour (1949)	Frank Thomas, Jr.
Cliff Barbour (1949)	Billy Idelson
Cliff Barbour (1949–1952)	James Lee
Jack Barbour (1949–1950)	Arthur Cassell
Jack Barbour (1951–1952)	Richard Wiggington
Mac (1950–1952)	Tony Randall

The Life of Riley

First Broadcast: October 4, 1949
Last Telecast: August 22, 1958
Network: NBC

The Life of Riley was one of several blue-collar, ethnic sitcoms popular in the 1950s. (After the show was canceled in 1958, television viewers wouldn't see another blue-collar comedy series until the 1970s.) As with many of television's other early sitcom families, *The Life of Riley* had it's beginnings on radio. The role of Chester A. Riley was originally created in 1943 by popular actor William Bendix. When the time came to make the transition to television, Bendix was too busy with movie commitments to take on the role.

A pilot for the televised version of *The Life of Riley* starred Herb Vigran and was broadcast on NBC in 1948. Then a young Jackie Gleason, with Rosemary DeCamp as his long-suffering wife, Peg, took over the title role in 1950. Unfortunately, Gleason's portrayal of the lovable yet bumbling hardhat was not a big hit with viewers, and the show was summarily canceled after only one season. At the time Gleason was making $500 per episode in what was to be his first television series.

Three years later, the show was brought back to the small screen with an entirely new cast, headed by the original Riley, William Bendix, and with Marjorie Reynolds as Peg. The "new" series had a successful five-year run. From the moment the show hit the airwaves, William Bendix immediately became typecast as Chester A. Riley, despite all his other previous acting accolades.

Chester A. Riley was the breadwinner of an Irish-American family living at 1313 Blue Bird Terrace in suburban Los Angeles. As with all sitcoms of the era, Chester earned the family's single paycheck while Peg maintained the household. Gainfully employed as a riveter at the fictional Stevenson Aircraft Company, he struggled to support Peg and their two teenage children, Babs and Junior, on a salary of $59.20 a week. While Chester was competent at work, at home he was far from being the respected and revered alpha male father figure of the day. Instead, he was a lovable, bumbling buffoon who always deferred to long-suffering wife Peg's better judgment in solving the daily trials and tribulations. In Riley's case, father never knew best, and he unwittingly made a mess out of the most innocent of situations. Riley was a bit of a pushover with the kids and although he meant well, usually faltered in his efforts to be a good husband and father. High schooler Babs' most ardent plea to her mother was usually, "What can we do to keep Daddy from interfering in my affairs?" Wisecracking, prepubescent Junior took every advantage of his father's inept parenting skills whenever the opportunity presented itself. Peg, on the other hand, was firm yet compassionate with both Riley and the children.

The basis for every episode was Riley's sorry attempt at trying to do the right thing, with the situation usually backfiring on him. His stock response to his inability to handle the current weekly dilemma was always, "What a revoltin' development this is!" Peg was wise enough to know that he tried his best, and although she would have to admonish her husband for his errors in judgment, she'd always started out by saying, "Riley, I know you meant well..."

Riley's place among the frustrated blue collar class echoed the feelings of many postwar families and allowed for some jabs at the frustrations of factory work and the ostentation of the upper classes. During the show's run, the sitcom title entered the American vocabulary as the ultimate expression of a lazy, inactive lifestyle.

The Life of Riley was the first show filmed especially for broadcasting. It was shot with a single camera on 35 mm film which was then reduced to 16 mm. In 1950, the show won an Emmy for Best Filmed Series.

BROADCAST HISTORY

NBC

October 1949–March 1950	Tuesday, 9:00–9:30
January 1953–September 1956	Friday, 8:30–9:00
October 1956–December 1956	Friday 8:00–8:30
January 1957–August 1958	Friday 8:30–9:00

CAST (1949–1950)

Chester A. Riley	Jackie Gleason
Peg Riley	Rosemary DeCamp
Junior	Lanny Rees
Babs	Gloria Winters
Jim Gillis	Sid Tomack
Digby "Digger" O'Dell	John Brown

CAST (1953–1958)

Chester A. Riley	William Bendix
Peg	Marjorie Reynolds
Junior	Wesley Morgan
Babs	Lugene Sanders
Jim Gillis(1953–1955, 1956–1958)	T.E. D'Andrea
Honeybee Gillis (1953–1955, 1956–1958)	Gloria Blondell
Egbert Gillis (1953–1955)	Gregory Marshall
Cunningham	Douglas Dumbrille
Dangle	Robert Sweeney
Riley's Boss	Emory Parnell
Waldo Binney	Sterling Holloway
Otto Schmidlap	Henry Kulky
Calvin Dudley (1955–1956)	George O'Hanlon
Belle Dudley (1955–1956)	Florence Sundstrom
Don Marshall (1957–1958)	Martin Milner

The Goldbergs

First Broadcast:	January 10, 1949
Last Broadcast:	October 19, 1954

The Goldbergs, a close-knit, middle-class Jewish family, were first introduced to a radio audience in 1929, just three weeks after Black Friday. One might surmise that the show was chicken soup for the audience's soul during that hard, Depression era. At the time, there was fierce competition for new potential hits on radio.

The show's star and driving force, Gertrude Berg, came from an entertainment background. (Berg's family owned the Fleischmann's resort in the Catskills.) As a teenager, she entertained guests with the sketches she wrote and in the mid–1920s began submitting radio scripts for consideration. After several years of rejection, she was offered a one-month contract at $75 a week, from which she paid the cast of a show she called "The Rise of the Goldbergs." Berg's show went on the air unsponsored because no one wanted to be first to sponsor a Jewish program. By 1932, *The Goldbergs* was one of the two or three most popular shows on radio. Until the late 1930s, Berg herself wrote all the scripts, five to six fifteen-minute stories per week, and even after hiring outside writers, continued to act as producer. She performed the role of the main character herself throughout the show's thirty year history on radio and television. *The Goldbergs* pioneered the character-based domestic sitcom format that would become television's most popular genre.

In 1936, the show moved from evenings to days and ended its radio run March 30, 1945. It resurfaced four years later for a brief radio encore. Moving to television in January 1949 and continuing through October 1954, it was broadcast live. In 1955, a filmed version was produced for syndication to local stations, and in that last incarnation, the family had moved from the Bronx to the small rural town of Haverville. Unfortunately, their life in the country lasted only one season.

The fictional Goldberg family was comprised of husband Jake, who owned his own clothing business, their son Sammy and daughter Rosalie. They lived in apartment 3-B at 1030 Tremont Avenue in the Bronx. Also in residence was the family patriarch, Uncle David. Molly was a housewife who, when she wasn't running the family with an iron fist, spent a lot of time gossiping with her neighbors across the inside courtyard of their apartment building. Molly's resounding call to her neighbor, "Yoo hoo, Mrs. Bloom," became her trademark. The first season's scripts dealt with such issues as the difficulties of raising children in an American environment that sometimes clashed with old world traditions and the immigrant family's striving for economic success and security. While Molly, Jake, and Uncle David spoke with a heavy Yiddish accent, the children were Americanized. Much of *The Goldbergs*' audience could relate to the trials and tribulations of children assimilating and casting aside the old ways since between 1924 and 1947, well over 2 million immigrants had arrived in the United States.

A typical Jewish mother in every sense of the word, Molly was a *yenta*, a matchmaker, head of household and the voice of reason. She had a theory and solution for all problems. When things didn't exactly go her way, she'd philosophically sigh, "Come will and come may, I must face it." Her broken English was peppered with endearing old world malapropisms. For example, after a long, hard day, she'd wearily turn to her husband and say, "It's late, Jake, and time to expire."

In addition to running her television family with an iron fist, Berg ran the show in just the same way. Actor Arnold Stang, who played neighbor Seymour Fingerhood on the TV series, recalled in an interview that while she was very tyrannical in many ways, she showed affection and had marvelous judgment. Stang claimed to have learned more from her than any other director.

Berg's iron fist was truly put to the test when, in September 1950, her co-star, Philip Loeb, a veteran actor with an affinity for left-wing causes, landed his name in the communist-hunting magazine *Red Channels*. That caused the show's sponsor, General Foods, to drop the show at season's end in 1951. Berg, like her problem solving alter ego, did what she could to solve the problem. Seven nerve-wracking months later, NBC said it would pick up the show with Vitamin Corp. of America as its sponsor. NBC said it didn't know if Loeb would return as Jake, and it was Berg herself who finally confirmed that Loeb was out. "There are 20 people depending on the show for a living, and their savings are dwindling," she said. "It's unfortunate that after doing what I did, waiting for the situation to clear, that I have to go along without him." In 1952, Harold J. Stone took over the part, followed by Robert H. Harris for the last three years of the show's run. It was three years before Philip Loeb found work again, and then it was Off-Broadway. In 1955, Loeb's final performance involved checking into a New York hotel room, hanging a *do-not-disturb* sign on his door and swallowing several dozen sleeping pills. Fade to black.

Throughout the show's run, Berg never lost sight of the ethnic Jewish background that made *The Goldbergs* unique in network radio and television, but most plot lines avoided direct discussion of anti–Semitism or world politics. She opted for having Molly Goldberg supervise her family's activities, deal with Jake's business setbacks and successes, and guide Rosalie and Sammy as they grew up, got married, and went off to war, just as most other traditional American families were following a similar path. The one exception was an unprecedented episode focused entirely on Yom Kippur, complete with a six minute Kol Nidre scene in a synagogue. The year was 1954. America would not see another leading Jewish character in a prime time series for 18 years.

Broadcast History

January 1949–February 1949	CBS Monday 8:00–8:30
March 1949–April 1949	CBS Monday 9:00–9:30
April 1949–June 1951	CBS Monday 9:30–10:00
February 1952–July 1952	NBC Monday/Wednesday/ Friday 7:15–7:30
July 1953–September 1953	NBC Friday 8:00–8:30
April 1954–October 1954	DuMont Tuesday 8:00–8:30

Cast

Molly Goldberg	Gertrude Berg
Jake Goldberg (1949–1951)	Philip Loeb
Jake Goldberg (1952)	Harold J. Stone
Jake Goldberg (1953–1956)	Robert H. Harris
Sammy Goldberg (1949–1952)	Larry Robinson
Sammy Goldberg (1954–1956)	Tom Taylor
Rosalie Goldberg	Arlene McQuade
Uncle David	Eli Mintz
Mrs. Bloom (1953)	Olga Fabian
Dora Barnett (1955–1956)	Betty Bendyke
Carrie Barnett (1955–1956)	Ruth Yorke
Daisy Carey (1955–1956)	Susan Steel
Henry Carey (1955–1956)	Jon Lormer
Seymour Fingerhood	Arnold Stang

2

The 1950s

The 1950s was the quintessential decade for TV families. In addition to viewers getting a glimpse into the lives of the Nelsons, the Williamses, the Andersons and the Cleavers, television itself was gathering steam. Viewers on the West Coast began receiving kinescopes of live New York productions. Bob Hope became the first major radio comic to appear on television when he portrayed a gun-toting cowboy on *Star Spangled Review,* and NBC originated the informal talk show format with *Broadway Open House* hosted by Jerry Lester and Morey Amsterdam. Robert Montgomery became the first Hollywood star to defect to the small screen with his new show, *Robert Montgomery Presents.* Game shows such as *Beat The Clock, You Bet Your Life,* and *What's My Line* all made their debuts, and ABC pioneered Saturday morning children's programming with *Animal Clinic,* a show for kids about the care and training of pets.

Many of radio's favorite personalities decided to try their luck in the new medium as well. *The George Burns and Gracie Allen Show, The Ed Wynne Show* and *The Jack Benny Show* became instant hits. Milton Berle's *Texaco Star Theater*, which originated in 1948, earned him the coveted Emmy for Most Outstanding Kinescope Personality. The following year, Berle was signed to the industry's longest contract, a 30 year deal that reportedly ran into seven figures.

On June 4, 1950, at the Boston University graduation ceremonies, university President Daniel Marsh warned seniors, "If the television craze continues with the present level of programs, we are destined to have a nation of morons." Comedian Danny Thomas had similar feelings about the small screen when he first tried his luck on NBC's *All Star Review*. His nightclub act was a dismal failure on TV and he blasted the new medium as being suitable "only for idiots!" While his opinionated statement was a

The Andersons of Springfield (*front,* Robert Young, Jane Wyatt; *rear,* Lauren Chapin, Elinor Donahue, Billy Gray) strove to impart the message that while father knew best most of the time, he was only human after all.

bit over the top, there were some incidents in the ensuing years that might have leant some credence to his prophecy. *Queen for a Day* emcee Jack Bailey was stabbed in the leg with a fingernail file by a woman who was angered by the fact that she was not a winner. Professional wrestler Freddie Blassie was stabbed 21 times and even had acid thrown at him by angry fans who couldn't distinguish between make-believe and reality.

In 1952, movie attendance was down nearly 50 percent from previous years, thanks to exciting new TV shows like *Dragnet, This Is Your Life, Our Miss Brooks* and *The Jackie Gleason* Show. Why should moviegoers pay a whopping 47 cents admission plus six cents on refreshments when they could watch television for free? Studio moguls were compelled to come up with a way to compete with television. By the end of the year, movie audiences found themselves hanging onto their seats while viewing a realistic roller coaster ride in the film *This Is Cinerama*, and by donning a pair of ten-cent throwaway glasses, they could enjoy "dramatic" effects of 3-D.

By 1954, the television industry had reached a turning point when its gross income ($593 million) became greater than that of radio. By the end of the decade, there were more television and radio sets in the U.S. than people.

Despite its great success, in May of 1955, television had its first major casualty when one of the four major networks, the DuMont Network, ceased operation.

I Love Lucy

First Broadcast: October 15, 1951
Last Broadcast: September 24, 1961

In 1952, when *I Love Lucy* had been on the air for one incredibly successful season, someone asked Lucille Ball how the show was created. Referring to her well-publicized marital woes with husband Desi Arnaz, she replied, "We decided that instead of divorce lawyers profiting from our mistakes, we'd profit from them."

The saga of Lucy and Desi had its beginnings in radio in the guise of *My Favorite Husband*, starring Lucille Ball and a very American Richard Denning. Audiences enjoyed the whimsical look into the married lives of two people with extremely different temperaments. The show was so successful, it was rumored that it might move to television, thanks to an offer from CBS. Little did they know at the time that the two people who would ultimately star in the television version would be more different than they could possibly imagine and be married to each other in real life as well. Studio executives initially rejected the notion of Desi Arnaz as the actor to play Lucy's on-screen husband. In the first place, the network and prospective sponsors balked at the casting of Arnaz because they feared his Cuban accent would alienate television viewers. Secondly, they didn't think people would believe that a typical American girl would be married to a Cuban bandleader. "What do you mean nobody'll believe it?" Lucy retorted. "We *are* married!"

To placate the naysayers, Lucy and Desi put together a first-rate husband and wife vaudeville act and took it on the road to see how audiences would accept this unlikey couple. They were met with resounding success. A TV pilot was shot and sent to New York, where it was met with less than enthusiastic response. But thanks to Philip Morris cigarettes assuming full sponsorship, the show was sold, and the rest, as they say, is show biz history.

Lucy and Ricky Ricardo were a young married couple living in a converted brownstone on East 68th Street in the upper east side of Manhattan. Unlike the husband figures in family shows of the past, Ricky Ricardo was not a bumbling, inept husband, but he did live with a wacky wife whom he often referred to as "that crazy redhead." When he got exasperated with Lucy, Ricky reverted to his native language to utter the now famous phrase, "Mira que tiene cosa la mujer esta!" meaning "What a thing this woman is!"

Ricky was the breadwinner, the head of household, and tried hard to rule roost. He instead became the target of Lucy's constant scheming to get into show business, which made life extremely difficult for the hotheaded husband. When Ricky would dismiss her pleas to be in his latest show, Lucy would usually cry, pout, or sometimes even threaten, "If you don't let me be in your show at the Palladium, I'll give you such a punch, you'll talk funnier than you do now!" Or, "I'm not gonna lift a little finger to help you any more. You can answer your own phone, shine your own shoes, type your own lyrics, light your own cigarettes and knock off your own ashes. And if you want another roast pig, you can crawl in the oven yourself, you big ham!"

In the show's first season the Ricardos were childless, and plot lines mostly revolved around Lucy's frustrating show business aspirations and the relationship between the Ricardos and their landlords—also their best friends—Fred and Ethel Mertz. The second season's story lines changed drastically when Lucille Ball found out that she was pregnant in real life. That situation almost brought the enormously popular show to a premature end. In the 1950s married television couples didn't even share a bed, much less have babies. With the word "pregnant" on top of the list of words that could never be uttered on the air, incorporating Lucille's real life pregnancy with Lucy's *delicate condition* was a daunting task. It was considered daring to put a pregnant woman on television, and this would be the first time an expectant mother was to portray a mother-to-be. Desi was sure the network and the sponsors would never let them get away with it, but after much thinking on the subject, it was universally agreed that they could get the necessary humor out of the situation and still stay well within the bounds of good taste. Great lengths were taken that viewers not be offended in any way, and a priest, rabbi and minister attended the filming of the first episode.

The first seven of the second season's episodes dealt with Lucy's pregnancy. Then, on January 19, 1953, the day that Lucille Ball actually gave birth to her son, Desi Jr., a viewing audience estimated at 44 million witnessed Lucy and Ricky Ricardo's becoming parents as well. On April 3, 1953, the first issue of *TV Guide* featured baby Desi on the cover.

Despite what many believe, Little Ricky's birth was not a television first. The domestic sitcom *Mary Kay and Johnny* (1947–50) starred real-life married couple Mary Kay and Johnny Stearns as a newlywed couple who lived in New York's Greenwich Village. True to the sitcom formulas of the early days of television, Mary Kay was a zany, trouble-prone wife, and Johnny Stearns was the responsible, levelheaded husband who rescued her from comic mix ups. The Stearns had a child in real life in December 1948 and within a month of the birth, the baby was written into the script. This predated the historic birth of Little Ricky/ Desi Arnaz, Jr., by five years.

With the addition of Little Ricky to the cast, plot lines focused more often on the couple's adjustment to being parents—particularly the question of how motherhood would affect Lucy's show business ambitions. In one memorable episode, after Ricky explains that motherhood is far more wonderful than being a star she bemoans, "Just think ... when Little Ricky goes to school and some of his playmates ask who his parents are, just what is he going to say? 'My father is Ricky Ricardo, the internationally known entertainer ... and then there's my mother, whose name escapes me for the moment.'"

While the family dynamic was altered with the addition of a child, Lucy continued her zany antics at home, but in the ensuing seasons also got the chance to wreak havoc in Florida, Hollywood, and throughout Europe. By the show's sixth season, the Ricardos opted to leave New York City and move to a house in Connecticut, which seemed make the Ricardos a more "normal" family that viewers could relate to. There was less emphasis on the show biz aspect, and story lines were altered to revolve around life in the country.

Even though the show was still number one in the ratings, by the 1956–1957 season, Lucy and Desi's real life marital woes were escalating, and both of them decided to cease production of a weekly series. That fall, the escapades of the Ricardos and Mertzes continued in the guise of a series of full-hour specials called *The Lucy-Desi Comedy Hour,* which featured popular guest stars of the day to join in the shenanigans.

The very last episode of *The Lucy-Desi Comedy Hour* starred the late Ernie Kovacs and his wife, Edie Adams. It seems appropriate that Desi Arnaz was the one to direct the final time Lucy and Ricky would be seen together. In real life, Lucy and Desi were now living apart and preparing to divorce. The very last scene called for a very long kiss, which, according to Arnaz, "would wrap up twenty years of love and friendship, triumphs and failures, ecstasy and sex, jealousy and regret, heartbreak and laughter ... and tears." After the kiss, the two stood there looking at each other, in tears for a very long time. Then Lucy said, "You're supposed to say 'cut.'" "I know," said Desi. "Cut, goddamn it!"

BROADCAST HISTORY

CBS

October 1951–June 1957	Monday 9:00–9:30
April 1955–October 1955	Sunday 6:00–6:30
October 1955–April 1956	Sunday 6:30–7:00
September 1957–May 1958	Wednesday 7:30–8:00
July 1958–September 1958	Monday 9:00–9:30
October 1958–May 1959	Thursday 7:30–8:00
July 1959–September 1959	Friday 8:30–9:00
September 1961	Sunday 6:30–7:00

CAST

Lucy Ricardo	Lucille Ball
Ricky Ricardo	Desi Arnaz
Ethel Mertz	Vivian Vance
Fred Mertz	William Frawley
Little Ricky (1956–1957)	Richard Keith
Jerry	Jerry Hausner
Mrs. Trumbull	Elizabeth Patterson
Caroline Appleby	Doris Singleton
Mrs. MacGillicuddy	Kathryn Card
Betty Ramsey (1957)	Mary Jane Croft
Ralph Ramsey (1957)	Frank Nelson

The Adventures of Ozzie and Harriet

First Broadcast: October 3, 1952
Last Broadcast: September 3, 1966

On March 26, 1954, *TV-Radio Life Magazine* begins an article on Ozzie and Harriet by asking, "Whatever became of the old-fashioned family unit? The one that used to be the backbone of our civilization?" The answer, of course, was the Nelsons, who, the article claims, "could have easily come off the face of an old-fashioned tintype. "

Ozzie Nelson created, produced, directed and co-wrote all the episodes of the low-budget show that turned out to be the longest-running sitcom in TV history—and became synonymous with white, middle-class America. One of the ways Ozzie kept the budget so low was by using his own family members on the show. It was the real-life Nelson family on the air depicting all the little adventures an American family might have on a weekly basis. The show had its roots in radio, starting in 1944. The boys' roles were played by professional actors until 1949, when Ozzie finally allowed his actual offspring to go on the air. David was 16 and Ricky was 13 when they made their debut. The Nelsons signed a long-term contract with ABC in 1949 that gave that network the option to move their program to television. Although never in the top ten rated programs, it did well throughout its run, appealing to the family viewing base targeted by ABC. The program picked up additional fans in April 1957, when Ricky sang Fats Domino's "I'm Walkin'" on an episode titled "Ricky the Drummer." That one show launched him into the instant status of teen idol.

The show focused on the Nelson family at home by chronicling the growing pains of the boys and dealing with such normal issues as hobbies, rivalries, schoolwork, and girlfriends. In early episodes the stories revolved around the four Nelsons, with only a few friends and neighbors featured, but as the boys began to get older, school friends, girlfriends and finally, their wives were added into the mix. The Nelsons lived at 822 Sycamore Road in the fictional town of Hillsdale. The house is said to have been an exact replica of the Nelsons' own home in the Hollywood foothills.

Unlike some of the era's sitcom dads who were portrayed as blundering fools, genial Ozzie was definitely the alpha male, but in a quiet, slightly bumbling manner. His word was always respected. He was the linchpin of the family, trying to point his young sons towards the proper path. But because his doting sons always took his advice to heart, sometimes it backfired, as in one episode where Ozzie decides to caution David on his overgenerous nature, and the well-meaning advice turns into a fiasco.

David and the Ricky's irrepressible repartee always furnished the high spots in the early episodes. They were typical teenage boys of the day with normal sibling rivalries, but instead of screaming, yelling and scuffles, the boys mimicked dignified Ozzie in that their confrontations always had a quiet civility to them. A typical exchange between the boys had Ricky complaining to David, "What about me? I'm your brother, you know."

David: Don't get maudlin.

Ricky: Well, if it weren't for me, you'd be an only child.

The household was held together by wise homemaker Harriet, who usually represented the voice of reason. She was the TV mother chosen as 1952's Hollywood Mother of the Year. As with other TV mothers of the day, Harriet was always clad in the elegant dresses that defined the 1950s housewife on television and more often than not could be found in the kitchen.

Ozzie Nelson was a hard worker in real life, becoming the nation's youngest Eagle Scout at the age of 13, an honor student and star quarterback at Rutgers, and a nationally known band leader in the 1930s with a law degree under his belt. On the show, however, he had no defined source of income. Unlike counterparts Jim Anderson or Ward Cleaver, who spent their days at work, Ozzie always seemed to be hanging around the house. While it was understood that Ozzie was indeed the breadwinner, nobody ever saw him work.

Broadcast History

ABC

October 1952–June 1956	Friday 8:00–8:30
October 1956–September 1958	Wednesday 9:00–9:30
September 1958–September 1961	Wednesday 8:30–9:00
September 1961–September 1963	Thursday 7:30–8:00
September 1963–January 1966	Wednesday 7:30–8:00
January 1966–September 1966	Saturday 7:30–8:00

Cast

Ozzie Nelson	Himself
Harriet Nelson	Herself
David Nelson	Himself
Eric "Ricky" Nelson	Himself
"Thorny" Thornberry (1952–59)	Don DeFore
Darby (1955–61)	Parley Baer
Joe Randolph (1956–66)	Lyle Talbot
Clara Randolph (1956–66)	Mary Jane Croft
Doc Williams (1954–65)	Frank Cady
Wally (1957–66)	Skip Jones
Butch Barton (1958–60)	Gordon Jones
June (Mrs. David) Nelson (1961–66)	June Blair
Kris (Mrs. Rick) Nelson (1964–66)	Kristin Harmon

Fred (1958–64)	James Stacy
Mr. Kelley (1960–62)	Joe Flynn
Connie Edwards (1960–66)	Constance Harper
Jack (1961–66)	Jack Wagner
Ginger (1962–65)	Charlene Salerno
Dean Hopkins (1964–66)	Ivan Bonar
Greg (1965–66)	Greg Dawson
Sean (1965–1966)	Sean Morgan

The Danny Thomas Show (aka Make Room for Daddy)

First Broadcast: September 29, 1953
Last Broadcast: September 2, 1971

Danny Thomas and television had an inauspicious beginning. In 1951, he signed on as one of the four revolving hosts of NBC's *Four Star Review*. The once a month gig was altered when the show evolved into *The Colgate Comedy Hour* and his hosting duties would be needed only two or three times a year. There was also the problem of Thomas' nightclub routines not working well on TV. A detailed storyteller by nature, the mere seven minutes he was allowed to do any of his famous routines, like "Ode to a Wailing Syrian" was barely enough time to set the story up, much less tell the whole tale, so he opted out and went back to his beloved saloons—as he called the nightclubs bitterly complaining that television was suitable "only for idiots" and vowed never to return.

While Thomas considered saloons his safe haven as far as his professional life was concerned, he was constantly complaining that he wanted to spend less time on the road and more time at home with his wife and kids. He was away so often, his children hardly knew him and used to call him "Uncle Daddy." When he traveled, his daughters, Marlo and Teresa, would move into the master bedroom and sleep with their mother. Upon Thomas' return, they had to move out to "make room for Daddy."

After a while, the thought of returning to television was less abhorrent, especially given the fact that ABC was hungry for shows, and a sitcom based loosely on his life as a performer might just be the way to go. A script was written, the pilot was shot and Thomas was elated. He had finally found a way to stay home with his family by doing a show about him and his family.

The character of Danny Williams was a hot-tempered but softhearted nightclub performer who lived at 505 East 50th Street, Apartment 542, in New York with his wife, Margaret, 11-year-old daughter Terry and

6-year-old son, Rusty. The household also included a maid, Louise, and frequent house guest Uncle Tanoose from Toledo, the offbeat patriarch of the Williams clan. Tanoose's nickname was "Hashush-al-Kabaar," which loosely translated means "The Man Who Made a Monkey Out of a Camel." His favorite foods were goat cheese and grape leaves, and he claimed his family descended from King Achmed the Unwashed.

With two bratty but lovable children, an outspoken maid and an uncle who constantly seemed to turn the household upside down, Danny was constantly upstaged. During the show's first three seasons, stories revolved around the home and working life of Danny Williams. Although his character wasn't on the road, his busy career often left little time to spend with his beloved family, and he was constantly at ends trying to strike a happy balance between family life and the entertainment business.

Because of tension on the set, Jean Hagen's character of Margaret was written out of the show at the end of the 1956 season, and shortly thereafter, Marjorie Lord appeared as Kathy, the new wife of "recently widowed" Williams. Kathy, also a widow, and Danny fall in love when Danny's son Rusty contracts the measles and Danny hires Kathleen, a beautiful registered nurse, to care for Rusty. While their wedding was not seen on the show, the start of the 1957 season had Danny and Kathy returning from their honeymoon with little Linda, Kathy's 5-year-old daughter by a previous marriage, in tow.

Like many real-life families in the same situation, the addition of a new wife caused quite a bit of turmoil in the Williams household at first, and much of the season's plot lines revolved around the new family's adjustment to each other. At first, Danny finds himself in the middle of a family controversy when daughter Terry begins to resent her new stepmother. Then, when Danny learns that his Uncle Tanoose is about to visit, he's afraid that the family patriarch might not approve of his new bride. Meanwhile, Rusty acquaints his new little sister with the methods used to soft-soap parents. Eventually, the newness of the situation happily resolves itself.

During the course of the show's 11-year run, the kids grew up, moved out, and got married. Many of the show's principals were reunited for two *Make Room for Daddy* specials, airing in 1967 and 1969, and in 1970 reappeared in a new sitcom, *Make Room for Granddaddy.* In its latest incarnation, Rusty was now a married med student, Linda was now at boarding school, and Terry, the mother of a young son and wife of a serviceman, left young Michael in the care of Danny and Kathy while she set off to visit her husband who was stationed in Japan.

Unlike some actors who preferred not to have children around the set, Danny Thomas loved the kids on the show. He said, in a way, he had two families at one time — his own kids at home at night and his show-kids for several hours in the daytime.

BROADCAST HISTORY

September 1953–June 1956	ABC Tuesday 9:00–9:30
October 1956–February 1957	ABC Monday 8:00–8:30
February 1957–July 1957	ABC Thursday 9:00–9:30
October 1957–September 1964	CBS Monday 9:00–9:30
April 1965–September 1965	CBS Monday 9:30–10:00
September 1970–January 1971	ABC Wednesday 8:00–8:30
June 1971–September 1971	ABC Thursday 9:00–9:30

CAST

Danny Williams	Danny Thomas
Mrs. Margaret Williams	Jean Hagen
Mrs. Kathy Williams	Marjorie Lord
Rusty Williams	Rusty Hamer
Terry Williams (1953–1958)	Sherry Jackson
Terry Williams (1959–1960)	Penny Parker
Linda Williams	Angela Cartwright
Louise (1953–1954)	Louise Beavers
Louise (1955–1964)	Amanda Randolph
Uncle Tenoose	Hans Conried
Phil Brokaw	Sheldon Leonard
Pat Hannigan	Pat Harrington, Jr.
Uncle Charley Halper	Sid Melton
Bunny Halper	Pat Carroll
Jose Jimenez	Bill Dana
Mr. Daly	William Demarest

Life with Father

First Broadcast: November 22, 1953
Last Broadcast: July 5, 1955

Clarence Day, Jr., grew up to be a biographer and essayist. Educated at St. Paul's School, Concord, N.H., and at Yale University, Day became a member of the New York Stock Exchange in 1897 and joined his father's brokerage firm as a partner. His autobiography *Life with Father* was the longest running play in the United States at the time, from 1940 to 1950, and his autobiographical articles about life with his father, Clarence, Sr., appeared in *Harper's Magazine* and later in *The New Yorker*. In Day's understated, matter-of-fact style, he explained how his father tangled with such challenges as holiday accommodations, the newly-invented telephone, illnesses, his sons' attempts to play musical instruments and hiring a new cook. After their success on Broadway, the stories were made into a movie in 1935 before inevitably coming to the small screen in the early 1950s.

The television version starred Leon Ames as the prim and proper Wall Street banker and benevolent despot of his 1880s New York City household. Clarence Day, Sr., was a stern traditionalist, but he was also loving and well respected by wife Vinnie and four redheaded sons. In the manner of the day, Vinnie outwardly had no more common sense than a butterfly, but was the real head of the household.

The family resided on West 48th Street in Manhattan, where stories focused on the struggles of a middle-class American family who were plagued by the stubbornness of a Victorian father who refuses to accept the progress attributed to a changing world. In Clarence Day's way of thinking, nothing had been right in the world since Grover Cleveland was elected president.

A staunch Republican with a short temper, Clarence, Sr., was not an easy man to live with. He was the type who wanted to buy a cemetery corner plot to be buried in "so I can get out," and demanded his life be just so. Woe to the family member, servant or tradesperson who disarranged his perfectly ordered existence. Clarence blusters at his wife, his cook, his horse, shopkeepers, servants, and, of course, his children and their inability to live up to his preposterous standards. Yet, the more he rants, the more comical he becomes, and the more he seems to endear himself to his beleaguered and bemused family.

At the insistence of Mrs. Clarence Day, Jr., who filled the position of special consultant on the show, all of the members of the television family had to have red hair like the real Day family, even though the show was broadcast in black and white.

Broadcast History

CBS

November 1953–May 1954	Sunday 7:00–7:30
August 1954–December 1954	Tuesday 10:00–10:30
January 1955–July 1955	Tuesday 8:00–8:30

Cast

Clarence Day, Sr.	Leon Ames
Vinnie Day	Lurene Tuttle
Clarence Day, Jr. (1953–1954)	Ralph Reed
Clarence Day, Jr. (1954–1955)	Steven Terrell

Whitney Day (1953–1954)	Ronald Keith
Whitney Day (1954–1955)	B.G. Norman
Whitney Day (1955)	Freddie Ridgeway
Harlan Day	Harvey Grant
John Day (1953–1954)	Freddie Leiston
John Day (1954–1955)	Malcolm Cassell
Margaret	Dorothy Bernard
Nora	Marion Ross

Father Knows Best

First Broadcast October 3, 1954
Last Broadcast: April 5, 1963

The fictional Anderson clan was the typical American family that everyone wanted to be a part of. The show stood out from other family shows of the period because both parents were portrayed as responsible, intelligent adults. Starting out as an NBC radio series in 1949, the character of Jim Anderson was similar to many other fictional fathers of the day. He was a bit of a bumbler and slightly inept, but by the time the show made the transition to television, he was much wiser and more paternal. Robert Young was the only member of the radio cast to continue on in the television series.

The Andersons lived at 607 South Maple Street in the fictional midwestern town of Springfield. Jim Anderson sold insurance for the General Insurance Company. Wife Margaret was the average American housewife but was nobody's fool. The children, 17-year-old Betty, 14-year-old Bud and 9-year-old Kathy seemed to live in an idyllic world where no matter what went wrong, they'd always have understanding parents to offer advice, comfort, and a shoulder to cry on.

Often referred to as "the original family sitcom," the show was the brainchild of series star Robert Young, and his longtime friend, producer Eugene B. Rodney. The partner's production company, Rodney-Young Enterprises, brought the series to television in 1954. They based the show on experiences each had with their own wives and children. To them, the scripts represented "reality," and because of this, father *didn't* always know best. Jim Anderson was not perfect. He could lose his temper and make the occasional error in judgment.

Every evening like clockwork, Jim would come home from the office, take off his jacket, put on his comfortable sweater, and deal with the everyday problems of a growing family. Whenever a crisis would arise, Jim would calmly offer up sensible advice. Because Young and Rodney were candid about their attempts to provide moral lessons throughout the series, the scripts allowed that parents make mistakes, and so did the kids, but by the end of each episode, love prevailed and their family was secure.

The TV series was not particularly successful at first, possibly because it was scheduled at 10:00 P.M. on Sunday nights, when very few children could watch it. Because of low ratings, CBS canceled the show in March 1955. A flood of viewer protests demanded that the program be reinstated and moved to an earlier time slot so that the whole family could enjoy it, which prompted NBC to change the following season's time slot to 8:30 P.M. *Father Knows Best* prospered for the next five years.

In 1960, Robert Young grew tired of the role he had been playing on radio and television for 11 years. He felt the family had outgrown the original premise of the show. When eldest daughter Betty got married and Bud decided to join the Army, they called it quits.

Broadcast History

October 1954–March 1955	CBS Sunday 10:00–10:30
August 1955–September 1958	NBC Wednesday 8:30–9:00
September 1958–September 1960	CBS Monday 8:30–9:00
October 1960–September 1961	CBS Tuesday 8:00–8:30
October 1961–February 1962	CBS Wednesday 8:00–8:30
February 1962–September 1962	CBS Monday 8:30–9:00
September 1962–December 1962	ABC Sunday 7:00–7:30
December 1962–April 1963	ABC Friday 8:00–8:30

Cast

Jim Anderson	Robert Young
Margaret Anderson	Jane Wyatt
Betty Anderson (Princess)	Elinor Donahue
James Anderson, Jr. (Bud)	Billy Gray
Kathy Anderson (Kitten)	Lauren Chapin
Miss Thomas	Sarah Selby
Ed Davis (1955–1959)	Robert Foulk
Myrtle Davis (1955–1959)	Vivi Jannis
Dotty Snow (1954–1957)	Yvonne Lime
Kippy Watkins (1954–1959)	Paul Wallace
Claude Messner (1954–1959)	Jimmy Bates
Doyle Hobbs (1957–1958)	Roger Smith
Ralph Little (1957–1958)	Robert Chapman
April Adams (1957–1958)	Sue George
Joyce Kendall (1958–1959)	Roberta Shore

December Bride

First Broadcast: October 4, 1954
Last Broadcast: April 20, 1961

The premise of this well-received comedy was quite a head-turner at first. The show centered around the life of an attractive widow, Lily Ruskin, who lived quite happily with her daughter, Ruth, and son-in-law, Matt Henshaw, in Westwood, California. The character of Lily Ruskin was based on series creator Parke Levy's own mother-in-law.

Although Lily was very popular with her peers and had a full life outside the home, Lily's life was centered around her adult children. With her sweet demeanor, Lily was a rare flower because unlike the usual stereotypical mother-in-law, she brought great joy to the household.

While Ruth and Matt were glad to have Lily around, they felt she should have a man in her life and were always looking for suitable marriage prospects for Lily, as was her cantankerous best friend, Hilda Crocker, who also happened to be the mother-in-law next door neighbor Pete couldn't stand. Pete, was often seen around the Henshaw household. Despite the fact that Pete constantly complained about his wife during his many visits to the Ruskin household, Gladys was never seen on the program. In one episode she did make an appearance with her husband but she was dressed in a gorilla costume. Like Niles Crane's wife, Maris, on *Frasier* and Norm's wife on *Cheers*, Pete's wife, Gladys, was often referred to, but never seen, until Pete and Gladys got their own spinoff in 1960. The zany redheaded comedienne Cara Williams was cast to play the part of Pete's sincere but scatterbrained wife.

Spring Byington had a long and successful stage and movie career before the television series began and was 61 years old when she took on the daunting task of a weekly television series. When asked how she liked doing television, she commented, "Television keeps me young because it keeps me busy, keeps my mind alert, my senses sharp, and my interest up." Although the role called for her to be gushy and fluttery, giggly and silly, actress Spring Byington had a charming personality, and created a most endearing character.

Broadcast History

CBS

October 1954–June 1958	Monday 9:30–10:00
October 1958–September 1959	Thursday 8:00–8:30
July 1960–September 1960	Friday 9:30–10:00
April 1961	Thursday 7:30–8:00

CAST

Lily Ruskin	Spring Byington
Ruth Henshaw	Frances Rafferty
Matt Henshaw	Dean Miller
Hilda Crocker	Verna Felton
Pete Porter	Harry Morgan

Leave It to Beaver

First Broadcast: October 4, 1957
Last Broadcast: September 12, 1963

The Cleaver family of Mayfield were pretty much the typical family of the day, and it's been said that the show played an important role in bridging the gap between the waning of radio comedy and the blossoming of the television sitcom. The premise of *Leave It to Beaver* was life through the eyes of an innocent young boy. Given the era in which the series ran, the scripts were very much ahead of their time because from time to time they touched on rather controversial subjects for the 1950s, such as alcoholism and divorce. The series also broke ground when it became the first television program to show a visible toilet in the house. The writers fought for ten weeks to get the commode past the censors, giving *Leave It to Beaver* the distinction of being the first television show to admit to having a functioning bathroom.

Strangely enough, as popular as the show was, and given the fact that some 50 years later it still is shown in reruns, *Leave It to Beaver* was never rated in the top ten.

The pilot script was entitled *Wally and Beaver*, but the sponsor, Remington Rand, felt this might be mistaken for title of a nature program, so the name was changed. To help explain young Theodore Cleaver's odd nickname, it was explained early on that after baby Theodore was born, brother Wally had difficulty pronouncing Theodore, and it came out sounding like "Tweeter." Parents Ward and June modified the sound to the slightly more dignified "Beaver."

Ward Cleaver was an accountant by day and a patient, stern, but caring father figure at home. A strict disciplinarian with no qualms about handing out necessary punishment, he rarely lost his temper, had the patience of a saint and was more prone to long lectures than a swift kick in the butt. His harshest admonishing comments would be in the guise of, "Beaver, your mother and I are very disappointed in you."

June was a devoted and nurturing stay-at-home mom. She kept a spotless house, always served meals on time, made sure Beaver always washed behind his ears, and always did the housework in a dress, pearls, and high heels. June could be considered overprotective at times, but always deferred to Ward when it came to disciplining the boys. "What will you do, Ward?" was her mantra.

Preteen Wally was pretty much the all–American kid. He was popular, a good student, good-looking and athletic. He usually referred to his younger brother as "ya little squirt" and hated to have him tag along when he went out with his friends, especially the smarmy Eddie Haskell. Eddie was the wise guy you'd love to hate. Always mouthing off to his friends, he'd change his tune in a heartbeat if a parent happened to stroll by. For example, one afternoon in Wally's bedroom when he and Eddie were planning to go out, Eddie didn't want Beaver to tag along. He began a tirade by warning, "Wally, if your dumb brother tags along, I'm gonna.... Oh, good afternoon, Mrs. Cleaver! I was just telling Wallace how pleasant it would be for Theodore to accompany us to the movies."

The Beaver was the typical little boy who idolized Wally, respected his parents, and was an average student in school. He had a wide-eyed innocence, was very impressionable, and while he knew right from wrong, Beaver was prone to errors in judgment, especially when left to his own devices to solve the problem of the week. The two most common catch phrases attributed to Beaver were, "Gee, Wally" or, "Hi Mom, hi Dad" as he come in the door.

The Cleavers lived a seemingly idyllic suburban, middle-class life, and each week the plot usually revolved around the Beaver's escapades. The show's creators, Joe Connely and Bob Moser, had 11 kids between them and all the story lines of *Leave It to Beaver* were taken from real life. Connelly's 8-year-old son, Ricky, was the inspiration for Beaver; his 14-year-old son, Jay, the model for Beaver's older brother, Wally. The duo attempted to depict situations with which the audience could easily identify, as in the trials and tribulations of changing residences when the Cleavers moved from a modest, picket-fenced house at 485 Maple Drive to a larger abode at 211 Pine Street.

Forty years later, *Leave It to Beaver* reruns still are showing on a regular basis and not just in the United States. The series has the distinction of being shown in 80 countries and in 40 languages as well.

When Jerry Mathers was asked in an interview a few years back if he ever got tired of being referred to as "The Beaver" all the time, his comment was, "No. It's nice to be a part of the Golden Age of television. It's one of the pinnacles of my career and it's something I'm very proud of."

Broadcast History

October 1957–March 1958	CBS Friday 7:30–8:00
March 1958–September 1958	CBS Wednesday 8:00–8:30
October 1958–June 1959	ABC Thursday 7:30–8:00
July 1959–September 1959	ABC Thursday 9:00–9:30
October 1959–September 1962	ABC Saturday 8:30–9:00
September 1962–September 1963	ABC Thursday 8:30–9:00

Cast

June Cleaver	Barbara Billingsley
Ward Cleaver	Hugh Beaumont
Beaver (Theodore) Cleaver	Jerry Mathers
Wally Cleaver	Tony Dow
Eddie Haskell	Ken Osmond
Miss Canfield (1957–1958)	Diane Brewster
Miss Landers (1958–1962)	Sue Randall
Larry Mondelo (1958–1960)	Rusty Stevens
Whitey Whitney	Stanley Fafara Clarence
"Lumpy" Rutherford (1958–1963)	Frank Bank
Mr. Fred Rutherford	Richard Deacon
Gilbert Bates (1959–1963)	Stephen Talbot
Richard (1960–1963)	Richard Correll

Bachelor Father

First Broadcast: September 15, 1957
Last Broadcast: September 25, 1962

While single-parent families would become all the rage in the late 1960s, *Bachelor Father* was the first of its kind in the '50s to depict a happy home life without the benefit of a two-parent family.

Bentley Gregg was a suave, handsome, successful, unmarried man about town. A Hollywood attorney with a large and successful law practice, Gregg lived at 1163 Rexford Drive in Beverly Hills with his Oriental house boy, Peter Tong. His life was seemingly idyllic, and most nights Bentley could be found out on the town with a different stunningly beautiful woman on his arm. That carefree life was suddenly interrupted when he became the legal guardian to his newly orphaned 13 year old niece.

Kelly Gregg was a typical, rambunctious teenager, and most episodes revolved around Uncle Bentley's trial-by-fire leap into fatherhood while trying to run a successful law practice and maintain his bachelor status. Peter, a jack-of-all-trades, was indispensable in running the Gregg home, especially after the arrival of Niece Kelly.

Bentley suffered through all the typical parental dilemmas, such as getting Kelly her own phone, waiting up for her after her first date, and teaching her to drive, with good grace. He also had to deal with the fact that Kelly encouraged her uncle to spend his evenings out, and she spent a great deal of time playing matchmaker, trying to find him a suitable wife.

As Kelly got older, teen rearing got harder, especially when she got interested in boys. In Bentley's mind, nobody was good enough for his niece. Her ultimate choice of a boyfriend, Howard Meecham, was a bit of a disappointment to Bentley. All of Kelly's friends liked Uncle Bentley, so they spent a whole lot of time at the house. A few even thought he was "dreamy." Actress Linda Evans, a teenager herself at the time, made a guest appearance in an episode of the show as one of Kelly's friends. Twenty years later, Evans found herself cast as John Forsythe's wife on *Dynasty*. Other up and coming stars of the day to appear on the show included Bill Bixby, Mary Tyler Moore and Ryan O'Neal. Established stars such as Gisele MacKenzie, Jack Benny, and singer Patti Page were also featured from time to time.

Bachelor Father took viewers out of Beverly Hills occasionally when the Greggs had an opportunity to visit Rome, London and Paris.

By series' end, Kelly had entered college and had fallen in love with Warren Dawson, one of Bentley's junior partners at the law firm. Bentley was still looking for the perfect woman. Forsythe was nominated for an Emmy for his first television role as the unlikely father figure.

Broadcast History

September 1957–June 1959	CBS Sunday 7:30–8:00
June 1959–September 1961	NBC Thursday 9:00–9:30
October 1961–September 1962	ABC Tuesday 8:00–8:30

Cast

Bentley Gregg	John Forsythe
Kelly Gregg	Noreen Corcoran
Peter Tong	Sammee Tong
Ginger	Bernadette Withers
Howard Meechim	Jimmy Boyd
Cousin Charlie Fong	Victor Sen Yung
Warren Dawson	Aron Kincaid

The Real McCoys

First Broadcast; October 3, 1957
Last Broadcast: September 22, 1963

Despite the eventual success of *The Real McCoys*, this was a show that almost wasn't. Grandpappy Amos was the head of the clan, as the show's theme song explains. His character roared like a lion but was gentle as a lamb. Veteran actor Walter Brennan also did a great deal of roaring when he was approached to star in this unlikely sitcom about a mountain family who moves from rural Smokey Corners, West Virginia, to California's San Fernando Valley when patriarch Amos inherits his brother's ranch. Brennan wanted no part of the show, claiming that he wasn't a comic actor. The networks didn't want the show, either, and experts said it would never appeal to anyone other than, perhaps, people living in rural areas.

The show's creators, Irving and Norman Pincus, got the last laugh. After obtaining financing from Danny Thomas Productions and finally convincing Brennan to do the part, *The Real McCoys* turned into a big hit and had the distinction of pioneering a rural comedy trend. It became the inspiration for other rural comedies such as *The Andy Griffith Show, The Beverly Hillbillies* and *Petticoat Junction*. During its successful run, *The Real McCoys* became the first sitcom in ABC's history to reach the top ten.

Widower Amos McCoy was a gruff, cantankerous geezer with a heart of gold who couldn't help but stick his nose into everyone else's business. He was ornery, often times incorrigible, and did what he could to get his own way. He lived with his grandson, Luke, Luke's little brother, Little Luke, Luke's little sister, Hassie, and Luke's wife, Kate. Rounding out the extended family was Pepino, the Mexican farmhand who "came with the house." The greatest love of Amos' life was his Model T Ford, Gertrude.

There was always a weekly conflict between Grandpa and modern society, Grandpa and the young 'uns, or Grandpa and the neighbors, especially archrival and best friend, crusty George MacMichael. His old-fashioned ways caused many a row, and the fact that Grandpa could neither read or write, and wouldn't admit it to anyone outside the family, caused him problems in everyday life as well.

In the show's final season, Luke returned to the series as a widower. Three of the five principal characters, Kate McCoy, Hassie McCoy, and Little Luke McCoy, were written out, and now that Luke was an eligible bachelor, he had women galore trying to get his attention. His major new love interest came in the guise of a young widow, Louise Howard, who moved in next door. Louise's aunt, who joined the cast a month later, spent a great deal of time trying to play matchmaker. Meanwhile, Amos had his own romantic trials to deal with. First, there was Flora MacMichael, George's spinster sister, who had always had a yen for Amos. Other widows in town also vied for Amos' attention, but his real challenge came when the men of the house needed a new housekeeper after Kate's demise. Three marriage-minded, elderly widows applied for the job. Grandpa encouraged their interest just enough to promote some free housecleaning chores and got more than he didn't pay for.

BROADCAST HISTORY

October 1957–September 1962	ABC Thursday 8:30–9:00
September 1962–September 1963	CBS Sunday 9:00–9:30

CAST

Grandpa Amos McCoy	Walter Brennan
Luke McCoy	Richard Crenna
Kate McCoy	Kathleen Nolan
Hassie McCoy	Lydia Reed
Little Luke McCoy	Michael Winkelman
Pepino Garcia, hired hand	Tony Martinez
George MacMichael	Andy Clyde
Flora Mac Michael	Madge Blake
Mac Maginnis	Willard Waterman
Hank Johnson	Lloyd Corrigan
Harry Purvis	Charles Lane
Mr. Taggart	Frank Ferguson

Blondie

First Broadcast: January 4, 1957
Last Broadcast: January 9, 1969

Probably the must bumbling father of them all, Dagwood Bumstead, came to light as a newspaper comic strip created by cartoonist Chic Young at the outset of the Great Depression in 1930. The strip was so well received, a series of 28 movies were produced in the 1940s before the show came to television twice, first in 1957, and again in 1968.

Blondie was such a big success at the time because it dealt with universal themes: love, marriage, parenthood, work, relaxation, eating and sleeping. Like many American families of the era, the Bumsteads lived in a rented house, Dagwood caught a bus to work, and they rarely went out for entertainment.

The Bumstead household was comprised of husband Dagwood, wife

Blondie, young son Alexander, also known as Baby Dumplin', and his older sister, Cookie. Dog Daisy, a "purebred mongrel," and her pups were also on board. Twenty-six episodes were produced in the 1957 version of the series, despite the fact that it only ran from January to September. Dagwood was played by Arthur Lake, the same actor who had assumed the role in movies and radio over the previous 20 years. Pamela Britton was chosen to take the role of Blondie for TV, replacing the movie's Penny Singleton.

In the comic strip, Blondie Boopadoop was a flighty flapper. At first she dated playboy Dagwood Bumstead, son of the millionaire J. Bolling Bumstead, who was a railroad magnate, along with several other boyfriends. The comic strip floundered until Young decided to have the couple fall deeply in love. Desperate to wed Blondie, in spite of his father's objections to her lowly social status, Dagwood went on a hunger strike until the elder Bumstead grudgingly acknowledged their relationship. He did, however, refuse to continue to support his son. The couple married and Dagwood, now disinherited, stripped of his wealth and family connections, was nonetheless blissfully happy with his sparkling, vivacious, yet unfailingly practical new bride. Once married, Blondie ceased to be flighty and became the guiding force of the Bumstead household. She became known as an all-American housewife and received thousands of letters a year from women asking her advice on everything from budgeting to cooking.

The predictable story lines revolved around the bumbling Dagwood. Most episodes had Blondie trying to make sure that Dagwood wasn't late for work, and watching him rush out the door, only to crash into their beleaguered mailman. Blondie, who had an energetic sunniness and deep affection for her husband, constantly tried to bolster his ego so that he would assert himself with his boss, Julius Dithers.

Dagwood was a typical '50s male who rarely set foot in the kitchen except to make himself a humongous, extremely thick sandwich piled high with a variety of meats, cheeses, condiments and lettuce. It was the only thing that Dagwood knew how to prepare. Typically, he would bring his sandwich out to his favorite chair, nearly sit down, and before he could sit get his first bite, some sort of comic situation would interrupt his "snack." This mountainous pile of dissimilar leftovers, precariously arranged between two slices of bread, is still referred to today as a Dagwood. The "Dagwood sandwich" has been memorialized in the American lexicon.

Broadcast History

January 1957–September 1957	NBC Friday 8:00–8:30
September 1968–January 1969	CBS Thursday 7:30–8:00

CAST (1957)

Dagwood	Arthur Lake
Blondie	Pamela Britton
Cookie	Ann Barnes
Alexander	Stuffy Singer
J.C. Dithers	Florenz Ames
Herb Woodley	Hal Perry
Mr. Beasley	Lucien Littlefield

CAST (1968)

Dagwood Bumstead	Will Hutchins
Blondie	Patricia Harty
J.C. Dithers	Jim Backus
Alexander	Peter Robbins
Cookie	Pamelyn Ferdin
Cora Dithers	Henny Backus
Tootsie Woodley	Bobbi Jordan
Mr. Beasley	Bryan O'Bourne

The Donna Reed Show

First Broadcast: September 24, 1958
Last Broadcast: September 3, 1966

Another wholesome family-centered comedy, *The Donna Reed Show* was first telecast on ABC at 10:00 P.M. opposite Milton Berle's *Texaco Star Theater*, and drew terrible ratings. It was only after the wife of the chairman of the board of Campbell Soup, the sponsor, used her influence and got the show moved to Thursdays that it found its audience.

The Stone family lived in the fictional suburban town of Hilldale. They helped solidify the notion that 1950s America was chock full of two-parent households, beautifully coiffed moms, wise and handsome fathers and delightful children. The story lines tried to mimic real life, and dealt with subjects that most people could identify with. Donna, a registered nurse by profession, tried hard to become the perfect housewife. She not only administered to the children, but also lent an occasional hand to husband Alex, a pediatrician, who ran his thriving practice out of an office located just off the Stones' living room.

Unlike many television families of the time, Alex was neither bumbling nor inept, and both parents shared the child rearing duties of teenage daughter Mary, portrayed by Shelly Fabares, and preteen son Jeff, portrayed by Paul Petersen. Donna was portrayed as smart, intelligent, and a great role model for the children because even though she was sweet, polite and charming, she was also outspoken, a free thinker and even a bit of an activist. When Jeff comes home with a black eye after fighting a boy who mocked Donna's acting in a local play, it's Donna, not Alex, who tries to teach Jeff how to defend himself. When housewives are mocked on a radio show, Donna gets up on her soapbox and defends homemakers like herself as being more than "just a housewife!" And when she gets what she feels is an unfair parking meter violation, she insists on a jury trial rather than paying a $2 fine. She bristles at being referred to as "the ideal wife and mother," and goes on a rampage and purposely loses her temper at people to prove that she has just as many imperfections as the other wives.

In the 1962 season, daughter Mary goes off to college, and her character is written out of the series. Trisha, an eight-year-old orphan who "adopted" the Stone family, was brought in to fill the void. Trisha was played by Paul Petersen's real-life little sister, Patty.

While *The Donna Reed Show* did quite well in the ratings, it was boosted even more by frequent guest appearances by baseball greats Don Drysdale, Willie Mays and Leo Durocher, as well as the likes of Buster Keaton, Cloris Leachman, DeForest Kelley, Gale Gordon, Hans Conried, Ted Knight and Tony Martin.

The show made recording stars out of its two teenage stars. The hit rock song "She Can't Find Her Keys" premiered on a 1962 episode in a dream sequence in which Jeff Stone imagined himself as a teen recording idol. Paul Peterson followed this hit song with the 1963 song "My Dad" dedicated to his TV father Alex Stone. The series had earlier spawned another hit song, "Johnny Angel," sung by Shelley Fabares.

The series was a family affair in more ways than just on the screen, as in addition to Patty Petersen coming on board, the show was produced by Donna Reed's real-life husband, Tony Owen.

Broadcast History

ABC

September 1958–September 1959	Wednesday 9:00–9:30
October 1959–January 1966	Thursday 8:00–8:30
January 1966–September 1966	Saturday 8:00–8:30

Cast

Donna Stone	Donna Reed
Dr. Alex Stone	Carl Betz
Mary Stone	Shelley Fabares

Jeff Stone	Paul Petersen
Midge Kelsey	Ann McCrea
Dr. David Kelsey	Bob Crane
Smitty	Darryl Richard
Herbie Bailey	Tommy Ivo
Scotty Simpson	Jimmy Hawkins
Karen Holmby	Janet Landgard
Bibi	Candy Moore
Trisha Stone	Patty Petersen

Dennis the Menace

First Broadcast: October 4, 1959
Last Broadcast: September 22, 1963

Dennis Mitchell, the blond, blue-eyed holy terror, was created as a comic strip in 1950 by cartoonist Hank Ketcham, who based the character on his own son, Dennis. Although Ketcham turned the active reins of his comic strip over to longtime assistants Ron Ferdinand and Marcus Hamilton in 1994, he supervised the work on his favorite kid until his death in June 2001. The television show aired on CBS from 1959 through 1963, and then was later picked up by NBC and aired for two years in reruns.

Dennis and his parents lived at 627 Elm Street, in the middle class suburban town of Hillsdale, right next door to their long-suffering neighbor, "Good Old Mr. Wilson," a man hoping to enjoy his golden years far from noisy children and yapping dogs. George Wilson shared his home with his wife, Martha, and their little dog Fremont. Dennis' dad, Henry, was an aeronautical engineer. Because Henry left home early each morning, he avoided many of his son's misadventures. He did, however, receive the occasional "SOS" call from his wife Alice, when the situation got too far out of hand.

Dennis was quite a mischievous little boy, whose best friends were Tommy and their nemesis, Margaret. His heart was always in the right place, but whenever Dennis meant to do good, chaos ensued. Being inquisitive and imaginative frequently landed him in situations that he couldn't control. Stories depict Dennis' disastrous attempts to assist people he believes are in trouble, especially when it came to Mr. Wilson. Dennis never set out to find trouble; it just seemed to always find him.

Although often harried and flustered, Alice had patience, energy, logic and love to spare. Like all other television housewives of the day, she proudly kept her small house clean and tidy, despite having a rambunctious little boy, and his big hairy dog, Ruff, underfoot. Most days, Alice couldn't wait for Henry to arrive home from the office so he could spend a little quality time with his son and let her off the hook.

Actor Joseph Kearns, who played the part of Mr. Wilson, passed away toward the end of the third season. Gale Gordon was introduced as his brother, John Wilson, a guest of Mrs. Wilson's. At the start of the fourth and final season, John Wilson, and his wife, Eloise, had moved into the house, and Dennis had another Mr. Wilson to torment.

In 1993, the series had a new incarnation, this time as a feature film starring Mason Gamble as Dennis, and crusty Walter Matthau in the role of the beleaguered Mr. Wilson.

Broadcast History

CBS

October 1959–September 1963	Sunday 7:30–8:00

Cast

Dennis Mitchell	Jay North
Henry Mitchell	Herbert Anderson
Alice Mitchell	Gloria Henry
George Wilson	Joseph Kearns
Martha Wilson	Sylvia Field
Tommy Anderson	Billy Booth
Seymour	Robert John Pittman
Margaret Wade	Jeannie Russell
Mrs. Lucy Elkins	Irene Tedrow
Miss Esther Cathcart	Mary Wickes
Mr. Quigley	Willard Waterman
Sgt. Theodore Mooney	George Cisar
John Wilson	Gale Gordon

Bonanza

First Broadcast: September 12, 1959
Last Broadcast: January 16, 1973

Set in the 1860s, *Bonanza* was the saga of the Cartwright clan, who lived on the Ponderosa, a sprawling ranch encompassing nearly 600,000 acres just outside of Virginia City, Nevada. Although *Bonanza* aired for 14 years as a first-run show and was syndicated to nearly every country in the world, it was far from being an instant hit. For its first two seasons, the show struggled in the ratings and was kept on the air mainly because it was filmed in color.

Widower Ben Cartwright was a wealthy rancher who had three adult sons, each born from a different wife. Because of this, the boys were as different as night and day. Adam, the eldest, was the brooding intellectual. Middle son Hoss was a gentle giant, a man of incredible strength and size, with a heart of gold. Little Joe was happy-go-lucky and impulsive. Being a single father in the wild, woolly west was no easy task. While Ben often had to rely on sheer will and a bit of luck to keep his sons on the right path, he had a little help at the ranch in the guise of Hop Sing, his Chinese house boy, who spoke very broken English. Hop Sing was indispensable to the Cartwrights. He cooked, cleaned and was always there when they needed him.

Ben was a strong patriarch and father who would guide his three sons through both wise counsel and model behavior. David Dortort, a writer and the show's producer, wanted to create a show that he felt would counteract the image of the bumbling, inept male depicted on many TV shows in the '50s, and he succeeded.

Family aside and above all else, Ben loved the Ponderosa. "Well maybe I've never been to Heaven," said Ben, "and maybe I'm never going to get the chance, but Heaven is going to have to go some to beat the thousand square miles of the Ponderosa."

The show dealt with then-controversial issues, such as racial prejudice, wife abuse, psychological problems, and drug and alcohol abuse, but each week was not a serious cowboy shoot 'em up. One episode might be a compelling drama and the next week the episode would have comedic overtones. But no matter which way the plot lines went, good always triumphed over evil. Bonanza's emphasis was on wholesome values, family and good, clean fun.

Pernell Roberts, who played Adam, became disenchanted and left at the end of the sixth season. His departure didn't hurt the show's ratings. Producers simply expanded the roles of the other characters. But when Dan Blocker suddenly died in 1972, the loss of Hoss was a devastating blow to both the cast and the show's fans.

Bonanza was the second-longest running western in television history after *Gunsmoke*, which starred James Arness as Marshal Matt Dillon.

Broadcast History

NBC

September 1959–September 1961	Saturday 7:30–8:30
September 1961–September 1972	Sunday 9:00–10:00

May 1972–August 1972	Tuesday 7:30–8:30
September 1972–January 1973	Tuesday 8:00–9:00

CAST

Ben Cartwright	Lorne Greene
Adam Cartwright (1959–65)	Pernell Roberts
Eric "Hoss" Cartwright (1959–72)	Dan Blocker
Joseph "Little Joe" Cartwright	Michael Landon
Hop Sing	Victor Sen Yung
Sheriff Roy Coffee (1960–72)	Ray Teal
Jamie Hunter–Cartwright (1970–73)	Mitch Vogel
"Candy" Canaday (1967–1970, 1972–1973)	David Canary
Griff King (1972–1973)	Tim Matheson
Deputy Clem Foster (1962–73)	Bing Russell
Dusty Rhoades (1970–72)	Lou Frizzell
Doc Martin (1968–73)	Harry Holcombe
Marshall	Slim Pickens

The Many Loves of Dobie Gillis

First Broadcast: September 29, 1959
Last Broadcast: September 18, 1963

It wasn't until *The Many Loves of Dobie Gillis* came along in September 1959 that there was a show centered around the lives of teenagers. Dobie and his friends started out in high school at the show's premiere and throughout the years they graduated, got drafted into the Army (briefly), then headed to college where they were taught by the same teacher they had in high school. Small world?

Dobie Gillis was a typical girl-crazy teenager and perpetual daydreamer. When it came to girls, it didn't matter if they were long, tall, dark, or small. Dobie just wanted a girl to call his own.

In early episodes, Dwayne Hickman as Dobie sat and meditated in a park with his elbow on his knee, chin resting on his fist, mirroring the statue of Rodin's *The Thinker* which stood directly behind him. As the camera zoomed in, Dobie told the TV viewers what was on his mind. In the show's first episode, he introduced himself by saying, "My name is Dobie Gillis and I like girls. What am I saying? I love girls! Love 'em! Beautiful, gorgeous, soft, round, creamy girls. Now, I'm not a wolf, mind you.

No, you see a wolf wants lots of girls, but me? Well, I just want one. One beautiful, gorgeous, soft, round, creamy girl for my very own. That's all I want! One lousy girl! But I'll tell you a sad, hard fact. I'm never gonna get a girl. Never. Why? Because to get a girl you need money. And standing between me and money is a powerful obstacle: a POWERFUL obstacle!"

The Gillis family lived above the family grocery store at 285 Norwood Street, Central City, where Dobie often worked after school. His father, Herbert T. Gillis, was always hopeful that Dobie would grow up, get smart, and take over the family business, which was something Dobie really didn't want. Father and son were constantly at odds, and an exasperated Herbert often uttered his famous catchphrase, "I gotta kill that boy, I just gotta." Mother Winifred had a better understanding of her son and often played peacemaker between the two men in her life. Stories usually dealt with Dobie's continual thoughts about the future, his running battle with his father over the prospect of acquiring work, his endless romantic heartaches, and his relationship with his "good buddy" Maynard G. Krebs, a beatnik with a severe allergy to work. Whenever anyone used the word "work" within listening distance of this bearded bohemian, it caused Maynard to flinch and cry out in pain: "Work!"

Aside from not being able to find his soul mate, Dobie had two real nemeses in life. First was the intelligent but unattractive Zelda Gilroy, who was constantly trying to get herself married to Dobie. She figured that with her brains and his sweetness, they could produce the perfect child. She would drive him crazy when she'd wrinkle up her nose in a certain way which would instinctively cause him to do the same. She would laughingly point out that his inability to resist copying this gesture was proof that he was totally under her spell. Then there was millionaire Chatsworth Osborne, Jr., a spoiled brat who flaunted his social status and his money to catch all the attractive girls who wouldn't give Dobie the time of day.

In the series' first episode, called "Caper at the Bijou," Dobie and Maynard conspire to rig the raffle at the local movie theater so that Dobie can win enough money to take the beautiful Thalia Menninger (Tuesday Weld) to the prom. For the final show of the series, entitled "The Devil and Dobie Gillis," writer Max Shulman chose to rework the very first episode, using the same plot device of the rigged raffle. Despite the self-plagiarism, this is a fine episode with a splendid speech by Herbert and an excellent dream sequence featuring Chatsworth Osbourne, Jr., as the devil.

Broadcast History

CBS

September 1959–September 1962	Tuesday 8:30–9:00
September 1962–September 1963	Wednesday 8:30–9:00

Cast

Dobie Gillis	Dwayne Hickman
Maynard G. Krebs	Bob Denver
Herbert T. Gillis	Frank Faylen
Winnie Gillis	Florida Friebus
Maynard G. Krebbs	Bob Denver
Zelda Gilroy	Sheila James
Thalia Menninger	Tuesday Weld
Chatsworth Osborne, Jr	Steve Franken
Dr. Leander Pomfritt	William Schallert
Davey Gillis	Darryl Hickman
Duncan Gillis	Bob Diamond
Virgil T. Gillis	Roy Hemphill
Jerome Krebs	Michael J. Pollard
Milton Armitage	Warren Beatty

3

The 1960s

Lucy and Desi got divorced. CBS, NBC and ABC become virtually all-color networks. The Beatles rocked *The Ed Sullivan Show*. Alan Shephard's sub-orbital flight attracted some 30 million TV viewers, and millions of Americans toured the White House with first lady Jacqueline Kennedy. On November 22, 1963, Walter Cronkite interrupted the Friday broadcast of *As the World Turns* with the following news bulletin: "In Dallas, Texas, three shots were fired at President Kennedy's motorcade in downtown Dallas. The first reports say that President Kennedy has been seriously wounded by this shooting."

All three networks immediately canceled regular weekend programming. It has been said that by focusing on national grief, TV finally came into its own. News coverage switched from the strict interpreting of events to witnessing history. With technology recently developed primarily for sporting events, networks were able to replay Jack Ruby shooting Lee Harvey Oswald.

On November 9, 1965, the worst blackout in history shut down every television station in New York City. In their greatest hour since the advent of television, about half the radio stations in the city remained on the air with auxiliary power, and their announcers earned much of the credit for preventing citywide panic.

Several new family shows appeared on the TV schedule. The "Swinging '60s" was a decade of diversity for television viewers. By 1960, all ethnic domestic comedies had disappeared, and in tune with rising divorce rates in the nation, many shows featured families run by a single father or mother. The early '60s started out with TV families similar to those of the '40s and '50s, with the solid family unit of *The Dick Van Dyke Show*. By 1969, *The Brady Bunch* took the cue of combined families that seemed to be becoming the norm in society.

Single parent Steve Douglas (Fred MacMurray) and his three sons (Stanley Livingston, Barry Livingston and Don Grady) mimicked many of the single parent households cropping up during the 1960s.

In a departure from previous programming, imaginations were stretched by the different breed of family portrayed by *The Addams Family* and *The Munsters,* which debuted within a week of each other. Maybe not so coincidentally, both shows were canceled the same week the following year. Not quite as unusual, but certainly still in the fantasy realm, were the Stephens family of *Bewitched* fame. Additionally, prime-time cartoon families such as *The Flintstones* and *The Jetsons* gave audiences a fictional portrayal of family life in the Stone Age and in the twenty-first Century. A little more down-to-earth were the Clampetts, aka *The Beverly Hillbillies.* And the Taylor family from Mayberry.

Television lost a good many early pioneers in the '60s as well. Edward R. Murrow, generally regarded as the greatest newscaster in radio and television, died in 1965. During the '50s he was seen regularly on TV with *See It Now* and *Person to Person*. Each Friday night, Murrow would visit with two celebrities in their homes. The interviews were done live with Ed seated in a comfortable chair in the studio while the subject showed him around his or her home via live television. Television pioneer Ernie Kovacs; veteran actress Gertrude Berg, best known for her starring role in *The Goldbergs*; Walt Disney, whose *Mickey Mouse Club* helped raise a generation of baby boomers; and *Lucy*'s Fred Mertz, William Frawley, are among those who died in the 1960s, but will live on, thanks to the advent of television reruns.

The Flintstones

First Broadcast: September 30, 1960
Last Broadcast: September 2, 1966

The Flintstones was the first prime-time cartoon series made especially for television. Because up until the 1960s cartoons were produced as "shorts" rather than full programs, the show was groundbreaking in that each episode contained only one story that lasted a full half hour.

The premise of the show was patterned after Jackie Gleason's *The Honeymooners*, and Gleason was none too pleased. Jackie's lawyers told him he could probably have *The Flintstones* canceled if he wanted to, but in the same breath also asked, "Do you want to be known as the guy who yanked Fred Flintstone off the air? The guy who took away a show that so many kids love, and so many of their parents love, too?" Apparently Jackie thought it over and decided to leave well enough alone.

Set in the prehistoric town of Bedrock, sometime in the Stone Age, *The Flintstones* claimed to be a "modern stone age family." They didn't speak in grunts or marvel at the wonder of fire. Each week, the story lines revolved around the same family issues their modern day viewers were experiencing.

Fred Flintstone was a dinosaur crane operator at the Rock Head & Quarry Cave Construction Company. He was kindhearted, loud, sometimes obnoxious and a bit of a dolt. Whenever Fred was happy, he uttered his famous, "Yabba Dabba Do!" Not unlike his *Honeymooners* counterpart, Ralph Kramden, Fred was always willing to blindly jump into any crazy scheme that he thought could better his station in life and land him in the lap of luxury. Predictably his schemes usually ended in disaster.

Long-suffering and patient wife Wilma was the typical Stone Age cavewife, enjoying many modern conveniences of the time. She had a baby elephant vacuum cleaner, a hungry creature under the sink to act as a garbage disposal, a bird-powered fan to keep the cave cool and an elephant-powered dishwasher. She was the levelheaded one in the family and was usually there to help get Fred out of the messes he always got himself into.

Rounding out the family were infant daughter Pebbles and the family pet Dino, the dogasaurus. Dino acted like an overgrown puppy, greeting Fred every evening when he came home from work by jumping up on him, knocking him down, then slobbering all over his face.

Fred and Wilma enjoyed the company of best friends and neighbors Barney and Betty Rubble. Barney was fairly dimwitted and just as gullible as Fred, but while Fred was a hothead, Barney was quite amiable and saw the humor in most situations. They both belonged to the Loyal Order of the Water Buffaloes. Betty, like Wilma, took pride in her cave, but also enjoyed civic and cultural activities. The Rubbles' infant son, Bamm Bamm, was Pebbles' best friend.

Many famous individuals— some voiced by real-life celebrities, some impersonated— showed up in Bedrock at one time or another. They included movie stars "Stony" Curtis, Ann-"Margrock," and Jimmy "Darrock"; and TV celebs Ed "Sullystone" and Perry "Masonry."

The Flintstones is presently seen in 22 languages in more than 80 countries around the world and is on somewhere every minute of the day.

Broadcast History

ABC

September 1960–September 1963	Friday 8:30–9:00
September 1963–December 1964	Thursday 7:30–8:00
December 1964–September 1966	Friday 7:30–8:00

Cast (Voices)

Fred Flintstone	Alan Reed
Wilma Flintstone	Jean Vander Pyl
Barney Rubble	Mel Blanc
Betty Rubble (1960–1964)	Bea Benaderet
Betty Rubble (1964–1966)	Gerry Johnson
Dino the Dinosaur	Mel Blanc
Pebbles (1963–1966)	Jean Vander Pyl
Bamm Bamm (1963–1966)	Don Messick

Special appearances

Hoagy Carmichael (Hoagy Carmichael)
Tony Curtis (Stony Curtis, in "The Return of Stony Curtis")

James Darren (James Darrock, in "Surfin Fred")
Ann-Margret (Ann-Margrock, in "Ann-Margrock Presents")
Elizabeth Montgomery (Samantha from *Bewitched*, "Samantha")
Jimmy O'Neill (Jimmy O'Neilstone, "Shinrock-A-Go-Go" 1964)
Dick York (Darrin from *Bewitched*, "Samantha")

The Andy Griffith Show

First Broadcast: October 3, 1960
Last Broadcast: September 16, 1968

Sheriff Andy Taylor and the town of Mayberry were first introduced to TV viewers as an episode on the TV hit *The Danny Thomas Show*. Since the trend at the time leaned toward rural comedies, Danny Thomas Productions came up with an innovative gimmick to see if audiences would be interested in Sheriff Taylor on a weekly basis. Instead of spending money to finance the pilot for *The Andy Griffith Show*, they invented the "spin-off." In one episode of his hit show, Danny and family travel by car through a small town named Mayberry, where Thomas is arrested for speeding by the local sheriff, played by Andy Griffith. In the scenes that ensued, the entire background of Sheriff Taylor is explained, and the characters of Mayberry introduced. On the basis of that one Danny Thomas episode, *The Andy Griffith Show* was sold.

The town of Mayberry was based upon Andy Griffith's real hometown of Mount Airy, North Carolina, and this was one of the reasons that many viewers got a feeling that Mayberry was a real place. The show was so popular that it never dropped below seventh place in the seasonal Nielsen rankings, and it was number one the year it stopped production.

Andrew Jackson Taylor was a widower with a young son, Opie. They lived with Andy's maiden Aunt Bee, who took care of both the house and her two "boys." Although Aunt Bee makes a comfortable home for Andy and Opie, she has many other hobbies and interests as well. She enjoys cooking and every Sunday would make either her famous fried chicken or roast beef for dinner. She also enjoyed gardening, was president of the Garden Club, member of the Ladies' League and committee head for the beautification of Elm Street. Even though she led a full life, she let nothing interfere with the care and feeding of Andy and Opie. Not even stardom. When approached by a local television station to be the star of her own daily cooking show, Bee is torn between the lure of fame and the fact that she won't be home every night to cook dinner. Assured by Andy and Opie that they'll manage just fine, Bee reluctantly agrees. Her newfound fame is short-lived when she realizes that the boys are not faring too well on their own.

Andy was a fair-minded and easygoing lawman, which was easy to be in a town that was virtually without crime. His main duties included giving out parking tickets, helping kids cross the street, and putting lids on trash cans. His homespun and old-fashioned wisdom applied both on the job and when it came to raising his young son. Life lessons abounded in the Taylor household, and everything revolved around family.

The residents of Mayberry were more than just friends and neighbors. All the townfolk, from Deputy Sheriff Barney Fife and Floyd the barber to the town drunk, Otis, were an extension of the Taylor clan and all abided by "The Mayberry Rules for a Happy Life," which were: *Don't play leapfrog with elephants; Don't pet a tiger unless his tail is wagging; and never, ever mess with the Ladies' Auxiliary.*

Broadcast History

CBS

October 1960–July 1963	Monday 9:30–10:00
September 1963–September 1964	Monday 9:30–10:00
September 1964–June 1965	Monday 8:30–9:00
September 1965–September 1968	Monday 9:00–9:30

Cast

Andy Taylor	Andy Griffith
Opie Taylor	Ronny Howard
Barney Fife (1960–65)	Don Knotts
Ellie Walker (1960–61)	Elinor Donahue
Aunt Bee Taylor	Frances Bavier
Clara Edwards	Hope Summers
Gomer Pyle (1963–64)	Jim Nabors
Helen Crump (1964–68)	Aneta Corsaut
Goober Pyle (1965–68)	George Lindsey
Floyd Lawson	Howard McNear
Otis Campbell (1960–67)	Hal Smith
Howard Sprague (1966–68)	Jack Dodson
Emmett Clark (1967–68)	Paul Hartman
Thelma Lou (1960–65)	Betty Lynn Warren
Ferguson (1965–66)	Jack Burns
Mayor Stoner (1962–63)	Parley Baer
Jud Crowley (1961–66)	Burt Mustin

My Three Sons

First Broadcast: September 29, 1960
Last Broadcast: August 24, 1972

Until 1960, most television families were centered on strictly nuclear groupings comprised of a mom, dad and biological children. But when creator Don Fedderson was approached by Chevrolet to develop a program that was "representative of America," *My Three Sons* became the forerunner of what was to become a popular trend in television: the widowed parent raising a family. *My Three Sons* is credited for its redefinition of the composition of the television family. These single-parent shows would dominate television's comedy schedule for the next decade with offerings such as *Family Affair* and *The Courtship of Eddie's Father*.

Steve Douglas was a mild-mannered aerodynamics engineer living at 837 Mill Street in Bryant Park, a small midwestern town. He became a widower when his wife, Louise, passed away the night before their youngest son Chip's first birthday. His busy work schedule prohibited him from being home long enough to effectively take care of his rambunctious brood, so his father-in-law, the grouchy "Bub" O'Casey, was called to duty to become the family's chief cook, bottle washer and full-time keeper of the clan. Bub got his name because the Douglas boys couldn't pronounce "Grandpa." Rounding out this family of men was a big, shaggy dog named Tramp, a mixed Briard.

When the show first went on the air, Steve's three sons, Mike, Robbie and Chip, were ages 18, 14 and 7, and story lines revolved around the growing pains of the three boys and how a family survives without a mother. By the second season, the shows became more of a situation comedy with normal kid problems and Steve's constantly having to fend off the ladies in his continuing search for Mrs. Right.

Three seasons in, eldest son Mike became a little long in the tooth and was married off and moved away. Needing a third son to keep the show's title true, the Douglas family adopted Chip's friend (and real-life brother) Ernie, after his parents were killed in a car accident. Elderly William Frawley, who portrayed Bub, left the series the next year for health reasons and was replaced by his fictional brother, Uncle Charley O'Casey, a no-nonsense, crusty ex-sailor with a tough exterior and soft heart. Frawley's departure was explained by saying that Bub went to Ireland for his Aunt Kate's 104th birthday, then never returned. Steve then invited Bub's brother, Uncle Charley O'Casey, to live with them and take over Bub's duties as chief cook and housekeeper.

From the third season on, the show appeared more heavily moralistic but also gave a lighthearted look at generational and gender conflicts. And as the years went by, the size of the Douglas family swelled and separated into individual households. In 1967, the show's setting was moved to the West Coast when Steve was transferred to North Hollywood, California. While attending college, Robbie, the middle son, meets, falls in love with, and marries Katie Miller, and soon they become the parents of triplets.

Three years later, Ernie encounters difficulty with a new teacher, Barbara Harper, a widow and mother of a young daughter, Dodie. Attempting to resolve the difficulty, Steve meets, falls in love with, and marries Barbara. Shortly thereafter, Chip, who is attending college, meets, falls in love with, and marries Polly Williams. Chip and Polly elope, then honeymoon at the same Mexican hotel where Steve wed Barbara. Adopted son Ernie was the only son not to marry.

Fred MacMurray had the opportunity to play a double role in the series in 1972 when he also appeared as Steve's look-alike cousin Lord Fergus McBain Douglas, a Scottish nobleman traveling to America in search of a bride. He lived with Steve and family for a time.

The show is the second-longest running TV sitcom, topped by *The Adventures of Ozzie and Harriet* which ran for 435 episodes. *My Three Sons* ran for 380 episodes over 12 years. Before Fred MacMurray agreed to star on the series, he negotiated a 65 nonconsecutive day shooting schedule in any one season that shot all the scenes in which he needed to appear. Consequently, all episodes were written far in advance and filmed out of sequence. MacMurray would, for example, tape all the year's scenes set in the living room in one afternoon. The cast would then shoot their scenes around the "missing" MacMurray weeks later and then through the miracle of some tricky editing, the TV viewers never knew that Fred and his fellow actors were talking to each other weeks apart. This technique was dubbed "The MacMurray Method" and was later adopted by other stars like Brian Keith, Henry Fonda and Bill Bixby.

On November 25, 1977, Fred MacMurray and other cast members resurfaced in the ABC reunion special *The Partridge Family/My Three Sons Thanksgiving Special.*

Broadcast History

September 1960–September 1963	ABC Thursday 9:00–9:30
September 1963–September 1965	ABC Thursday 8:30–9:00
September 1965–August 1967	CBS Thursday 8:30–9:00
September 1967–September 1971	CBS Saturday 8:30–9:00
September 1971–December 1971	CBS Monday 10:00–10:30
January 1972–August 1972	CBS Thursday 8:30–9:00

CAST

Steve Douglas	Fred MacMurray
Mike Douglas (1960–1965)	Tim Considine
Robbie Douglas (1960–1971)	Don Grady
Chip Douglas	Stanley Livingston
Michael Francis "Bub" O'Casey (1960–1965)	William Frawley
Uncle Charley O'Casey (1965–1972)	William Demarest
Ernie Thompson Douglas (1963–1972)	Barry Livingston
Sally Ann Morrison Douglas (1963–1965)	Meredith MacRae
Katie Miller Douglas (1967–1972)	Tina Cole
Dodie Harper Douglas (1969–1972)	Dawn Lyn
Barbara Harper Douglas (1969–1972)	Beverly Garland
Terri Dowling (1971–1972)	Anne Francis
Polly Williams Douglas (1970–1972)	Ronne Troup

The Dick Van Dyke Show

First Broadcast: October 3, 1961
Last Broadcast: September 7, 1966

The Dick Van Dyke Show had an inauspicious beginning and was canceled after its first season. Carl Reiner, the show's creator and original writer, based many of the episodes on his experience as a writer for the comedy series *Your Show of Shows*. In fact, Reiner played the part of Rob Petrie in the pilot episode of the show, called *Head of the Family*. Originally intended as an acting vehicle for himself, Reiner's pilot failed to sell. However, Danny Thomas Productions' producer Sheldon Leonard liked the idea and said it had potential if it were recast—which was Leonard's nice way of saying, "Keep Reiner off camera." Broadway star Dick Van Dyke auditioned for the role and so impressed the network brass that he was cast as the lead and the show was renamed.

Robert Petrie was boyish, charming and witty. Admittedly allergic to chicken feathers and cats, Rob was the head writer for the fictional *Alan*

Brady Show. His ability to be both wildly spontaneous and professionally disciplined make him perfect for this prestigious position. He works with a colorful group of co-workers, who are also good friends. Buddy Sorrell is a human joke machine who takes great pleasure in insulting the show's producer, the humorless Mel Connely, who also happens to be Alan Brady's brother-in-law. Sally Rogers is great at her job as a comedy writer but disappointed in her personal life. She lives alone with her cat, Mr. Henderson, and although she has a steady relationship with dull mama's boy Herman Glimpshire, she is always on the lookout for a new man.

For for the first two seasons of the program audiences were in the dark as to who the tyrannical Alan Brady was, because they only saw the back of his head. The most common shots of his mysterious pate were from behind his large office desk or barber chair when he was talking to bumbling Mel. Two years after the series debuted, Alan Brady was finally revealed on the episode entitled "The Alan Brady Show." It was none other than the series creator himself, Carl Reiner.

Rob commutes to work in Manhattan from the suburb of New Rochelle, where he lives on Bonnie Meadow Road with his attractive wife, Laura, and their son, Richie. Rob is a very loving husband and father; he shows affection quite openly, although in his high-profile job, many women become attracted to him over the years. This presents a continuing dilemma for Laura, who is prone to jealousy despite Rob's constant fidelity.

Nineteen years old at the time, Laura met Sgt. Robert Petrie of Company A at Camp Crowder Army Base in Joplin, Missouri, while she was entertaining the troops as a dancer in a UNS show. Rob tried to make a good impression, but instead, broke her toes during a dance. Despite the injury, she falls in love with the klutz and they marry shortly thereafter. It doesn't take long before the Petries send out birth announcements for their new son, Ritchie.

Laura's a clever, stylish woman who takes pride in her appearance, her home, and her family. While she is her own woman, Laura is not beyond sobbing, "Oh, Rob!" whenever things seem to go wrong, which happens regularly. In contrast to other television mothers of the day, Laura had a mind of her own and was downright sexy. Gone were the full-skirted, floral print dresses, high heels and pearl necklaces. Laura wore capri pants, and that caused a big brouhaha with the sponsors, Procter and Gamble, because it was their position that a woman wearing pants on television was quite brazen, even though that's what women around the country were wearing around their own homes. The issue was settled when it was decided that Laura could wear pants in one scene per show, and Carl Reiner promised the sponsor that by using careful camera angles; Laura's trousers would not be shown "cupping under."

Unlike most '60s sitcoms where it was often unclear what television dads did for a living, *The Dick Van Dyke Show* allows the viewer to spend an equal amount of time with the father at home and at work. While the show deals with the subject of a typical suburban family, it focused much more on Rob and Laura than on Ritchie. Ritchie seemed to be the ideal child. He rarely came out of his bedroom and if he did, would only say a few lines before retreating back.

In May 2004, the surviving cast members, including Dick Van Dyke, Mary Tyler Moore, Rose Marie and Carl Reiner, reunited for a much anticipated and long overdue prime time television special on CBS.

Broadcast History

CBS

October 1961–December 1961	Tuesday 8:00–8:30
January 1962–September 1964	Wednesday 9:30–10:00
September 1964–September 1965	Wednesday 9:00–9:30
September 1965–September 1966	Wednesday 9:30–10:00

Cast

Rob Petrie	Dick Van Dyke
Laura Petrie	Mary Tyler Moore
Sally Rogers	Rose Marie
Maurice "Buddy" Sorrell	Morey Amsterdam
Ritchie Petrie	Larry Mathews
Melvin Cooley	Richard Deacon
Jerry Helper	Jerry Paris
Millie Helper	Ann Morgan Guilbert
Alan Brady	Carl Reiner
Stacey Petrie	Jerry Van Dyke

Hazel

First Broadcast: September 28, 1961
Last Broadcast: September 5, 1966

Veteran actress Shirley Booth starred in the title role as the outspoken housekeeper to the Baxter clan. The show had its early beginnings as a comic strip created by Ted Key in 1943. While in most households the maid was usually seen and not heard, Hazel was just the opposite. She not only ran the household, she ran the home.

Hazel's boss, George Baxter, was a conservative laywer living in a suburban home at 123 Marshall Road, Hydsberg, New York, with his gorgeous wife, Dorothy, and their young son, Harold. The show followed the tradition of many glamorous TV moms whose work often gets done by the maid.

Despite George's efforts to hold on to the head of household status, Hazel often undermined his authority. While she wore a uniform and did all the expected housekeeping chores, Hazel took her duties to the next level by becoming an indispensable part of the family. Hazel had her nose in everyone's business and often preempted George's authority, but in doing so, the family soon came to realize that she was very often right and had a ready solution to most problems. Hazel was forever warning "Mr. B" about the dangers of domestic life while undercutting his authority at every opportunity. On rare occasions when things didn't exactly go her way, she'd shrug and admit defeat by saying, "Well, Mr. B, it ain't up to my usual!"

In the show's fifth and final season, George and Dorothy were "transferred" to the Middle East for George's work, so Hazel took Harold with her and started working for George's brother and his family. Brother Steve, a real-estate salesman, his wife, Barbara, a housewife, and their daughter, Susie, were soon the recipients of Hazel's good advice and meddling ways.

Shirley Booth garnered two Emmys for her role. When associates deplored her doing the sitcom as demeaning her talents, she gently took issue with them. "Why not enjoy Hazel's success?" she said to a colleague. "I'm as pleased as I can be. I like my work."

Broadcast History

September 1961–July 1964	NBC Thursday 9:30–10:00
September 1964–September 1965	NBC Thursday 9:30–10:00
September 1965–September 1966	CBS Monday 9:30–10:00

Cast

Hazel Burke	Shirley Booth
George Baxter (1961–1965)	Don DeFore
Dorothy Baxter (1961–1965)	Whitney Blake
Rosie	Maudie Prickett
Harvey Griffin	Howard Smith
Harold Baxter	Bobby Buntrock
Harriet Johnson (1961–1965)	Norma Varden
Herbert Johnson (1961–1965)	Donald Foster
Deidre Thompson (1961–1965)	Cathy Lewis

Harry Thompson (1961–1965)	Robert P. Lieb
Mona Williams (1965–1966)	Mala Powers
Millie Ballard (1965–1966)	Ann Jillian
Steve Baxter (1965–1966)	Ray Fulmer
Barbara Baxter (1965–1966)	Lynn Borden
Susie Baxter (1965–1966)	Julia Benjamin

The Jetsons

First Broadcast: September 23, 1962
Last Broadcast: September 8, 1963

While this cartoon series only lasted one year in prime time, its original 24 episodes have been rebroadcast over and over. In 1985, in order to make the show more viable for syndication, 41 new episodes were produced.

George and Jane Jetson were the typical middle class family of the future. The show takes place late in the 21st century, when people like to vacation on Venus, and a typical work week is three days long. The Jetsons live in the Skypad Apartments in Orbit City on the planet Earth, and George works at Spacely Space Sprockets.

George Jetson is a loving if inept family man who always seems to make the wrong decision. He's bored with his humdrum 21st century life as a "digital index operator" (button-pusher). Jane is a loving wife and mother who is always seeking a new look and trying to find ways to make life as pleasant as possible for poor beleaguered George. She's a whiz around the house, pushing buttons to do chores. George and Jane share their home with their boy, Elroy, a ten-year-old genius in all space sciences, and 16-year-old Judy, whose prime interests are boys, clothes, boys, dating, boys, going out with her friends, and boys.

With all the modern technology of the age, one would doubt that there would be the need for a maid. After all, how hard is it to push a button and have your dinner pop out piping hot and ready to eat? But each generation is more spoiled than the one before it, so the Jetsons utilize the services of Rosie the robot, a *Hazel* clone. She is an outdated model, but the Jetsons love her anyway and would never trade her for an upgrade. Rounding out the clan is the family dog, Astro. As one might imagine, it's rather hard to walk a dog when you live high up in outer space and have no backyard, but in the 21st century, dogs are walked on outside treadmills.

Even though the cartoon version of the 21st century is visually different than the one we're currently living in, family life remains pretty much the same. Traffic is always a problem, especially considering the 500 mph speed limit. The kids are constantly embarrassed by their parents. George is always having problems at work with his boss, the mean-spirited Mr. Spaceley, and when life in the big city drives the Jetson family mad, they dream of packing up and moving to an empty moon. George constantly schemes for greater riches, because according to George, "A thousand dollars a week doesn't stretch very far these days."

BROADCAST HISTORY

ABC

September 1962–September 1963 Sunday 7:30–8:00

CAST

Astro	Don Messick
Cogswell	Daws Butler
Cosmo G. Spacely	Mel Blanc
Elroy Jetson	Daws Butler
George Jetson	George O'Hanlon
Henry Orbit	Howard Morris
Jane Jetson	Penny Singleton
Judy Jetson	Janet Waldo
Rosie the Robot	Jean Vander Pyl

The Beverly Hillbillies

First Broadcast: September 26, 1962
Last Broadcast: September 7, 1971

Another in the line of burgeoning rural situation comedies, *The Beverly Hillbillies* was one of CBS's longest running shows, even though the critics hated it. *Newsweek* called it "the most shamelessly corny show in years" and social critic David Susskind was so alarmed by the show's subject matter, he called upon "the few intelligent people left" to write their congressman and complain. The critics' outcries fell on deaf ears, and television viewers embraced the Clampett family with open arms.

The story begins back home in the Ozarks, when dirt-poor mountain man Jed Clampett was out hunting for the family dinner. He didn't strike his prey, but his badly aimed buckshot hit the ground and struck oil. When John Brewster of the OK Oil Company presented Jed with a $25 million check, the Clampett family packed up their 1921 Oldsmobile truck and moved to a sprawling mansion at 518 Crestview Drive in the Hills of Beverly. Jed deposited his money at the Commerce Bank of Beverly Hills under the watchful eye of greedy banker and next-door-neighbor Milburn Drysdale. Upon their Beverly Hills arrival, the Clampetts are mistaken for a staff of backwoods servants. After settling in to their new lifestyle, the Clampetts find that the luxuries of their new mansion are a poor substitute for the comforts of their former mountain shack. To make things a bit more homey, Granny decides to start a vegetable garden on the grounds of the Clampett mansion, much to the neighbors' chagrin.

Widower Jed Clampett was the patriarch of the family and raised the clan with great gobs of homespun wisdom and the help of his ornery little spitfire mother-in-law, Daisy Moses, better known as Granny. Granny pretty much had the first and last word on all household matters. While she might have left the Ozarks kicking and screaming, once resigned to her fate of big city living, she tried to make the best of it. She spent a lot of time cooking up potions, like Granny's Spring Tonic, along with the usual fare of possum stew and hog jowls. Her goal in life was to try and find a suitable husband for Jed's beautiful tomboy daughter Elly Mae. The problem was that Elly Mae was a wee bit naive and cared more for her house full of critters than the long line of suitors who continually knocked at the mansion's opulent front doors. Cousin Jethro Bodine was big, strong, good looking, and thought himself to be quite the ladies' man. He was also dumb as a doorknob. When the show began, Jethro was in his early 20s and had a sixth grade education. It wasn't until the series was on the air for four years that he finally got his grade school diploma. His life's ambitions were to become a "Double naught spy, brain surgeon, movie producer, and guru."

Over the next nine years, several constants emerged. Jed never replaced his old worn hat or the family truck; Elly May never got a husband; Granny never got to move back to the hills; Jethro never got to keep the girl; and the uppity Mrs. Drysdale failed in her efforts to oust her hillbilly neighbors out of Beverly Hills.

Broadcast History

CBS

September 1962–September 1964	Wednesday 9:00–9:30
September 1964–September 1968	Wednesday 8:30–9:00
September 1968–September 1969	Wednesday 9:00–9:30
September 1969–September 1970	Wednesday 8:30–9:00
September 1970–September 1971	Tuesday 7:30–8:00

CAST

Jed Clampett	Buddy Ebsen
Daisy Moses (Granny)	Irene Ryan
Elly May Clampett	Donna Douglas
Jethro Bodine	Max Baer, Jr.
Milburn Drysdale	Raymond Bailey
Jane Hathaway	Nancy Kulp
Cousin Pearl Bodine (1962–63)	Bea Benaderet
Mrs. Margaret Drysdale (1962–69)	Harriet MacGibbon
Jethrene Bodine (1962–63)	Max Baer, Jr.
Sonny Drysdale (1962)	Louis Nye
Dash Riprock (nee Homer Noodleman)	Larry Pennell
Elverna Bradshaw (1969–71)	Elvia Allman
Shifty Shafer (1969–71)	Phil Silvers
Flo Shafer (1969–71)	Kathleen Freeman

The Patty Duke Show

First Broadcast: September 18, 1963
Last Broadcast: August 31, 1966

Every girl wanted to be Patty Lane, a typical American teenager, happily living in suburbia with her mom, Natalie, a housewife; dad, Martin, the managing editor of *The New York Chronicle*; and annoying, nerdy 12 year old little brother, Ross. Patty lived an idyllic, middle class life at 8 Remsen Drive, Brooklyn Heights, Brooklyn, New York. She was crazy about rock 'n' roll, slumber parties and her long-suffering boyfriend, Richard. Just when you thought life couldn't get any better for this perky lass, twin cousin Cathy, a sophisticated, ballet loving, mirror image of Patty, moves into the Lane household. Cathy will be living with them until she completes her high school education and is able to rejoin her father, Kenneth Lane, a foreign correspondent for *The Chronicle*. At first, Patty doesn't really understand her demure, soft-spoken cousin, and foreign-raised Cathy sometimes encounters difficulty as she tries to adjust to the American way of life. And while the two are as different as night and day, they form an alliance that makes for lots of fun for the twins and confusion for everyone else. The girls confused everybody in their middle-class neighborhood by mischievously switching personalities at critical moments.

The dual personalities Duke had to portray were a bit of a strain, both off camera and on. As a public relations gimmick, she had to use two separate dressing rooms, one for Patty and the other for Cathy. "It was really a pain," Duke recalls in her autobiography, "because I was always leaving in one room something I needed in the other. I kept begging the people in charge to knock down the cardboard wall between them so I could have one room and be comfortable, but the answer was always no."

Duke claims the success of the show was largely due to the strong family unit portrayed. "The kids would do outrageous things, much more preposterous than kids watching ever would, but in the end, everything was okay, the love was obvious, everyone was still together and strong. There was a security in that family, and that was wish fulfillment of a sort for the kids who sat with their TV trays and watched at home." Jean Byron, who portrayed the mother on the show recently commented, "I was always proud of the show. It was wholesome. It was family entertainment."

In 1999, the original cast members resurrected their characters for *The Patty Duke Show: Still Rockin' in Brooklyn Heights.* This time the family reconvenes in New York in order to surprise Patty and end up battling her old arch-nemesis Sue Ellen, who is intent on having the high school torn down. In the new movie, Ms. Duke's Patty still spends her days at Brooklyn Heights High School, where she is now a respected drama teacher. She continues to have a close relationship with her high-school steady, Richard (original cast member Eddie Applegate), although he's now her ex-husband. Cousin Cathy is a recent widow who lives with her bright 14-year-old son in her native Scotland. They are reunited when Cathy comes in for a special surprise for Patty.

Broadcast History

ABC

September 1963–August 1966	Wednesday 8:00–8:30

Cast

Patty/Cathy Lane	Patty Duke
Martin/Kenneth Lane	William Schallert
Natalie Lane	Jean Byron
Ross Lane	Paul O'Keefe
Richard Harrison	Eddie Applegate
J.R. Castle	John McGiver

Petticoat Junction

First Broadcast: September 24, 1963
Last Broadcast: September 12, 1970

Created by Paul Henning, who had previously brought *The Beverly Hillbillies* to television, *Petticoat Junction* was yet another rural comedy to take the airwaves by storm. The show was number four in the Nielsen ratings its first year and remained in the top 25 for five of its seven seasons despite its many cast changes.

The sitcom revolved around the lives of Kate Bradley, the widowed owner of the Shady Rest Hotel in Hooterville, and her three beautiful — and eligible — daughters: level headed Betty Jo, Bobbie Jo, a sexy bookworm and Billie Jo, who was not only the eldest, but the most boy crazy. Also in residence was cantankerous Uncle Jo Carson, who in addition to being the girls' uncle, was the lazy yet lovable manager of the hotel who could often be found at Sam Drucker's General Store playing checkers or leading rehearsals of the Hooterville Volunteer Fire Department Band. Joe was usually working on some grand money-making scheme that never panned out.

Kate was a very amiable type, and a friend to all in Hooterville. When not playing mother hen to her brood of girls or interfering in their love life, she was very civic minded and involved in her little hamlet, especially when it came to Homer Bedloe, the vice president of CF&W Railroad. Homer was determined to shut down operations of the Hooterville Cannonball, a steam driven locomotive that ran through Hooterville and stopped right outside of the Shady Rest to drop off passengers.

In the show's third season, the writers married off Betty Jo when handsome pilot Steve Elliott crashed his airplane outside of town and was nursed back to health by the girls at the hotel. He and Betty Jo moved into their own place close by and had a baby daughter, Kathy Jo.

Throughout the show's run, a number of cast changes took place. Three actresses portrayed Bille Jo and two portrayed Bobbie Jo. A big change came in the 1968–69 season when Bea Benaderet, who played Kate, unfortunately passed away. The producers brought in June Lockhart as Dr. Janet Craig to try and fill the gap, but it never quite worked.

Two years after *Petticoat Junction* premiered, CBS added *Green Acres* to its lineup, another rural offering set outside of Hooterville. It wasn't unusual for the characters from one show to appear on the other.

Broadcast History

CBS

September 1963–September 1964	Tuesday 9:00–9:30
September 1964–August 1967	Tuesday 9:30–10:00
September 1967–September 1970	Saturday 9:30–10:00

Cast

Kate Bradley (1963–1968)	Bea Benaderet
Uncle Joe Carson	Edgar Buchanan
Billie Jo (1963–1965)	Jeannine Riley
Billie Jo (1965–1966)	Gunilla Hutton
Billie Jo (1966–1970)	Meredith MacRae
Bobbie Jo (1963–1965)	Pat Woodell
Bobbie Jo (1965–1970)	Lori Saunders
Betty Jo	Linda Henning
Steve Elliott	Mike Minor
Dr. Janet Craig	June Lockhart
Floyd Smoot	Rufe Davis
Charlie Pratt	Smiley Burnette
Sam Drucker	Frank Cady
Homer Bedloe	Charles Lane

The Addams Family

First Broadcast: September 18, 1964
Last Broadcast: September 2, 1966

How can you not love a family whose credo is "Sic gorgiamus allos subjectatos nunc" (meaning, "We gladly feast on those who would subdue us")?

Starting out in the fertile imagination of cartoonist Charles Addams in *The New Yorker*, the members of the Addams Family actually were creepy, kooky, mysterious and spooky, but in many ways, this macabre family unit was just as wholesome as the Cleavers. They just had a funny way of showing it.

The family lived in an eclectically decorated, musty, dank mansion on North Cemetery Ridge. There was a swordfish head on the wall with a leg sticking out of it, an eight-foot stuffed polar bear that wasn't quite dead, and many small black boxes throughout the house in which "Thing" would pop out of whenever anyone in the family needed a disembodied helping hand.

Gomez Addams was the head of the household. A cigar smoking devotee of playing with model trains (he loved to blow them up), he ran his happy home with an iron manacle. Slinky, sexy Morticia was Gomez's wife and mother to their children, Wednesday and Pugsley. Kitty Kat was the family lion, and Morticia lavished lots of attention on her pet plant Cleopatra, a huge African strangler, whom she raised from a seedling. Morticia would spend hours lovingly hand-feeding Cleopatra yak meatballs. Rounding out the immediate family unit was Uncle Fester, a bald psychotic whose favorite party trick was turning on light bulbs with his mouth; Grandmama Addams, who, even though she was a witch, was probably the most normal of the clan; and Lurch, the six-foot-nine-inch butler who closely resembled the Frankenstein monster. A frequent house guest was dear Cousin Itt, a tiny hairball on legs who spoke gibberish that only the immediate family could understand, and whose only distinguishable articles of clothing were his bowler hat and a pair of sunglasses.

Morticia was a loving wife and doting mother, always looking after the welfare of her family. When she disapproves of the children's assigned schoolbooks because they portray giants, goblins and ghouls as the bad guys, she starts writing better stories such as "The Good Giant Slays Sir Lancelot" and "Cinderella, The Teenage Delinquent." When Pugsley abandons his pet octopus, adopts a puppy, wears a Boy Scout uniform, and decides to play baseball, Gomez and Morticia fear their child is becoming normal and seek the counsel of a child psychiatrist. And whenever the children go out to play (always after dark), she admonishes them to be careful and not stay out too long, lest they get a bad case of "moonburn."

One running gag on the show was Gomez's obsession with French. The French language drove him crazy with desire when spoken by his wife, Morticia. Gomez would say "Tish!, when you speak French, it drives me wild, Cara Mia!" He would then grab her arm and plant a trail of kisses from her hand up to her waiting lips. Morticia's French supposedly helped clear up a sinus condition Gomez had for 22 years.

Broadcast History

ABC

September 1964–September 1966 Friday 8:30–9:00

Cast

Morticia Frump Addams	Carolyn Jones
Gomez Addams	John Astin
Uncle Fester Frump	Jackie Coogan
Lurch	Ted Cassidy

Grandmama Addams	Blossom Rock
Pugsley Addams	Ken Weatherwax
Wednesday Addams	Lisa Loring
Cousin Itt	Felix Silla
Voice of Cousin Itt	Tony Magro
Mr. Briggs, the postman	Rolfe Sedan
Esther Frump, Morticia's mother	Margaret Hamilton
Mother Lurch	Ellen Corby
Thing	Ted Cassidy

The Munsters

First Broadcast: September 24, 1964
Last Broadcast: September 1, 1966

The Munster family was introduced to television audiences just one week after their ghoulish counterparts, *The Addams Family*, debuted on a rival network. *The Munsters* were probably one of the first "mixed marriage" shows on television. Herman Munster, a Frankenstein-like monster, was married to Lily, a vampire. The family was comprised of their son, Eddie, a little wolf boy, Lily's 350-year-old vampire father, Grandpa, their "poor unfortunate" beautiful niece, Marilyn, and Spot, the humongous fire-breathing family pet who lived under the stairs.

The Munsters lived in a spooky Victorian mansion at 1313 Mockingbird Lane, and considered themselves a typical, well-adjusted American family. In many ways, they were. Despite their supernatural heritage, they faced the same daily problems as their viewing audience. Sweet, gentle, bumbling Herman just didn't understand his wife, and although he tried to do the right thing by her, his best efforts were not always enough. He might have been huge in stature, but he was small of brain. He was a gravedigger for the Gateman, Goodman & Graves funeral home by trade, and while he was good at his menial job, he was a terrible head of household. When he was frustrated or just being contrite, Herman would throw a monster-sized temper tantrum, and Lily would have to step in and calm the situation down. She was also the problem solver and most level headed of the clan. Lily might have been the voice of reason and strong on the outside, but she shared many of the insecurities all stay-at-home mothers face. Fearing that she was not useful around the house, or to herself, Lily decided to go out and look for a job.

A typical mother hen, Lily was always looking out for her clan, but had a special spot in her heart for Marilyn, the black sheep of the family.

By normal, human standards, Marilyn was quite beautiful, but in the eyes of her immediate family, she was shockingly repellent. Because of this, Lily felt certain that Marilyn would never meet her Prince Charming.

Little Eddie seems to fit right in with the kids at school, despite his little fangs and werewolf-like appearance. He, like Marilyn, don't seem to notice that the Munster family are the oddballs, and when Eddie reads a school composition entitled "My Parents— An Average American Family" to his class, his teacher believes the boy is exhibiting symptoms of an overactive imagination.

The show was produced by two family show pioneers, Joe Connelly and Bob Mosher, who produced and wrote for *Leave It to Beaver* prior to producing *The Munsters.*

Broadcast History

CBS

September 1964–September 1966 Thursday 7:30–8:00

Cast

Herman Munster	Fred Gwynne
Lily Munster	Yvonne DeCarlo
Grandpa Munster	Al Lewis
Eddie Munster	Butch Patrick
Marilyn Munster (1964)	Beverly Owen
Marilyn Munster (1965–1966)	Pat Priest

Bewitched

First Broadcast: September 17, 1964
Last Broadcast: July 1, 1972
Network: ABC

An extremely popular show that earned several Emmys, *Bewitched* was the biggest hit series produced by ABC up to that time. Imaginative and well-written, the show consistently found itself in Nielsen's top 12. By 1968, its reruns had sold for $9 million. *TV Guide* honored the show as one of the greatest shows of all time, and the episode *Divided He Falls* was named by *TV Guide* as one of the greatest episodes in television history.

Set in Westport, Connecticut, the show focused on the trials and tribulations of a "mixed" marriage—a mortal, Darrin Stephens, who worked as an advertising executive, and his beautiful wife, Samantha, a witch. The couple were married on the first show and from that point on, all similarities to a normal relationship were forever abandoned. To please her husband, Samantha made an earnest attempt to abandon her witchcraft and to become a suburban "mortal" housewife. (Samantha generally exercised her powers by either casting whimsical verbal spells or by twitching her nose and mouth, known on the show as the "witch twitch.") But with regular visits from her large, bewitched family, none of whom approved of her marriage or her desire to try and live a mortal life, Samantha's wishes were deemed virtually impossible.

The stories usually involved disruption created by either Samantha's or Darrin's family. Samantha's mother, Endora, enjoyed using meddling witchcraft to complicate her daughter's marriage. And busybody "mortal" neighbor Gladys Kravitz was among the many who kept the Stephens household in a virtual vortex. Darrin's neurotic boss Larry Tate, Samantha's look-alike cousin, Serena (played by Montgomery herself), mischievous Uncle Arthur, bumbling Aunt Clara, eccentric "witch doctor" Dr. Bombay and Samantha's warlock father, Maurice, helped round out the stellar cast.

It was the adult members of the cast who caused the ruckus the first two seasons. The portrayal of a typical nuclear family was again stretched to the limits when, in the show's third season, because of Elizabeth Montgomery's real life pregnancy, Samantha and Darrin had a daughter, Tabitha. When Montgomery again became pregnant in 1969, a son, Adam, was written into the show. Both children, to Darrin's dismay, displayed witchly powers. The trials and tribulations of a mortal father trying to hinder those powers in very young children (who could unwittingly turn him into a stuffed toy or nursery rhyme character) generated Darrin's main plight in the episodes that focused on the youngsters.

The show saw a few major cast changes throughout its run, most notably the departure of Dick York in 1969, who was summarily replaced by Dick Sargent without as much as a word of explanation. The first Gladys Kravitz, Alice Pearce, passed away in 1966 and was replaced by Sandra Gould. Kasey Rogers replaced the original Louise Tate, Irene Vernon, in 1966. And Darrin's beleaguered father, Frank, was portrayed by both Robert F. Simon and Roy Roberts. None of these cast changes seemed to alter the show's appeal to viewers or rattle the production itself. Actor Bernie Kopell, who had a recurring role as the 100 year old apothecary, and appeared many other times as a guest star, recently said about the show, "The word *bewitched* just fits so nicely in describing my experiences on that show. If any aspect of the show was difficult or pressure-filled, it was never apparent on that 'happy set.'"

Elizabeth Montgomery's real-life husband was William Asher, the director of the series (who also directed *I Love Lucy*, *Danny Thomas*, and

Patty Duke). Asher and Montgomery owned a percentage of the profits of *Bewitched* as well as a percentage of the merchandising rights.

Bewitched set a precedent in being the first TV program to show a husband and wife sharing the same bed on a regular basis. Traditionally, all married TV couples in the 1950s and early 1960s were required to sleep in separate (twin) beds to uphold moral codes of the times, called the Hayes Code, a series of rules and regulations designed to moderate the action of Hollywood film industry directors and producers in the 1930s. The Hayes censorship guidelines dictated that a man and woman could never be seen in the same bed. If the situation occurred that a man and woman were on the same bed together, one of them had to keep a leg on the floor. A man could sit on the side of a bed and talk to a woman in the bed, but one of his legs had to maintain contact with the floor at all times.

Florence Henderson from *The Brady Bunch* claimed for years that she and her TV husband were the first couple to share a bed together, but reruns disprove her claim.

Broadcast History

ABC

September 1964–January 1967	Thursday 9:00–9:30
January 1967–September 1971	Thursday 8:30–9:00
September 1971–January 1972	Wednesday 8:00–8:30
January 1972–July 1972	Saturday 8:00–8:30

Cast

Samantha Stephens	Elizabeth Montgomery
Serena	Elizabeth Montgomery
Darrin Stephens (1964–68)	Dick York
Darrin Stephens (1969–72)	Dick Sargent
Endora	Agnes Moorehead
Larry Tate	David White
Phyllis Stephens	Mabel Albertson
Frank Stephens	Roy Roberts
Frank Stephens	Robert F. Simon
Maurice (1964–72)	Maurice Evans
Aunt Clara (1964–68)	Marion Lorne
Abner Kravitz (1964–72)	George Tobias
Gladys Kravitz (1964–66)	Alice Pearce
Louise Tate (1964–66)	Irene Vernon
Uncle Arthur (1965–72)	Paul Lynde
Gladys Kravitz (1966–72)	Sandra Gould

Tabitha Stephens (1966–72)	Diane Murphy
Tabitha Stephens (1966–72)	Erin Murphy
Louise Tate (1966–72)	Kasey Rogers
Dr. Bombay (1967–72)	Bernard Fox
Esmeralda (1969–72)	Alice Ghostley
Adam Stephens (1971–72)	David Lawrence
Adam Stephens (1971–72)	Greg Lawrence
Apothecary	Bernie Kopell

My Mother the Car

First Broadcast: September 14, 1965
Last Broadcast: September 6, 1966

In spite of the fact that *My Mother the Car* had a terrific cast and stellar writers/creators, the show has been touted as probably the worst tripe that ever hit the airways and possibly the worst television series of all time. It's true that the series' premise was a bit strange, the critics hated it, and it ran for just one season, but the sometimes overlooked moral of this unusual story is: A mother's love never dies.

Dave Crabtree was a small town lawyer and family man with a wife and two children. One afternoon, while visiting his local car dealer to purchase a good, used station wagon for the family, the words "*buyer beware*" could not have been more prophetic. Because a small town lawyer earns a small town salary, Dave couldn't afford a late model car. Souring the lot, Dave came across an ancient 1928 Porter. Not only did it carry the right price tag, but he seemed inexplicably attracted to the old relic. Once he got behind the wheel for a test drive, the reason for his attraction became abundantly clear. When he turned on the car's radio to see if it was in working order, Dave was shocked to hear his long-dead mother Agnes' voice. "Hello Davey, it's your mother."

Those five simple words turned Dave's life upside down. As a dutiful son, he was, of course, compelled to buy the car, but then had to face the consequences at home when he showed up with it. In typical sitcom fashion, Dave was the only one who could hear his mother and the only one allowed to drive the car. When he tries to convince his family that the car wasn't just a car, they thought he was nuts. It didn't help matters when, as Dave tried to convince his family of the benefits of a car that talked, he enthusiastically cried "Honey, the kids will finally meet their Grandma!"

Dave tried to get his mother to talk to his wife to prove his sanity, but Mom steadfastly refused. "Honey," she said, "the world isn't ready for a talking car. They'd cart me off and I'd be playing auto shows, maybe even the Smithsonian Institute. And you know how drafty those marble floors get." Dave asked again, "So you won't talk?" but Mom held firm and said "Only to you, son ... only to you."

As if that wasn't enough to contend with, enter the diabolical Captain Bernard Manzini, a ruthless car collector who wanted the car for his personal collection. Dave obviously couldn't sell his mother to this ruthless man, who throughout the show's run devised a number of plots to get the car into his clutches. When not dodging Manzini's schemes, Mom had quite a few adventures on her own. She got amnesia when she bumped her bumper, won an appearance on a TV game show, did a brake company TV commercial and even discovered a plot to assassinate a foreign leader.

But first and foremost, she was Mom. Whenever Dave had a problem he visited the garage and talked to his mom. Before Dave left his mom for the night, he placed a blanket over her radiator to keep her warm. And on Mother's Day, Dave gave the car a lovely bouquet of flowers.

In actuality, the 1928 Porter was designed by Barris Kustom Industries (remember the Batmobile?) and powered by a 283ci Chevrolet V-8 and a Powerglide automatic transmission. The car's body was made up from various vehicles including a Model T Ford, a Maxwell, a Hudson and pieces of a Chevrolet. To make it appear that the car was driverless (when Mom was getting around on her own), the rear floorboard was removed so that a second driver could be placed out of sight of the viewing audience. He drove the car using a mirror.

Broadcast History

NBC

September 1965–September 1966 Tuesday 7:30–8:00

Cast

Dave Crabtree	Jerry Van Dyke
His Mother, the Car	Ann Sothern
Barbara Crabtree	Maggie Pierce
Cindy Crabtree	Cindy Eilbacher
Randy Crabtree	Randy Whipple
Captain Manzini	Avery Schreiber

Lost in Space

First Broadcast: September 15, 1965
Last Broadcast: September 11, 1968

CBS network executives gave Irwin Allen's *Lost in Space* a green light after his popular *Voyage to the Bottom of the Sea* took off in the ratings in 1964. One of the few television families that did not fit into the sitcom genre, *Lost in Space* took place 30 years in the future, in the late 1990s. It was the story of the space age Family Robinson, who were on a five-year voyage of exploration to the Alpha Cenaturi star system, when their spaceship, the *Jupiter II*, was sabotaged by Dr. Zachary Smith, a smarmy foreign government agent and doctor of intergalactic environmental psychology who wasn't supposed to be on board in the first place. The pioneer family got lost somewhere in the stars and were forced to battle weird creatures and face the day to day survival needs of their various hostile environments.

Father John Robinson was tough, cheerful, reliable and a good father. Mother Maureen was compassionate and tried to remain cheerful and hopeful. She was at first shocked when John proposed the idea of becoming the first family to colonize Alpha Centauri, but finally consented to the voyage. Eldest daughter Judy didn't want to join her family on the mission, either. She changed her mind when dreamy Major Donald West, a military psychologist, was selected to be *Jupiter II*'s pilot. Sweet and cheerful, youngest daughter Penny is a bit of a tomboy and loves animals of whatever species. Precocious son Will was intensely curious, which often got him in trouble. Will was very devoted to the Robinsons' B-9 environmental control robot, Robbie, and used his skill with electronics to keep the robot functioning at a high level. He was frighteningly brilliant and could cobble almost anything together from a $10 electronics kit.

Although staunch and adventurous, Major West was not always as cheerful and optimistic as the rest. His dislike of Dr. Smith was so strong that he continually threatened to beat Smith's brains out. Dr. Smith was notorious for his unique verbosity when doling out insults, particularly to Robbie the Robot. He would often admonish him by calling him a bumbling bag of bolts, a mechanized misguided moron or a presumptuous popinjay. In the beginning, Smith was cold, vicious and just plain nasty, then suddenly transformed into a bumbling, greedy cretin, whose idiotic complacency and incredibly large ego constantly brought trouble to the family. "Oh the pain, the pain," he often moaned.

The robot is the most colorful and fascinating member of the crew. Misprogrammed at the start by Smith, Robbie begins as a hulking bad guy, then slowly transforms into the most lovable member of the cast. Robbie is best remembered for his arm-flailing alert, "Warning! Warning! Alien presence!"

With such a wide variety of personalities clashing in this extended family unit, and all the alien beasties they had to contend with on their journey, its a wonder that they ever made it back to Earth in one piece.

BROADCAST HISTORY

CBS

September 1965–September 1968 Wednesday 7:30–8:30

CAST

Professor John Robinson	Guy Williams
Maureen Robinson	June Lockhart
Judy Robinson	Marta Kristen
Will Robinson	Billy Mumy
Penny Robinson	Angela Cartwright
Don West	Mark Goodard
Dr. Zachary Smith	Jonathan Harris
Robbie the Robot	Bob May
Robbie's Voice	Dick Tufeld

The Big Valley

First Broadcast: September 15, 1965
Last Broadcast: May 19, 1969

The Big Valley was the first and only Western TV series built around a strong female character. Barbara Stanwyck once said of her character, Victoria Barkley: "I'm just playing Lorne Green in a Mother Hubbard."

Widow Victoria Barkley was the matriarch of the Barkley clan, and nobody's fool. She was smart, strong-willed and determined. It was no walk in the park being a single woman in the wild, woolly West, constantly finding it necessary to protect her dynasty from those who would steal the family's land, livestock, and everything else that wasn't nailed down. She also had to be a loving, nurturing mother at the same time.

Victoria and her three grown sons and one grown daughter lived at the Barkley Ranch in California's San Joaquin Valley in the 1870s. The Barkleys were the richest and most powerful family in the Valley and their massive 30,000 acre spread included holdings from mines to logging camps, citrus groves, and the cattle with which they got their start.

Eldest son Jarrod is a prominent lawyer with offices in both Stockton and San Francisco. Middle child Nick is the more hotheaded and outspoken member of the family. Then there's Audra, the youngest and the only daughter among very protective brothers. Heath is quiet and thoughtful, the illegitimate son of Victoria's late husband Tom, but one whom she has accepted as, and loves as, one of her own. They share joy and laughter, heartache and pain, and everything in between. From land disputes, squatters, bank robbers, and horse thieves, to anthrax, injuries, illness, and even the occasional kidnapping, the Barkleys have more than their fair share of both troubles and adventures.

Storylines followed Murphy's Law to a T. Everything that could possibly go wrong, did. The Barkleys lead the resistance when the Coastal and Western Railroad hire bullyboys to force farmers to give up their land for a pittance. When a young man named Heath appears claiming to be Tom Barkley's bastard son, Victoria starts brooding about how her husband could have truly loved her if he was once unfaithful to her and fathered a bastard child. She journeys to Heath's hometown to try to find the truth about Tom's relationship with Heath's mother. Nick is bitten by a rabid wolf and Victoria is kidnapped by outlaws who think she's the local schoolteacher. The reason is unusual: the gang leader wants her to teach him how to read. The Barkleys are plagued by neighbors who claim a boundary changed when a stream changed course.

The Barkelys were a tough but loving lot, loyal to each other no matter what. And despite the odds, they always came out on top.

Broadcast History

ABC

September 1965–July 1966	Wednesday 9:00–10:00
July 1966–May 1969	Monday 10:00–11:00

Cast

Victoria Barkley	Barbara Stanwyck
Jarrod Barkley	Richard Long
Nick Barkley	Peter Breck
Heath Barkley	Lee Majors
Audra Barkley	Linda Evans
Silas	Napoleon Whiting

Family Affair

First Broadcast: September 12, 1966
Last Broadcast: September 9, 1971

Family Affair was an updated version of *Bachelor Father* ... with a twist. Instead of the uncle ending up with one orphaned, teenage child on his posh doorstep, Bill Davis ends up with a teenager and two tiny twins. Their parents, Bill's brother and sister-in-law, died in an accident, and the other relatives felt that Bill could best provide for them. Instead of having three children land on the Davis doorstep at the same time, which might prove to be a shock, in the program's first episode, viewers were introduced to the twins, Buffy and Jody. Cissy arrived the following week.

Both Davis and Bentley Gregg were financially secure, gainfully employed, carefree bachelors with an Oriental house boy and a very proper gentleman's gentleman, respectively, to take care of them. Neither of these swinging singles was prepared to take on parenthood. While Gregg was a successful Beverly Hills attorney, Davis was a highly paid consulting engineer who lived in an elegant apartment off Fifth Avenue in Manhattan. Gregg had an Oriental houseboy, and Bill Davis had Mr. French, a very British, prim and proper gentleman's gentleman, to watch over his household.

Awkward situation notwithstanding, Bill and Mr. French become very attached to the children and have to adjust their lifestyles to accommodate the new members of the household. A stickler for neatness and order, Mr. French has the hardest adjustment to make since he is with the children all the time. Uncle Bill is either at work or out of town on assignments a great deal of the time.

Eldest child Cissy was a typical teenager, whose life revolved around school and boys. Buffy and Jody were rambunctious 6-year-olds who really did try to be good, but it didn't always work. All three were brought up right, had good manners and respected their elders. They also idolized their Uncle Bill.

Most episodes revolve around the usual TV family-type crises, blending comical dilemmas and heartfelt family values. Cissy wants to be a hippie, much to Bill's chagrin. Buffy's hamster runs away in the park, or Bill worries about modern influences on the children. Many of the show's comical and heartwarming scenes are due to the delightful acting skills of veteran actor Sebastian Cabot, who finds it necessary to loosen his stuffy ways when dealing with Buffy and Jody.

The show's star, Brian Keith, had a bit of practice playing a father of twins. Prior to the television series, he starred with Maureen O'Hara and Hayley Mills in Disney's smash hit *The Parent Trap* in 1961.

Broadcast History

CBS

September 1966–September 1969	Monday 9:30–10:00
September 1969–September 1971	Thursday 7:30–8:00

Cast

Bill Davis	Brian Keith
Mr. Giles French	Sebastian Cabot

Buffy	Anissa Jones
Jody	Johnnie Whitaker
Cissy	Kathy Garver

The Mothers-in-Law

First Broadcast: September 10, 1967
Last Broadcast: September 7, 1969

It's always been advisable to try to love one's neighbors. But in the case of the Hubbards and the Buells, that advice had to be taken literally to keep the peace because they were in-laws.

The Mothers-in-Law starred Kaye Ballard as Kay Buell and Eve Arden as Eve Hubbard, two longtime next-door neighbors who become in-laws when their kids, Eve and Herb's daughter, Suzie, and Roger and Kaye's son, Jerry, get married. The Hubbards were respectable and highbrow. Eve Hubbard was the country club housewife-type and her husband Herb an uptight lawyer. Roger and Kay Buell, on the other hand, were a little lower brow. Roger was a television comedy writer who worked at home and Kay was a loudmouth and lazy housewife. They were also Italian, which led to lots of ethnic jokes.

The situations that arise on the series are just what one would expect when two families collide. The conflicts begin immediately when a fight breaks out between the Hubbards and the Buells about their children's wedding plans. Then, the newlyweds' honeymoon is over before it starts when the Hubbards and the Buells show up at their resort hotel.

Kaye and Eve promise not to interfere in their kids' lives when Suzie and Jerry move into their apartment above the Hubbards' garage, but it's a promise they can't keep, forcing the kids to create a fake divorce to teach their mothers a lesson about butting in. The kids are also forced into making a decision about possibly moving out when their mothers' interference in their lives becomes too much for them to endure. Then, when Suzie gives birth to twins, fights erupt between the families about what they will be named.

The show was produced by Desilu productions, and Desi Arnaz was the executive producer. Thinking that it might help the ratings, he guest-starred on a few episodes of the show as bullfighter Raphael Del Gado.

Arnaz pulled together the best talent available on the Desilu lot—Madelyn Pugh Davis and Bob Carroll, Jr., who wrote so many of the classic *I Love Lucy* episodes, penned the pilot and continued on as writers for the series. Additionally, as with *I Love Lucy*, many popular guest stars were brought in as well, including Rob Reiner, Paul Lynde, Ozzie Nelson, Jimmy Durante and Don Rickles.

BROADCAST HISTORY

NBC

September 1967–September 1969 Sunday 8:30–9:00

CAST

Eve Hubbard	Eve Arden
Herbert Hubbard	Herb Rudley
Kaye Buell	Kaye Ballard
Roger Buell (1967–68)	Roger Carnel
Roger Buell (1968–69)	Richard Deacon
Jerry Buell	Jerry Fogel
Suzie Hubbard Buell	Deborah Walley
Raphael del Gado	Desi Arnaz

The Courtship of Eddie's Father

First Broadcast: September 17, 1969
Last Broadcast: June 14, 1972

Based on the novel by Mark Toby and also made into a 1963 movie starring Glenn Ford and Ronny Howard, *The Courtship of Eddie's Father* follows magazine publisher Tom Corbett, a widowed father raising a 7-year-old son with the aid of his Asian housekeeper, Mrs. Livingston, who shares the responsibility of running a motherless household and offers tidbits of sage "Oriental" wisdom to her employer and his son. *Eddie's Father* was one of the earliest programs that featured a Japanese American occupying a central role.

The Corbetts manage quite well overall, but Eddie is obsessed with the idea that his father needs a wife and has a penchant for getting his dad romantically involved with prospective brides. Try as he may, by the series' end, Tom remains a single father.

As with most single parents, Tom spends as much time as he can with Eddie, but often wonders if the demands of his job are diminishing their relationship. Eddie experiences the same problems most kids go through, like the first day of school, having to deal with a bully, and first case of puppy love.

The show followed *The Andy Griffith Show* format, where Tom would teach a lesson, and Eddie would apply it incorrectly, forcing Tom to confront the problems and straighten it all out. A heart-to-heart talk at the end of each episode would resolve the issue, and Eddie and his Dad would talk about the lesson learned.

In a *Los Angeles Times* article in 1984, Bill Bixby described the show: "An adult, family reality comedy is what is it is. We're dealing with situations which, depending on your outlook, could be classified as controversial problems. For example, in one segment, I fall in love with a lady, but she's not emotionally prepared for motherhood. And, because I have a son, we have to part. That's a real problem for many people. Ours is a show dealing with 'today' and with love on many levels.

"I knew the emotional potential of *Eddie's Father*. It dealt with feelings. You'd laugh one minute and you were touched the next. But it wasn't sugary. It was children relating to parents as well as parents dealing with children. It wasn't perfect, but TV in a half hour format is an awesome challenge. We gave one answer; we didn't preach."

BROADCAST HISTORY

ABC

September 1969–September 1970	Wednesdays 8:00–8:30
September 1970–September 1971	Wednesdays 7:30–8:00
September 1971–January 1972	Wednesdays 8:30–9:00
January–June 1972	Wednesdays 8:00–8:30

CAST

Tom Corbett	Bill Bixby
Eddie Corbett	Brandon Cruz
Mrs. Livingston	Miyoshi Umeki
Norman Tinker	James Komack
Tina Rickles	Kristina Holland
Joey Kelly	Jodie Foster
Crissy Drummond	Tippi Hedren
Etta	Karen Wolfe

The Brady Bunch

First Broadcast: September 26, 1969
Last Broadcast: August 30, 1974

The Brady Bunch creator, Sherwood Schwartz, claims that the idea for the show came from a newspaper story he'd read in 1966. It said that at that time, almost 30 percent of marriages involved a spouse who had at least one child from a previous marriage. "Now, in 1966, this was a new phenomenon, and I realized that there really was a whole new kind of family springing up. Y'know, television was loaded with happily married couples, and single widows and widowers, but there wasn't any show that revolved around the marital amalgamation of two pre-existing families." Though the series is now a cultural icon, when it premiered on ABC in 1969, *The Brady Bunch* garnered mostly negative reviews.

The premise of the show was a simple one. When architect Mike Brady, a widower, met his future wife Carol, a widow, they were each raising three children as single parents. When Mike and Carol fell in love and decided to marry, it was necessary to blend their families into one. How six children and two adults can happily coincide in a four-bedroom, two-bathroom home is anybody's guess, but the Bradys muddled through it quite well, with a little help from Alice, the Bradys' housekeeper. The only question is, if the children shared one upstairs bathroom, and Mike and Carol shared the master bath, what did poor Alice, who lived in the maid's room off the kitchen, do when she had to "go"?

The first season's story lines dealt mainly with the family adjusting to living together, which was no easy task. In many instances, it was the men versus the women, with Bobby, Peter and Greg one one side and Marcia, Cindy and Jan hunkering down on the other. The two sets of kids fought like cats and dogs, and each group thought their parent was the only one worth paying attention to. While still often at odds with each other, the initial resentments of a blended family slowly transformed into the normal growing pains of adolescence and sibling rivalry for the remainder of the show's run.

This was the first show of its time to attempt to resolve the *broken home syndrome* that TV viewers had been exposed to for many years. And, even though America was in the throes of the "Make Love Not War" counterculture of the '60s when the show premiered, it became one of the few series that was a throwback to the '50s by touting more traditional family values. They ignored the political and social issues of the day, and even though the kids made an attempt to be *hip* and *with it*, they were just too wholesome to pull it off effectively.

After the show went off the air, it not only spawned one spin-off, *The Brady Kids*, but also *The Brady Bunch Hour, The Brady Brides* and *The Bradys*.

Broadcast History

ABC

September 1969–September 1970	Friday 8:00–8:30
September 1970–September 1971	Friday 7:30–8:00
September 1971–August 1974	Friday 8:00–8:30

Cast

Mike Brady	Robert Reed
Carol Brady	Florence Henderson
Alice Nelson	Ann B. Davis
Marcia Brady	Maureen McCormick
Jan Brady	Eve Plumb
Cindy Brady	Susan Olsen
Greg Brady	Barry Williams
Peter Brady	Christopher Knight
Bobby Brady	Mike Lookinland

4

The 1970s

Television was changing, as was the world. A blue-collar bigot named Archie Bunker hit the airways with an earsplitting impact. It was just the beginning of the new wave of TV shows that brought up issues never before dealt with on the small screen: abortion, rape, interfaith marriages, poverty, and, in the case of *M*A*S*H*, antiwar sentiment. We were living in a time when PLO hijackers were taking over airplanes, campuses across the country were erupting in protest, farm workers were striking and the United States was slowly extricating itself from Vietnam. Simon & Garfunkle's "Bridge over Troubled Water" won three Grammy Awards, and both Jimi Hendrix and Janis Joplin died of drug overdoses.

On January 2, 1971, cigarette advertising ended on U.S. television, relegating the rugged Marlboro Man to print media. In June of the same year, in the first step of a modernization plan, CBS canceled *The Ed Sullivan Show* just two weeks short of its twenty-third year on the air. The industry estimated that 50 percent of American households owned color TVs. Television viewers were mourning the passing of Jack Benny, Ed Sullivan, and Ozzie Nelson.

The country was in turmoil and so were network executives when it came to trying to figure out how to portray the all–American family. Because of the rising black middle class, the Jeffersons were breaking racial barriers. Archie Bunker was testing the freedom of speech barrier, and Mary Tyler Moore broke the stereotypical gender barrier in her portrayal of Mary Richards, an unmarried woman, neither divorced or widowed, living by herself and making it on her own.

The Ewings of *Dallas* weren't television's first dysfunctional family, but they were certainly the most reprehensible. In the mid–1960s, *Peyton Place* was the first nighttime soap opera to captivate audiences, and even though *Dallas* got off to a slow start in 1978, it soon became the most popular series on network television, laying the groundwork for many other prime time soaps to come.

The Waltons reminded audiences of a time and mindset long ago left behind on Walton's Mountain. *The Jeffersons* of New York and the Evans

With actors Ralph Waite, Michael Learned, Will Geer, and Ellen Corby at the helm, the nostalgic Walton clan reminded viewers of a time gone by when families worked hard to stay together by using liberal doses of love and respect.

family on the lower east side of Chicago offered a view into both ends of the black family experience. But it was the Cunninghams of Milwaukee who would be the harbingers of the next era in prime-time family television. Under pressure from the FCC and various groups protesting TV sex and violence, all three networks reluctantly agreed to make 8:00 to 9:00 P.M. the "family hour." The debut of *Happy Days* in 1974 not only complied with the protest groups, but brought back a wave of nostalgia for TV audiences who were looking for a way to relive that kinder, gentler era of the '50s.

The Partridge Family

First Broadcast: September 25, 1970
Last Broadcast: August 31, 1974

The real-life inspiration behind *The Partridge Family* were the Cowsills, a family comprised of teen siblings Bill, Bob, Barry, John, Susan and Paul. In tandem with mom Barbara, they were one of the biggest pop acts of the late 1960s, with a series of hits including "The Rain, the Park and Other Things." In 1969, the group scored their biggest chart entry with the title song from the rock musical *Hair*. Around that same time Columbia Pictures' television division sent a group of screenwriters to observe the Cowsills' daily lives for a possible series based on their story, but the show never panned out. By the time *The Partridge Family* hit the airwaves in 1970, the Cowsills' career was on the decline, and in the wake of the 1971 LP "On My Side," the group disbanded.

Music played an integral role in the lives of most teenagers in the 1970s and the Partridge kids, who lived at 698 Sycamore Road, San Pueblo, California, were no exception. Like many of their peers, they decided to form their own rock 'n' roll band. Their only problem was they didn't have a vocalist, so on a lark, they asked their widowed mother to sit in one afternoon on an impromptu recording session. (According to the pilot episode, Shirley's husband, whose first name has never been revealed, "died suddenly six months previously." His cause of death was also never revealed and he was rarely mentioned again.) Surprisingly, they sold the song, "I Think I Love You" to a record company, and the fatherless suburban family of six became an overnight success.

In real life, Barbara Cowsill had been convinced to join her children's group by a Mercury Records producer to enhance the group's wholesome family image. The Partridge clan, with their new agent, Reuben Kinkaid, an irritable man who really didn't like children at all, set off to perform across the country in a psychedelic bus, a used 1957 Chevrolet school bus from Al's Used Cars, with a sign that read "Careful, Nervous Mother Driving" prominently displayed in the back window.

Keith, the eldest child, was a teen heartthrob. Idealistic eldest daughter Laurie was the girl with a social conscious. Middle child Danny was a con man, whose special nemesis was Reuben Kinkaid. The youngest of the group were son Chris and daughter Tracy. Under the guidance of '70s supermom Shirley Partridge, the five kids survived various capers that almost always culminated in successful concerts.

Several *Partridge Family* songs became genuine hits, including the theme, "Come On, Get Happy," and "I Think I Love You," which sold four million copies. On the *Partridge Family* albums, Jones and Cassidy sang their own parts, but studio artists supplied background vocals and music.

BROADCAST HISTORY

ABC

September 1970–June 1973	Friday 8:30–9:00
June 1973–August 1974	Saturday 8:00–3:30

CAST

Shirley Partridge	Shirley Jones
Keith Partridge	David Cassidy
Laurie Partridge	Susan Dey
Danny Partridge	Danny Bonaduce
Christopher Partridge (1970–1971)	Jeremy Gelbwaks
Christopher Partridge (1971–1974)	Brian Forster
Tracy Partridge	Suzanne Crough
Reuben Kinkaid	David Madden
Ricky Stevens (1973–1974)	Ricky Segall
Alan Kinkaid (1973–1974)	Alan Bursky

All in the Family

First Broadcast: January 12, 1971
Last Broadcast: January 25, 1992

Norman Lear's blue-collar family caused quite a revolution in television and was the most influential sitcom in the history of broadcasting since *I Love Lucy*. Just as "Lucy" pioneered the three-camera filming process, *All in the Family* pioneered videotaping before a live audience. It was also the first situation comedy to deal openly with prejudice, politics and bigotry.

It's been jokingly reported that every family had one Archie Bunker in its realm, but he was the one nobody ever admitted to. Now here was everyone's "Uncle Archie," out in the open, spewing his colorful racial epithets, reactionary views and male chauvinism.

Based on the British series, *Till Death Do Us Part*, the show wasn't an instant hit when it debuted. In fact, there was a strong possibility of cancellation. It took viewers well into the first season to get over the shock of the show's blunt and outrageous humor. From then on, *All in the Family* remained the number one program on television for five years.

The show revolved around the lives of the Bunkers, a lower-middle class family who lived at 704 Hauser Street in Queens, New York. The Bunker family was more akin to the blue collar family of the '50s than to their contemporaries in the liberal '70s. In Archie's mind, women were second-class citizens, born to breed and care for their families. A woman's place was in the home, and men were the breadwinners. A dock foreman for the Pendergast Tool and Dye Company by trade, when money was tighter than usual, Archie also moonlighted as a cab driver for his pal, Munson. If it took two jobs to keep food on the table, so be it.

His wife, Edith, whom Archie repeatedly referred to as "Dingbat," was even tempered, tolerant of his tirades, a bit confused at times, but able to cope with the changes that day-to-day life required. She tried her best to be the perfect housewife, with dinner on the table every night at six sharp. The Bunkers had one child, a young-adult daughter named Gloria who, to Archie's chagrin, married Mike Stivic, who was not only a "Pole," but an educated, liberal one at that. On their wedding day, Archie's only comment was, "It looks like we lost a daughter, but we gained a meathead." Because Mike was going to college, studying for a degree in sociology, he and Gloria lived with Archie and Edith. Archie was Mike's polar opposite. He was uneducated, extremely prejudiced, quite outspoken and completely intolerant of anyone's views on any subject, if they didn't mesh with his own. In other words, an arch-conservative. Archie constantly blasted every minority group, be it racial or religious. Needless to say, this caused quite a bit of grief for Mike, who was nicknamed "Meathead" by the intolerant Archie. Loud arguments between the two men were commonplace in the Bunker household, with Edith trying in vain to play peacemaker, and Gloria wailing in the background, frustrated at the need to stick up for her husband and at the same time, not betray her father's love.

While the show incredibly managed to get by the censors on many daring issues, during the episodes built around Archie's newborn grandson, Joey, it was deemed unfit by CBS for Carroll O'Connor to be shown changing little Joey's diapers. They did it anyway, with discreet angles, and not a single viewer objected.

A former writer of the show, the late Stanley Ralph Ross had his own take on the show's censors. "Some of the censors got very silly ... it's like they were trying to justify their jobs. They'd look to find things. But in the sixties," Ross explained, "if you were with a hit show, you could get away with anything. For example, we would deliberately put things in the show that we knew they would find, and we'd say, 'Ok, we'll take that out, but you've got to let us have the other thing.' So it was sort of like a trade off."

"I was the first writer on *All in the Family*, and even in the beginning, Norman Lear was afraid to make Rob Reiner's character Polish. He wanted him to be Czechoslovakian, and I told him there was nothing funny about being Czechoslovakian, Yugoslavian, or Serbo-Croatian. "Polack" is funny, and I pushed and pushed and pushed him to get that. I wrote five or six episodes the first year, but my favorite was the second episode of the season when Archie got into an automobile accident with a Jewish woman. In spite of all the anti–Semitic remarks he made, Archie hired three Jewish attorneys (Rabinowitz, Rabinowitz and Rabinowitz) to handle the case." The episode got an Emmy nomination and a Writer's Guild Award.

Throughout its run, the show went through several changes. First, Mike and Gloria had a child and moved next door. Then, in the 1977–78 season, Archie gave up a secure paycheck and opened his own business with his friend Murray — a neighborhood bar, Kelsey's, which he renamed Archie's Place. At the end of that season, Sally Struthers and Rob Reiner both announced they were leaving the show, and the final episode saw them moving to California. To make up for their absence, the Bunkers took in their young niece, Stephanie, who had been abandoned by her father. The next year, Jean Stapleton felt that she had exhausted the potential of her character and asked to be phased out. In the first episode of the following season, Archie was seen grieving over Edith's unexpected death from a stroke.

In spite of all the changes, *All in the Family* remained one of the top hits in television and four spin-offs emerged from the show. *Maude* grew out of Beatrice Arthur's appearance as Edith's cousin in 1971. *The Jeffersons*, starring Sherman Hemsley, Isabel Sanford and Mike Evans, were Archie's black neighbors who moved on up to the East side. *Good Times* was the first spinoff of a spinoff that happened when Maude's maid, Florida (Esther Rolle), moved to Chicago for her own series. And finally, *Archie Bunker's Place* debuted in 1979. Carroll O'Connor was the only member of the original *All in the Family* cast to remain.

Broadcast History

CBS

January 1971–July 1971	Tuesday 9:30–10:00
September 1971–September 1975	Saturday 8:00–8:30
September 1975–September 1976	Monday 9:00–9:30
September 1976–October 1976	Wednesday 9:00–9:30
November 1976–September 1977	Saturday 9:00–9:30
October 1977–October 1978	Sunday 9:00–9:30
October 1978–March 1983	Sunday 8:00–8:30
March 1983–May 1983	Monday 8:00–8:30
May 1983	Sunday 8:00–8:30
June 1983	Monday 9:30–10:00
June 1983–September 1983	Wednesday 8:00–8:30
June 1991	Sunday 8:30–9:00
June 1991–July 1991	Sunday 8:00–8:30
September 1991–January 1992	Friday 8:30–9:00

Cast

Archie Bunker	Carroll O'Connor
Edith Bunker (1971–80)	Jean Stapleton
Gloria Bunker Stivic (1971–78)	Sally Struthers
Mike Stivic (Meathead) (1971–78)	Rob Reiner
Lionel Jefferson (1971–75)	Mike Evans
Louise Jefferson (1971–75)	Isabel Sanford
Henry Jefferson (1971–73)	Mel Stewart
George Jefferson (1973–75)	Sherman Hemsley
Irene Lorenzo (1973–75)	Betty Garrett
Frank Lorenzo (1973–74)	Vincent Gardenia
Bert Munson (1972–77)	Billy Halop
Tommy Kelsey (1972–73)	Brendon Dillon
Tommy Kelsey (1973–77)	Bob Hastings
Justin Quigley (1973–76)	Burt Mustin
Barney Hefner (1973–83)	Allan Melvin
Jo Nelson (1973–75)	Ruth McDevitt
Stretch Cunningham (1974)	James Cromwell
Teresa Betancourt (1976–77)	Liz Torres
Stephanie Mills (1978–83)	Danielle Brisebois
Harry Snowden (1977–83)	Jason Wingreen
Hank Pivnik (1977–81)	Danny Dayton
Murray Klein (1979–81)	Martin Balsam
Mr. Van Ranseleer (1978–83)	Bill Quinn

Veronica Rooney (1979–82)	Anne Meara
Jose (1979–83)	Abraham Alvarez
Linda (1980–81)	Heidi Hagman
Raoul (1980–83)	Joe Rosario
Ellen Canby (1980–82)	Barbara Meek
Polly Swanson (1980–81)	Janet MacLachlan
Ed Swanson (1980–81)	Mel Bryant
Billie Bunker (1981–83)	Denise Miller
Gary Rabinowitz (1981–83)	Barry Gordon
Bruce (1982–83)	Bob Okazaki
Marsha (1982–83)	Jessica Nelson

The Waltons

First Broadcast: September 14, 1972
Last Broadcast: August 20, 1981

Another of the very few non-sitcom television families, *The Waltons* brought wholesome entertainment and a warm family drama to the television airwaves in an era when the rest of the world seemed to be topsy-turvy. When the series began, the people of Walton's Mountain were finding life to be very hard during the Great Depression, and as the show continued, the viewers saw how World War II affected people in the small, close-knit community.

The show's creator, Earl Hamner, Jr., based the series on his autobiographical novel, *Spencer's Mountain*, which had been made into a feature film of the same name and subsequently adapted as a CBS-TV holiday special, *The Homecoming*, in 1971. Hamner was one of eight children, living near Schuyler, Virginia, and left home in the late 1930's to become a professional writer.

The initial public reaction to the special was so overwhelming that executives Lee Rich and Bob Jacks of the newly-formed Lorimar Productions convinced CBS to continue it as a series, with Hamner as co-executive producer and story editor.

The Waltons were a large, tight-knit family, living up on the fictional Walton's Mountain in the Blue Ridge Mountains of Virginia, during the Depression. The family was comprised of feisty Grandma Esther and mischievous Grandpa Zeb Walton, their son, John, his wife, Olivia, and their seven children. John runs his own sawmill, but given the depressive economic status of the era, the family was poor. But what they lacked in money, they abundantly made up for in love. The message of this show was family unity, and the respect and reverence of elders. Even in the case of the eccentric Baldwin sisters, spinster neighbors who innocently brewed moonshine in their stately home, or Ike Godsey's snobbish socialite wife, Cora Beth, the children never talked back, disobeyed or were disrespectful. Old fashioned family values were played up in the series.

Zeb Walton is the patriarch of the Walton family and has been married to Esther Walton for over 50 years. He works with John in the family lumber mill, enjoys fishing, walking on his mountain and enjoying an occasional sip of the Baldwin ladies' "recipe." His death is referred to at the beginning of the show's seventh season, but he lived on in spirit, frequently remembered out loud by family members. Grandma Esther is a very religious, strong, independent and determined woman. Gruff on the outside, she loves her family dearly. Ellen Corby, the actress who played Grandma, suffered a stroke which kept her out of the show for a season. In the script for that season, Grandma Walton had also suffered the same fate, and in the episode "Grandma Comes Home" she returned to the series on a limited basis, partially incapacitated.

John is not a church man, preferring to believe and worship his own way and has earned the reputation of being an honest, hard working, reliable and kind man. Olivia is very religious and finds great comfort in reading her Bible. She supports her husband in all that he does, and raises her brood in a firm, yet loving manner.

Each week the show followed the trials and tribulations of a tough and rugged family life with the narrative given from perspective of the oldest son, John Boy. While John Boy would never do anything to undermine his parent's expectations of him, he yearns to leave Walton's Mountain someday and pursue his dream of becoming a writer. When he graduates from the local high school he earns a scholarship to Boatwright University, where he majors in journalism. After getting his degree, he goes to the war zones to write for a large newspaper, and eventually marries Janet, a magazine editor from New York. Throughout the show's nine years on the air, all the children graduate from school, become productive citizens, get married and have children of their own.

The last scene of each episode featured a night view of the Walton homestead with its windows lit and someone in the family starting to say goodnight to the rest of the family. This started a cascade of responses as each member of the Walton family wished each other goodnight. According to a two-hour special, "TV Road Trip," hosted by John Ritter for *The Travel Channel*, the classic ritual was based on the real-life experiences of Earl Hamner. At one point in his life, Hamner's seven brothers and sister used to bid each other lengthy good-nights at bed time, sometimes taking up to ten minutes.

In 1982 the show was brought back for three *Waltons* specials, *A Wedding on Walton's Mountain, Mother's Day on Walton's Mountain,* and *A Day for Thanks on Walton's Mountain.* In the 1990s three more specials were produced: *A Walton Thanksgiving, A Walton Easter* and *A Walton Wedding,* all starring the original cast.

Broadcast History

CBS

September 1972–August 1981	Thursday 8:00–9:00

Cast

Narrator: Earl Hamner, Jr.	
John Walton	Ralph Waite
Olivia Walton (1972–1980)	Michael Learned
Zeb (Grandpa) Walton (1972–1978)	Will Geer
Esther (Grandma) Walton (1972–1979)	Ellen Corby
John Boy Walton (1972–1977)	Richard Thomas
John Boy Walton (1979–1981)	Robert Wightman
Mary Ellen Walton Willard	Judy Norton-Taylor
Jim-Bob Walton	David W. Harper
Elizabeth Walton	Kami Cotler
Jason Walton	Jon Walmsley
Erin Walton	Mary Elizabeth McDonough
Ben Walton	Eric Scott
Ike Godsey	Joe Conley
Corabeth Godsey (1974–1981)	Ronnie Claire Edwards
Mamie Baldwin	Helen Kleeb
Emily Baldwin	Mary Jackson
Verdie Foster	Lynn Hamilton
Rev. Matthew Fordwick (1972–1977)	John Ritter
Rosemary Hunter Fordwick (1973–77)	Mariclare Costello
Yancy Tucker (1972–1979)	Robert Donner
Flossie Brimmer (1972–1977)	Nora Marlowe
Maude Gormsley (1973–1979)	Merie Earle
Dr. Curtis Willard (1976–1978)	Tom Bower

Rev. Hank Buchanan (1977–1978)	Peter Fax
J. D. Pickett (1978–1981)	Lewis Arquette
Cindy Brunson Walton (1979 1981)	Leslie Winston
Rose Burton (1979–1981)	Peggy Rea
Serena Burton (1979–1980)	Martha Nix
Jeffrey Burton (1979–1980)	Keith Mitchell
Toni Hazleton (1981)	Lisa Harrison
Arlington Wescott Jones (Jonesy) (1981)	Richard Gilliland

Maude

First Broadcast: September 12, 1972
Last Broadcast: April 29, 1978

And then there's Maude ... the outspoken and anything but tranquil brash woman of the '70s, who shouts "God'll get you for that" at those who cross her. She was introduced to television audiences as Edith Bunker's cousin on *All in the Family*. She was so well received that the CBS brass came up with a spinoff of her own. According to show creator, Norman Lear, "Maude was the flip side of Archie Bunker; a 'flawed liberal.'"

The Findlay family lived in Tuckahoe, New York. Walter Findlay was owner of Findlay's Friendly Appliances and Maude's fourth husband. Most of the time, he was rather quiet and neutral. Also sharing the abode were Maude's divorced daughter, Carol, Carol's nine-year-old-son, Phillip, and, before they spun her off in 1974 to her own show, *Good Times*, Florida, the maid.

Even though the show was classified as a situation comedy, *Maude* was groundbreaking in that heretofore taboo topics such as menopause, abortion, plastic surgery, alcoholism, mental illness, race relations and marijuana laws were addressed. Compared to the white, middle-class families portrayed on television in the '50s and '60s, *Maude* was considered extremely controversial, and the issues frequently struck a chord with viewers.

The series started off with a bang, tackling some very testy subjects in its first two seasons. "Maude's Dilemma," a two-part episode, depicted the 45-year-old Maude finding herself pregnant and opting for an abortion. The show was boycotted by the Roman Catholic Church, stating that the promotion of abortion was unacceptable in a situation comedy. Two CBS affiliates canceled the episodes and 32 CBS affiliates were pressured by anti-abortion factions not to rerun the segments in the summer of 1973. The first time the show aired CBS received 7,000 letters; the second time around 17,000 letters of protest poured in. This program appeared at a time when the Supreme Court had not yet protected legalized abortion. Reportedly, pro-life groups mailed Norman Lear photographs of aborted fetuses in protest. The second airing of the program gave the show a 41 percent share with 65 million people tuning in.

Maude Findlay was also the first prime-time character to undergo a face lift. She justified her need for the operation by saying she felt "Like an old hen with a turkey's neck and crow's feet — I could be the centerfold for the Audubon Society." Her facial transformation was achieved by tape and makeup. The subjects of spousal abuse, alcoholism and mental illness were covered in another episode when Walter strikes Maude during a drunken rage and suffers a breakdown.

The socially controversial show represented a change in television sitcoms during the early 1970s. Having come from the era of civil rights, Vietnam protests and various forms of consciousness raising, baby boomers were open to new kinds of television.

Broadcast History

CBS

September 1972–September 1974	Tuesday 8:00–8:30
September 1974–September 1975	Monday 9:00–9:30
September 1975–September 1976	Monday 9:30–10:00
September 1976–September 1977	Monday 9:00–9:30
September 1977–November 1977	Monday 9:30–10:00
December 1977–January 1978	Monday 9:00–9:30
January 1978–April 1978	Saturday 9:30–10:00

Cast

Maude Findlay	Beatrice Arthur
Walter Findlay	Bill Macy
Carol	Adrienne Barbeau
Phillip (1972–1977)	Brian Morrison
Phillip (1977–1978)	Kraig Metzinger
Dr. Arthur Harmon	Conrad Blain
Vivian Cavender Harmon	Rue McClanahan
Florida Evans (1972–1974)	Esther Rolle
Henry Evans (1973–1974)	John Amos

Chris (1973–1974)	Fred Grandy
Mrs. Nell Naugatuck (1974–1977)	Hermione Baddeley
Bert Beasley (1975–1977)	J. Pat O'Malley
Victoria Butterfield (1977–1978)	Marlene Warfield

Apple's Way

First Broadcast: February 10, 1974
Last Broadcast: January 12, 1975

Produced by Earl Hamner, Jr., and Lee Rich of *The Waltons*, *Apple's Way* was another wholesome show, with decency and good moral and family values at its core.

While many urban families dream about packing up their hectic lives and moving away to a more soothing, rural setting, few can afford to do so. In the case of George Apple, a laid back, patient and successful Los Angeles architect, the call of his home town, Appleton, Iowa, was too overpowering. George decided to leave the rat race and take his family back home to his roots.

The small community of Appleton had been founded by George's ancestors, and the adjustment to a more tranquil life was quite a challenge to his four city bred children and wife.

George is a bit of an activist and tries to set a good example for his children. When he hears that an old, historic tree in town is about to be cut down, George goes up in the tree and sits there for days so that the tree can't be cut down which demonstrates to his kids that one should stand for the principles one believes in. Most of the show's episodes contained a moral lesson to be learned.

The general buzz at the time was that the show was an attempt to copy *The Waltons* with the main difference being that it took place in modern times, not during the Depression. Apparently not enough viewers wanted another dose of wholesome family values, and despite a strong cast and a good production team, the series was canceled after 24 episodes.

Broadcast History

CBS

February 1974–January 1975	Sunday 7:30–8:30

Cast

George Apple	Ronny Cox
Barbara Apple	Lee McCain
Paul Apple	Vincent Van Patten

Cathy Apple	Patti Cohoon
Patricia Apple (1974)	Franny Michel
Patricia Apple (1974–1975)	Kristy McNichol
Steven Apple	Eric Olson
Grandfather Aldon	Malcolm Atterbury

Happy Days

First Broadcast: January 15, 1974
Last Broadcast: July 12, 1984

The Cunningham family of Milwaukee was the quintessential '50s television family; more down-to-Earth than the Andersons, and funnier than the Cleavers, but maybe that's because viewers were introduced to the Cunninghams in the 1970s and given a "nostalgic look" back into yesteryear with a '70s slant. The show came about when programmers were looking to cash in on the wave of 1950s nostalgia generated by the hit film *American Graffiti*.

The Cunninghams represented the middle class family values of the 1950s. Lessons were learned, but never preached. Howard Cunningham fit the bill of bumbling father, but he was not portrayed as stupid. He worked a 9 to 5 job as the owner of Cunningham Hardware and came home very night to find dinner on the table and a loving family to share it with. Howard spent his free time with his lodge brothers at the Leopard Lodge or bowling for a team called the Ten Pins. He cared deeply abut his family and always tried to comfort them in times of need. "Here, have a Life Saver," he'd say to Richie. "It'll make you feel better."

Instead of being the voice of reason as many '50s mothers were, wife Marion was a bit ditzy and scattered. She cooked, she cleaned, she catered to her family, and only rarely showed any backbone, but she certainly wasn't inept, and was fiercely protective of her family.

Eldest son Chuck only appeared briefly in the show's first season, then disappeared completely, without explanation. Second son Ritchie was a typical high school kid, and the show's story lines usually focused on the trials and tribulations of his teenage world. Kid sister Joanie was just 13 when the show started, and was the typical brat. Howard used to brag that Joanie's first word was "hardware." She spent much of her time hanging out with Jenny Picalo, whom the Cunninghams felt was a decidedly bad influence on their wholesome daughter. The kids typically hung out at Arnold's Drive-In with Richie's pals, Potsie Webber and Ralph Malph.

While the Cunninghams were a typical American family in almost every way, they shared their life with someone who would never have been accepted into the Cleaver household; a greasy haired, rough around the edges ex-hoodlum with a heart of gold, named Arthur Fonzarelli. Fonzie's dropout life revolves around his job at Bronco's Auto Repairs, his leather jacket, his motorcycle and girls, not necessarily in that order. When Fonzie is first introduced to the family, Howard is a bit appalled, but Marion sees through the tough facade and treats him like one of her own, eventually moving him into the apartment above the family garage. His thumbs-up gesture, "aaayyh!," and leather jacket would soon become his trademarks. He was always available to give Richie advice about life and, of course, girls, in his "office," the men's room at Arnold's.

Like many families of the era, everyone sat down to dinner and shared their day. As the editor of the school paper, Richie decided to do an article on "Why people are afraid of things." The kitchen table discussion that night had each member of the Cunningham family open up and reveal their vulnerabilities to each other by admitting their own fears. Richie was afraid of smelling flowers every since that "bumble bee incident." Marion feared taking a shower every since the movie *Psycho.* Joanie was afraid of the Boogie man; and Howard didn't like worms because they were squishy.

During the show's ten and a half year run, Richie and his pals graduated from high school, then attended the University of Wisconsin. The adult Potsie worked at Mr. Cunningham's hardware store. In the show's 1980 season, Richie and Ralph Malph joined the Army and were shipped off to Greenland. In the show's final years, Fonzie became co-owner of Arnold's, manager of Bronco's Auto Repairs, and a shop teacher at Jefferson High. Joanie blossoms into a young woman and pairs up with Fonzie's young cousin, Chachi Arcola. *Joanie Loves Chachi*, a spinoff, was created for the two young lovebirds in the show's 1982–1983 season. Chachi, his mom and new stepfather, Al, move to Chicago, where Chachi tries out a singing career. Joanie, the love of his life, shares the band's vocals and moves with the Arcolas. The often uttered phrase of exasperation "Sit on it!" became a national catch phrase, and also a commentary on how audiences felt about the show. Poor ratings canceled the show and had all cast members moving back to Milwaukee for the *Happy Days* final season.

Broadcast History

ABC

January 1974–September 1983	Tue 8:00–8:30
September 1983–January 1984	Tue 8:30–9:00

April 1984–May 1984	Tue 8:30–9:00
June 1984–July 1984	Thu 8:00–8:30

CAST

Richie Cunningham (1974–80)	Ron Howard
Arthur "Fonzie" Fonzarelli	Henry Winkler
Howard Cunningham	Tom Bosley
Marion Cunningham	Marion Ross
Warren "Potsie" Webber (1974–83)	Anson Williams
Ralph Malph (1974–80)	Donny Most
Joanie Cunningham	Erin Moran
Chuck Cunningham (1974)	Gavan O'Herlihy
Chuck Cunningham (1974–75)	Randolph Roberts
Arnold (Matsuo Takahashi) (1975–76, 1982–83)	Pat Morita
Alfred "Al" Delvecchio (1976–1982)	Al Molinaro
Charles "Chachi" Arcola (1977–84)	Scott Baio
Lori Beth Allen Cunningham (1977–82)	Lynda Goodfriend
Jenny Piccalo (1980–83)	Cathy Silvers
Roger Phillips (1980–84)	Ted McGinley
Officer Kirk	Ed Peck

Little House on the Prairie

First Broadcast: September 11, 1974
Last Broadcast: March 21, 1983

Based on the best-selling autobiographical series of books by the same name, author Laura Ingalls Wilder paints a colorful picture of life in the 1870s, and the problems a family could easily encounter trying to make a life for themselves in the untamed American West. The TV series came on the heels of a successful made-for-TV movie, which had aired in March 1974.

Laura's father, Charles Ingalls, was a homesteader struggling to make a living on a small farm near the town of Walnut Grove, Minnesota. The Ingalls had moved from Kansas in search of a future in a young and growing community. Wife Caroline was the typical frontier wife. She was hardworking, loving and devoted to her family. Even though Charles was a strict but loving father, and dispensed life lessons whenever necessary, it was often Caroline who passed out meaningful words of wisdom to her three daughters, Mary, Laura, and Carrie. To try and make ends meet, in addition to Charles working his farm, he also worked at the local sawmill.

Laura, affectionately called "Half Pint" by her father, was the headstrong middle child. She didn't necessarily go out and find trouble, but trouble would always find her. Curious about all things and impatient about most, one evening she was tired of studying and asked Caroline, "Ma? How long is all this leaning gonna take?" to which Caroline wisely replied, "We start learning when we're born, Laura. And if we're wise we don't stop until the Lord calls us home."

Older sister Mary was as quiet and polite as Laura was outgoing and rambunctious. An excellent student, Mary had aspirations of becoming a teacher. Then tragically, she lost her sight and was sent to a school for the blind.

The denizens of Walnut Grove were a close knit community that banded together against the harsh living conditions of frontier life. The Ingalls had their share of family catastrophes, like the death of a newborn son, daughter Mary's blindness, and all sorts of natural disasters which threatened both lives and livelihoods. With a little help from Doc Baker, Reverend Robert Alden, and their good friends and neighbors, the Ingalls managed to thrive as best they could.

While the Ingalls were inherently good, their nemesis, the Olesons, owners of the town's general store, were just the opposite. Harriet Oleson was a pompous, small-minded, mean-spirited gossip. Husband Nels was a quiet man whose fate was to put up with his overbearing wife. Their daughter Nellie was a carbon copy of her mother and lived, it seemed, to make Laura's life miserable. Nellie's younger brother, Willie, was just as mean as his sister, but not nearly as smart.

By the end of the series, Charles and Caroline became parents again to yet another daughter and an adopted son, Albert. Due to economic conditions in the area, Charles was forced to give up the farm and move to Burr Oak, Iowa, where he found gainful employment. Mary married her instructor at the blind school, Adam Kendall, and both were teaching sightless children at their own school in the Dakotas. Tomboy Laura also fell in love, married Almanzo Wilder and became a teacher herself, as well as a mother to young daughter Rose.

Michael Landon left the show in the 1982 season to devote more time to producing. Victor French returned to the show as a regular, playing the Ingalls' surrogate father. That same season, a very young Shannen Doherty became a cast regular as Laura's niece, and Michael Landon's daughter, Leslie, joined the cast as the new school teacher.

Broadcast History

NBC

September 1974–September 1976	Wednesday 8:00–9:00
September 1976–March 1983	Monday 8:00–9:00

Cast

Charles Ingalls	Michael Landon
Caroline Ingalls	Karen Grassle
Laura Ingalls Wilder	Melissa Gilbert
Mary Ingalls Kendall	Melissa Sue Anderson
Carrie Ingalls	Lindsay Greenbush/ Sidney Greenbush
Lars Hanson	Karl Swenson
Nels Oleson	Richard Bull
Harriet Oleson	Katherine MacGregor
Nellie Oleson Dalton	Alison Arngrim
Willie Oleson	Jonathan Gilbert
Dr. Baker	Kevin Hagen
Rev. Robert Alden	Dabbs Greer
Isaiah Edwards	Victor French
Jonathan Garvey	Merlin Olsen
Andy Garvey	Patrick Laborteaux
Alice Garvey	Hersha Parady
Eva Beadle Simms	Charlotte Stewart
Albert Ingalls	Matthew Laborteaux
Adam Kendall	Linwood Boomer
Grace Ingalls	Wendi Turnbaugh/ Brenda Turnbaugh
Hester Sue Terhune	Ketty Lester
Almanzo Wilder	Dean Butler
Eliza Jane Wilder	Lucy Lee Flippin
James Cooper Ingalls	Jason Bateman
Cassandra Cooper Ingalls	Missy Francis
Nancy Oleson	Allison Balson
Grace Snider-Edwards	Bonnie Bartlett
Andrew "Andy" Garvey	Patrick Laborteaux
Percival Dalton	Steve Tracy
Jenny Wilder	Shannen Doherty

Etta Plum	Leslie Landon
Rose Wilder	Jennifer Steffin/Michelle Steffin

Rhoda

First Broadcast: September 9, 1974
Last Broadcast: December 9, 1978

Rhoda Morgenstern was introduced to television viewers as Mary Richards' best friend and upstairs neighbor on *The Mary Tyler Moore Show*. When she got her own spin-off, she introduced herself to audiences thusly: "My name is Rhoda Morgenstern. I was born in the Bronx, New York, in December of 1941. I've always felt responsible for World War II. The first thing I remember liking that liked me back was food. I had a bad puberty; it lasted 17 years. I'm a high school graduate. I went to art school. My entrance exam was on a book of matches. I decided to move out of the house when I was 24. My mother still refers to this as the time I ran away from home. Eventually, I ran to Minneapolis, where it's cold and I figured I'd keep better. Now I'm back in Manhattan. [In a louder voice] New York, this is your last chance!"

Rhoda was single, slightly overweight, somewhat insecure and had a sharp tongue. Her parents, the overbearing Ida and soft spoken Martin, provided her with a typically New York (Bronx) Jewish upbringing; equally liberal amounts of food and guilt. Ironically, neither Nancy Walker, who played Ida, nor Valerie Harper, in the title role, was Jewish.

Rhoda worked as a window dresser at Hempel's Department Store in Minneapolis, and, like most single women, was always on the lookout for a significant other. By the time Rhoda reluctantly left Minneapolis for a dutiful trip home to New York to visit her family, she had slimmed down, updated her wardrobe, and had a lot more self confidence. All she expected from the trip home was aggravation from her overbearing, exasperating, Jewish guilt-queen mother, whose job in life was to feed her family, meddle in everyone's business and search for husbands for her daughters.

Instead, Rhoda met and fell in love with Joe Girard, the divorced owner of a wrecking company with a 10-year-old son. After meeting Joe, any thoughts about returning to Minneapolis flew out the window.

While the romance between Rhoda and Joe was blossoming, Rhoda moved into the tiny, cramped apartment of her dumpy and insecure younger sister, Brenda. She might have been more physically comfortable staying in her old room at her parents' apartment, but living again under the same roof with Ida was not an option. Besides, a mere eight episodes later, she and Joe tied the knot and moved into an apartment of their own in Brenda's building. While their much touted marriage only lasted for two seasons, the close-knit Morgenstern family played a big part in Rhoda's life. The interactions between Rhoda, Brenda and Ida are priceless, and this was the kind of a mother/daughter relationship that many viewers could relate to. Ida frequently made unexpected visits to her daughter's apartments, had a great sixth sense, and could always figure out when something was wrong with her children. Despite Ida's overbearing and meddlesome ways, she was the glue that held the family together.

Broadcast History

CBS

September 1974–September 1975	Monday 9:30–10:00
September 1975–January 1977	Monday 8:00–8:30
January 1977–September 1978	Sunday 8:00–8:30
September 1978–December 1978	Saturday 8:00–8:30

Cast

Rhoda Morgenstern Gerard	Valerie Harper
Brenda Morgenstern	Julie Kavner
Joe Gerard (1974–1977)	David Groh
Ida Morgenstern	Nancy Walker
Martin Morgenstern	Harold J. Gould
Carlton the Doorman	Lorenzo Music
Myrna Morgenstein (1974–1976)	Barbara Sharma
Gary Levy (1976–1978)	Ron Silver
Sally Gallagher (1976–1977)	Anne Meara
Johnny Venture (1977–1978)	Michael Delano
Nick Lobo	Richard Masur

Good Times

First Broadcast: February 1, 1974
Last Broadcast: August 1, 1979

As Jimmie Walker's character J.J. might say, this spin-off of *Maude* hit the airways and exploded like "Dy-No-Mite!"

Not aptly titled, *Good Times* followed the home life of Maude's maid, Florida Evans, who along with her husband and three children attempted to make the best of living in a high-rise government-funded ghetto apartment in Chicago's West Loop. In addition to the other tenants in the project, they also had to contend with roaches, winos, junkies and muggers. In other words, they had to make do.

While the Evans clan didn't have much materially, there was always lots of love to go around. Their ability to stay strong while facing nearly insurmountable odds was one of the show's underlying themes. Unlike other television families, they brought relevancy and realism of the African American experience to prime time. It would be ten years down the road before Bill Cosby and his fictional Huxtable clan would portray blacks as wealthy, well-educated professionals. Meanwhile, the Evans family skillfully tackled the subject of living in an urban slum with a measure of realism. Each day was an upward battle; fighting inflation, unemployment and racial bigotry. But in spite of their difficult situation, they never shirked their responsibility to teach values and morality to their children.

Florida's husband, James, was always in and out of work. Eldest son J.J. was in trade school and always looking for a get rich scheme. He was the comedian of the family, never passing up a chance to make light of a bad situation. "Mama can make a chicken last for three days!" he would boast. "Yeah! Day one, you swish it around in some boilin' hot water and we got chicken soup! Day two is the teaser, you take the wings, the thigh, and the neck, and you get somethin' that's so yummy, it tickles your tummy! Day three, you got the legs, the thigh, and the breasts. You got somethin' so light, we call it Chicken Dy-no-mite!"

Daughter Thelma, a year younger than J.J. , was still in high school, and a typical teenager. Her youngest brother, Michael, was the smartest of the trio. He was thoughtful, intelligent, and fascinated with African American history. Also frequenting the Evans' apartment was Florida's neighbor and best friend, Willona Woods, and the mean but inept building superintendent, Booker.

In the show's 1976–1977 season, the plot lines changed when James found a job out-of-state and was set to move the family to a better life in Mississippi . Unfortunately, his character was killed in an automobile accident and Florida became a widow, left to raise her children by herself. That scenario only lasted for one season. She subsequently found a new man, got married, and then the two of them left the show, leaving the kids to fend for themselves. By the time her character reappeared the following season, with her new husband, the show's ratings began to founder.

Broadcast History

CBS

February 1974–September 1974	Friday 8:30–9:00
September 1974–March 1976	Tuesday 8:00–8:30

March 1976–August 1976	Tuesday 8:30–9:00
September 1976–January 1978	Wednesday 8:00–8:30
January 1978–May 1978	Monday 8:00–8:30
June 1978–September 1978	Monday 8:30–9:00
September 1978–December 1978	Saturday 8:30–9:00
May 1979–August 1979	Wednesday 8:30–9:00

CAST

Florida Evans (1974–1977, 1978–1979)	Esther Rolle
James Evans (1974–1976)	John Amos
James Evans, Jr. (J.J.)	Jimmie Walker
Willona Woods	Ja'net DuBois
Michael Evans	Ralph Carter
Thelma Evans Anderson	BernNadette Stanis
Carl Dixon (1977)	Moses Gunn
Nathan Bookman (1977–1979)	Johnny Brown
Penny Gordon Woods (1977–1979)	Janet Jackson
Keith Anderson (1976–1979)	Ben Powers
Sweet Daddy (1978–1979)	Theodore Wilson

That's My Mama

First Broadcast: September 4, 1974
Last Broadcast: December 24, 1975

Clifton Curtis was a young, hip barber in a black middle-class neighborhood of Washington, D.C. He had inherited the family barber shop after the death of his father, and in a way, also inherited his mother, a loving, opinionated woman who lived with her single son, and a woman who was almost always right.

Clifton's younger sister, Tracy, was a sensible woman married to a boring, uptight accountant. Tracy would often side with Mama against Clifton's schemes.

Clifton liked his profession and his status as a carefree bachelor, but his Mama had different ideas. Because she only wanted the best for her son, in her mind, that meant a woman in his life, so she put a great deal of effort into trying to find him a suitable spouse.

Clifton hung out in the barber shop with Earl the postman, as well as with Josh and Wildcat, two older men who never seemed to need a haircut. They would philosophize and gossip about the goings-on in the neighborhood.

BROADCAST HISTORY

ABC

September 1974–September 1975	Wednesday 8:00–8:30
September 1975–December 1975	Wednesday 8:30–9:00

CAST

Clifton Curtis	Clifton Davis
Eloise "Mama" Curtis	Theresa Merritt
Earl Chambers (1974)	Ed Bernard
Earl Chambers (1974–1975)	Theodore Wilson
Tracy Curtis Taylor (1974–1975)	Lynne Moody
Tracy Curtis Taylor (1975)	Joan Pringle
Leonard Taylor	Lisle Wilson
Wildcat	Jester Hairston
Josh	DeForest Covan
Junior	Ted Lange

The Jeffersons

First Broadcast: January 18, 1975
Last Broadcast: July 23, 1985

The Jeffersons was another spin-off of *All in the Family,* conceived by producers Norman Lear and Bud Yorkin. This team's creation of highly successful and often controversial sitcoms during the 1970s and early 1980s helped to change television history.

George and Louise Jefferson were Archie Bunker's next-door neighbors in Queens. George was an opinionated black man, just as neighbor Archie was the opinionated white bigot. In fact, the show's writers had to tone down George's racism in order to appeal to a wider audience. The Jeffersons were struggling to get by until George opened up his own dry cleaning business and achieved the American dream. Much to everyone's surprise, the store was so successful that Jefferson Cleaners became a successful chain of seven stores, giving George, Louise and son Lionel a chance to move on up out of Queens and into a high-rise apartment on Manhattan's East Side.

George was loud, sometimes overbearing, cranky and full of himself. He was vain about money, and loudly flaunted his wealth to anyone who would listen. Louise, "Weezy," was the polar opposite of her husband, more levelheaded, and a strong woman who could put her husband in his place when need be, and that was more often than not. Louise was comfortable with their newfound and well-deserved wealth, but didn't allow it to go to her head. She managed the household and her neighbors quite well, but often had to play referee between George and Florence Johnston, the Jeffersons' sassy maid.

While George found a sparring partner in Florence, Louise had to contend with feisty Mother Jefferson, a frequent, uninvited guest who would never pass up an opportunity to put Louise down and remind her that she wasn't good enough for George.

George and Weezy's son, Lionel, is the apple of his parents' eyes and the first family member to go to college. While George is extremely proud of his son's academic accomplishments, he is less pleased with Lionel's romantic involvement with Jenny Willis, daughter of upstairs neighbors Tom and Helen Willis, and the product of a mixed marriage. Politically incorrect George often referred to the Willises as "the Zebras." He didn't have a whole lot of nice things to say about English neighbor Harry Bentley or Ralph the doorman, either.

George's worst nightmare happens when Lionel marries Jenny and makes in-laws of the Willises, and grandparents of George and Louise. The show made television history when *The Jeffersons* became the first television program to feature an interracial married couple.

Broadcast History

CBS

January–August 1975	Saturdays 8:30–9:00
September 1975–October 1976	Saturday 8:00–8:30
November 1976–January 1977	Wednesday 8:00–8:30
January 1977–August 1977	Monday 8:00–8:30
September 1977–March 1978	Saturday 9:00–9:30
April–May 1978	Saturday 8:00–8:30
June–September 1978	Monday 8:00–8:30
September 1978–January 1979	Wednesday 8:00–8:30
January–March 1979	Wednesday 9:30–10:00
March–June 1979	Wednesday 8:00–8:30
June 1979–September 1982	Sunday 9:30–10:00
September 1982–December 1984	Sunday 9:00–9:30
January–March 1985	Tuesday 8:00–8:30
June–July 1985	Tuesday 8:00–8:30

CAST

George Jefferson	Sherman Hemsley
Louise Jefferson	Isabel Sanford
Lionel Jefferson (1975, 1979–1981)	Mike Evans
Lionel Jefferson (1975–1978)	Damon Evans
Tom Willis	Franklin Cover
Helen Willis	Roxie Roker
Jenny Willis	Berlinda Tolbert
Harry Bentley	Paul Benedict
Mother Olivia Jefferson	Zara Cully
Florence Johnston	Marla Gibbs
Marcus Garvey	Ernest Harden, Jr.
Ralph the Doorman	Ned Wertimer
Allan Willis	Jay Hammer
Jessica Jefferson	Ebonie Smith
Charlie	Danny Wells

One Day at a Time

First Broadcast: December 16, 1975
Last Broadcast: September 2, 1984

Like most single mothers raising two teenage daughters on their own, Ann Romano had no other choice but to take things *One Day at a Time.* Her plight was similar to that of many American women at the time. While it wasn't the first show featuring a single mother, *One Day at a Time* was the first show to revolve around the life of a divorced mother. The series was produced by sitcom genius Norman Lear, who also produced *Happy Days, Laverne & Shirley, All in the Family, The Jeffersons* and *Maude.*

This topical and controversial series introduced audiences to the recently divorced mother of two teenage girls, who after 17 years of marriage, packed up her family and moved into a small apartment in her hometown of Indianapolis. Ann didn't have the luxury of being a stay-at-home mom, and found herself not only having to cope with a divorce and two headstrong teenagers, but because money was an issue, also having to face reentering the job market. During the show's second season, Ann's life got a little easier as she landed a well-paying job as an advertising account executive.

Ann was a feminist who tried to raise her girls in an honest and straightforward manner. The show didn't ignore the tough issues, such as teen suicide, birth control, or alcoholism, or tough love. When eldest daughter Julie ran away to live with her boyfriend Chuck, Ann went to see Julie and Chuck, who were renting a dingy motel room. Julie said to Ann that she would come back home if she let her do whatever she wanted—"either I live my life, or I don't come back." After a dramatic pause, Ann tells her, "all right Julie ... DON'T COME BACK!"

While moving back home to Indianapolis had its advantages, Ann soon found out that the close proximity to her sometimes overbearing mother, who paid frequent visits to the Romano apartment, was a bit unsettling, as was the constant presence of lothario Dwayne Schneider, the building superintendent.

Needing to be more than just a parent to her children, Ann reenters the dating scene. Her love interest early in the show was David Kane, who was considerably younger than Ann. It was an ill-fated romance and didn't last.

In the 1979 season, while still in college, eldest daughter Julie married her longtime boyfriend, Max Horvath, an airline flight steward. The scripts had the newlyweds move away from Indianapolis and out of the show. In real life, actress MacKenzie Phillips had developed a serious drug problem and needed to be written out of the show for rehabilitation.

Meanwhile, in the fall of 1980, Ann quit her job and started an advertising agency with Nick Handris, a single father. Business and romance bloomed between the two, but unfortunately, Nick was killed in a car accident during the 1981–82 season. After Nick's death in 1981, his son Alex moved in with Ann and Barbara, then in 1982, younger daughter, Barbara, married dental student Mark Royer, and Julie gave birth to a daughter, Annie.

Not to be left out in the marrying game, Ann finally ended up wed to architect Sam Royer, Barbara's father-in-law. The series wrapped up in 1984 with Ann and Sam moving overseas, where Ann had received a job offer.

Broadcast History

CBS

December 1975–July 1976	Tuesday 9:30–10:00
September 1976–January 1978	Tuesday 9:30–10:00
January 1978–January 1979	Monday 9:30–10:00
January 1979–March 1979	Wednesday 9:00–9:30
March 1979–September 1982	Sunday 8:30–9:00
September 1982–March 1983	Sunday 9:30–10:00
March 1983–May 1983	Monday 9:30–10:00
June 1983–February 1984	Sunday 8:30–9:00

March 1984–May 1984	Wednesday 8:00–8:30
May 1984–August 1984	Monday 9:00–9:30
August 1984–September 1984	Sunday 8:00–8:30

CAST

Ann Romano Royer	Bonnie Franklin
Julie Cooper Horvath	Mackenzie Phillips
Barbara Cooper Royer	Valerie Bertinelli
Dwayne Schneider	Pat Harrington, Jr.
Ed Cooper	Joseph Campanella
David Kane	Richard Masur
Ginny Wrobliki	Mary Louise Wilson
Mr. Jerry Davenport	Charles Siebert
Max Horvath	Michael Lembeck
Grandma Katherine Romano	Nanette Fabray
Nick Handris	Ron Rifkin
Alex Handris	Glenn Scarpelli
Francine Webster	Shelley Fabares
Mark Royer	Boyd Gaines
Sam Royer	Howard Hesseman
Annie Horvath	Lauren Maloney

Phyllis

First Broadcast: September 8, 1975
Last Broadcast: August 30, 1977

Phyllis Lindstrom was first introduced to the television audience as Mary Richards' busybody, self-centered, self-styled, know-it-all friend and landlady on *The Mary Tyler Moore Show.* At the time, Phyllis was married to dermatologist husband Lars, and the Lindstroms were raising a preteen daughter, Bess. Bess was a gifted child, who very often seemed to be the mother of the family. Given how modern and mature Phyllis wanted the mother-daughter relationship to be, Bess called Phyllis by name rather than calling her "Mom."

In this MTM spin-off, Phyllis finds herself a widow in her mid-forties. Like Rhoda before her, Phyllis packs her bags, and with precocious Bess in tow, leaves Minneapolis for her hometown of San Francisco. Unemployed and a bit unsettled, Phyllis and Bess move in with Lars' scatter-brained mother, Audrey, and Audrey's second husband, Judge Jonathan Dexter. It's not the ideal situation, especially when Judge Dexter's 87-year-old mother also moves into the apartment. For an old broad, Mother Dexter is sharp as a tack, and takes the lead when it comes to putting Phyllis down.

Phyllis eventually finds her way into the job market as an assistant to Julie Erskine at Erskine's Commercial Photography Studio. Given her busybody temperament and lack of experience, her gainful employment is short-lived. In the second season Phyllis is hired as administrative assistant to Dan Valenti, a member of the San Francisco Board of Supervisors.

As if Phyllis doesn't have enough to contend with, Bess is now maturing, spreading her wings, and giving her mother a few unwanted gray hairs; as when Phyllis calls Bess, who is on a skiing trip, to see how she is, and a man answers the phone; or when Phyllis finds out that Bess posed nude for the school paper to protest the firing of a teacher who once bared all in a men's magazine. The final blow comes when Bess meets and falls in love with Phyllis's boss's nephew, Mark, and elopes to Las Vegas.

Broadcast History

CBS

September 1975–Janaury 1977	Monday 8:30–9:00
January 1977–July 1977	Sunday 8:30–9:00
August 1977	Tuesday 8:30–9:00

Cast

Phyllis Lindstrom	Cloris Leachman
Bess Lindstrom	Lisa Gerritsen
Julie Erskine (1975–1976)	Liz Torres
*Julie Erskine (1975)	Barbara Colby
Leo Heatherton	Richard Schaal
Audrey Dexter	Jane Rose
Judge Jonathan Dexter	Henry Jones
Sally "Mother" Dexter	Judith Lowry
Leonard Marsh	John Lawlor
Harriet Hastings	Garn Stephens
Dan Valenti	Carmine Caridi
Arthur Lanson	Burt Mustin
Mark Valenti	Craig Wasson
Van Horn, park wino	Jack Elam

*Barbara Colby, who was originally signed for the role of Julie Erskine, was murdered soon after production began and was replaced by Liz Torres.

Family

First Broadcast: March 9, 1976
Last Broadcast: June 25, 1980

Before the arrival of such affluent television families as the Ewings or the Carringtons, the conventional, melodramatic Lawrence clan of South Pasadena, California, were the family du jour. Portrayed as a typical middle-class family of their time, they lived in a beautiful old home with all the trappings of an upper middle-class life. But their comfortable lifestyle didn't make them immune to the negativities of life.

Doug Lawrence is a successful lawyer and loving father who only wants the best for his children. That's why he and his 17 year old son Willie are constantly at odds. Willie seemingly doesn't share his father's traditional work ethic and drops out of college to pursue a writing career. Wife Kate is a levelheaded, no-nonsense housewife and mother. A throwback to an earlier era, Kate is always meticulously well groomed. Letitia, whose nickname, Buddy, better fits her personality, is the preteen baby of the family. Buddy's a tomboy who prefers jeans to dresses, and her favorite mode of transportation is a skateboard. Eldest daughter Nancy is an aspiring lawyer who lives in the family guesthouse with her baby son. She moved back home after discovering her husband in bed with one of her girlfriends.

The Lawrences are a close knit bunch, and deal with a wide range of problems, both social and personal. The show was meant to depict real life and openly dealt with such issues as to homosexuality, bigotry, and abortion. Doug's temporary blindness as the result of an automobile accident and Nancy's breast cancer diagnosis are wake-up calls to the family, and to viewers, about how fragile and unpredictable life can be.

Also touched upon briefly was the fact that Kate and Doug lost a son, Timmy, in a boating accident five years before the show began. Two years into the series, the family adopted Annie, an eleven-year-old girl whose parents had been killed in an automobile accident.

Both Sada Thompson and James Broderick were veteran actors when the series began; Thompson would not consider a weekly program until she was personally asked by producer Mike Nichols to play Kate Lawrence. In 1978, she won an Emmy Award for her portrayal of Kate Lawrence. James Broderick is best known to film-goers for his performance as Alice's husband in the 1969 film *Alice's Restaurant* and his role in the mini-series *Roots.* He was the father of contemporary film star Matthew Broderick, who paid homage to his dad by prominently displaying the elder Broderick's photograph in the 1990 film *The Freshman.*

BROADCAST HISTORY

ABC

March 1976–February 1978	Tuesday 10:00–11:00
May 1978	Tuesday 10:00–11:00
September 1978–March 1979	Thursday 10:00–11:00
March 1979–April 1979	Friday 8:00–9:00
May 1979	Thursday 10:00–11:00
December 1979–February 1980	Monday 10:00–11:00
March 1980	Monday 9:00–10:00
June 1980	Wednesday 8:00–9:00

CAST

Kate Lawrence	Sada Thompson
Doug Lawrence	James Broderick
Nancy Lawrence Maitland (1976)	Elayne Heilveil
Nancy Lawrence Maitland (1976–1980)	Meredith Baxter-Birney
Willie Lawrence	Gary Frank
Letitia "Buddy" Lawrence	Kristy McNichol
Jeff Maitland	John Rubinstein
Mrs. Hanley (1976–1978)	Mary Grace Canfield
Salina Magee (1976–1977)	Season Hubley
Annie Cooper (1978–1980)	Quinn Cummings
Timmy Maitland (1978–1980)	Michael David Schackelford

Eight Is Enough

First Broadcast: March 15, 1977
Last Broadcast: August 29, 1981

Based on the book *Eight Is Enough* by Thomas Braden, the show chronicles the lives of the Bradford family of Sacramento. Tom and Joan Bradford have been married for 25 years and are devoted to each other and their eight children, ages 8 to 23, when the series began. "Never try eating nectarines since juice may dispense" is the system the Bradfords devised to remember the names of their children: Nicholas, Tommy, Elizabeth, Nancy, Susan, Joannie, Mary, and David.

Tom, the father, was a newspaper columnist for *The Sacramento Register*. Joan stayed home and raised her brood. Story lines followed the trials and tribulations of the large Bradford clan. They were a loving, tight-knit family, but with so many children of various ages and distinct personalities, things were never dull at the Bradford home. Tom and Joan taught their children to be independent thinkers from an early age, and whenever a major problem arose in one of their lives, Tom didn't preach or tell his children how to solve it. He and the child usually sat down in his home office and talked things through.

Three episodes into the first season, Diana Hyland, the actress who portrayed Joan, was forced off the show due to a terminal illness. She was written out of the remainder of the season as "being away." The third episode of the show, entitled "Pieces of Eight," was broadcast just two days after her death. The second season opened with Tom being a recent widower and having the daunting task of raising the huge family on his own. His widower status changed shortly thereafter when Tom met Sandra Sue Abbot, a school teacher who had come to the house to tutor one of the children. By the end of the year, Tom and "Abby" were married in a special two hour telecast.

While most people didn't come from such large families, the issues the Bradfords tackled each week were similar to those of all families of the time: stepparents, sibling rivalry, school, dating, and drugs. Household problems might be as simple as youngest son Nicholas' guilty conscience when bad luck seems to run in the family after he breaks a chain letter, or as complex as a family crisis when son Tommy is hospitalized for a ruptured spleen.

Throughout the show's run, the kids grew and spread their wings. Other regulars were added to the cast when son David and daughter Susan got married, Joanie got engaged, and Elizabeth considered moving in with her boyfriend.

In the late 1980s, there were two reunion specials produced, *Eight Is Enough: A Family Reunion* and *An Eight Is Enough Wedding*. Tom's wife Abby is played by Sandy Faison in the *Wedding* show. She replaced *Family Reunion's* Mary Frann, who in turn had replaced the original Abby, Betty Buckley. Interesting to also note, like *Family Reunion, An Eight Is Enough Wedding* was telecast opposite the World Series on October 15, 1989, and like the earlier film, *Wedding* won its time slot in the ratings.

Broadcast History

ABC

March 1977–May 1977	Tuesday 9:00–10:00
August 1977–March 1981	Wednesday 8:00–9:00
March 1981–August 1981	Saturday 8:00–9:00

Cast

Tom Bradford	Dick Van Patten
Joan Bradford (1977)	Diana Hyland
Sandra Sue "Abby" Abbott Bradford	Betty Buckley
Nicholas Bradford (age 8)	Adam Rich
Tommy Bradford (age 14)	Willie Aames
Elizabeth Bradford (age 15)	Connie Needham Newton
Nancy Bradford (age 18)	Dianne Kay
Susan Bradford Stockwell (age 19)	Susan Richardson
Joannie Bradford (age 20)	Laurie Walters
Mary Bradford (age 21)	Lani O'Grady
David Bradford (Pilot Only)	Mark Hamill
David Bradford (age 23)	Grant Goodeve
Dr. Greg "Doc" Maxwell (1977–1979)	Michael Thoma
Daisy Maxwell (1977–1979)	Virginia Vincent
Donna (1978–1981)	Jennifer Darling
Merle "The Pearl" Stockwell (1979–1981)	Brian Patrick Clarke
Janet Bradford (1979–1981)	Joan Prather
Ernie Fields (1979–1981)	Michael Goodrow
Jeffrey Trout (1980–1981)	Nicholas Pryor
Jeremy Andretti (1980–1981)	Ralph Macchio

Soap

First Broadcast: September 13, 1977
Last Broadcast: April 20, 1981

While most family-oriented television shows in the late '70s were attempting to portray "normal" households with relatable plots, *Soap* took this concept to the extreme, and the show was nearly canceled before it even hit the air. Touted to be a satire on soap operas, story lines ran the gamut from the contentious to the ridiculous. ABC affiliates were picketed for planning to run the show, religious groups were up in arms, and the network received a myriad of hate mail. Controversial as it was, once the show hit the prime time schedule, it quickly gained a loyal audience.

Jessica Tate and Mary Campbell were sisters, living in Dunn's River, Connecticut. Jessica was as naive and ditzy as Mary was levelheaded and down-to-earth. Jessica was married to Chester, a wealthy, successful, philandering businessman. The Tates had three children, adult daughters Corinne, a sexpot; quiet and conservative Eunice; and Billy, a 14 year old spoiled brat. Rounding out the household were Jessica's shell-shocked father, "The Major," who always wore his old Army uniform from World War II because in his mind, the war was still being fought, and Benson, the family's disrespectful and outspoken black servant. His last name was never mentioned during the run of *Soap*, but was established as DuBois in the spinoff series, *Benson*. When Benson left the series, he was replaced by another butler, Sanders, played by actor Roscoe Lee Browne.

Across town, the blue-collar Campell clan was comprised of Burt, Mary's construction worker second husband; Mary's two sons, Jodie and Danny; and Burt's natural son, Chuck/Bob, so-named because Chuck and his ventriloquist dummy Bob were inseparable. Burt's son Jodie was a homosexual and the first outwardly gay character to appear on network television. Danny, who worked with his stepfather, was involved with organized crime. In the show's first episode, Burt had another natural son, Peter, a tennis pro, played by actor Robert Urich, who was quickly murdered off the series by Chester Tate. It's also mentioned in the show's first episode that Burt killed Mary's first husband.

Neither the Tate nor Campbell household could be considered normal by any stretch of the imagination, and mayhem was always the order of the day. Regularly the center of catastrophe was Jessica. When she had a problem, everybody got mixed up in it. Subject matter included murder, uninhibited sex, alien abduction, racketeering, homosexuality, infidelity, impotence, mental illness and even exorcism, when Corinne marries an ex-priest and gives birth to a baby possessed by the devil.

The series went off the air with a literal BANG. Jessica is taken hostage by her lover El Puerco's enemies, and faces a firing squad.

Broadcast History

ABC

September 1977–March 1978	Tuesday 9:30–10:00
September 1978–March 1979	Thursday 9:30–10:00
September 1979–March 1980	Thursday 9:30–10:00
October 1980–January 1981	Wednesday 9:30–10:00
March 1981–April 1981	Monday 10:00–11:00

Cast

Chester Tate	Robert Mandan
Jessica Tate	Katherine Helmond

Corrine Tate (1977–1980)	Diana Canova
Eunice Tate	Jennifer Salt
Billy Tate	Jimmy Baio
Benson (1977–1979)	Robert Guillaume
The Major	Arthur Peterson
Mary Dallas Campbell	Cathryn Damon
Burt Campbell	Richard Mulligan
Jodie Dallas	Billy Crystal
Danny Dallas	Ted Wass
The Godfather (1977–1978)	Richard Libertini
Claire (1977–1978)	Kathryn Reynolds
Peter Campbell (1977)	Robert Urich
Chuck/Bob Campbell	Jay Johnson
Dennis Phillips (1978)	Bob Seagren
Father Timothy Flotsky (1978–1979)	Sal Viscuso
Carol David (1978–1981)	Rebecca Balding
Elaine Lefkowitz (1978–1979)	Dinah Manoff
Dutch (1978–1981)	Donnelly Rhodes
Sally (1978–1979)	Caroline McWilliams
Detective Donahue (1978–1980)	John Byner
Alice (1979)	Randee Heller
Mrs. David (1979–1981)	Peggy Hope
Millie (1979)	Candace Azzara
Leslie Walker (1979–1981)	Marla Pennington
Polly Dawson (1979–1981)	Lynne Moody
Saunders (1980–1981)	Roscoe Lee Brown
Dr. Alan Posner (1980–1981)	Allan Miller
Attorney E. Ronald Mallu (1978–1981)	Eugene Roche
Carlos "El Puerco" Valdez (1980–1981)	Gregory Sierra
Maggie Chandler (1980–1981)	Barbara Rhoades
Gwen (1980–1981)	Jesse Welles

Diff'rent Strokes

First Broadcast: November 3, 1978
Last Broadcast: August 30, 1986

Wealthy widower Phillip Drummond was the president of Trans

Allied, Inc. in New York. He shared a huge, posh Park Avenue apartment with his teenage daughter, Kimberly. When it was found out that their longtime housekeeper was dying, Drummond promised to her that he'd look after her two young sons, Willis and Arnold. That didn't mean he'd keep a watchful eye on them from afar. Suddenly, two little black kids from Harlem found themselves leaving their familiar surroundings, moving into the Drummond apartment and living the good life.

It wasn't an easy transition. In the series' first episode, called *Moving In*, Drummond welcomed eight-year-old Arnold and twelve-year-old Willis into his lavish penthouse. Willis was suspicious and reserved, while Arnold, whose favorite catch phrase was, "What'chu talkin' 'bout Willis?," was eager to embrace his new lifestyle. Overanxious to make them feel at home, Drummond showered them with gifts and love — and was puzzled when he learned that the boys were planning to sneak from the lap of luxury back to Harlem. To the streetwise brothers the wealthy, white lifestyle was shockingly foreign. Drummond was eager to meet the boys' needs and keep them happy and had his heart in the right place, and while the cultural differences kept things on the edge for the first few episodes, it didn't take long before the boys began feeling more at home.

Not being able to handle the newly formed family on his own, Phillip hired a new housekeeper, Edna Garrett. Mrs. Garrett not only became indispensable to the running of the house, but became a surrogate mother to all three children.

As the series progressed, new characters were introduced while others departed. Mrs. Garrett made the move to her own spinoff, *The Facts of Life*, becoming the housemother at Eastland, the prestigious girl's school that Kimberly attended. It took two housekeepers to replace her. Then, in the 1984 season, Phillip met and fell in love with television show host Maggie McKinney. Maggie had a young son, Sam, and when she and Phillip tied the knot and moved in, Arnold and Willis got a new little brother.

No matter how the family dynamics might have changed, there was always a lot of love around and a few life lessons to be learned, for both the children and the adults. In one episode, Mr. Drummond's socialite snobbish mother arrives and finds that there is a lot she doesn't like about her son's new sons, but she soon learns a valuable lesson about what's really important in a person.

Among the show's many guest stars, then first lady Nancy Reagan appeared in a 1983 episode dealing with drug abuse.

BROADCAST HISTORY

November 1978–October 1979	NBC Friday 8:00–8:30
October 1979–October 1981	NBC Wednesday 9:00–9:30
October 1981–August 1982	NBC Thursday 9:00–9:30
August 1982–August 1985	NBC Saturday 8:00–8:30
September 1985–March 1986	ABC Friday 9:00–9:30
June 1986–August 1986	ABC Saturday 8:00–8:30

CAST

Philip Drummond	Conrad Bain
Arnold Jackson	Gary Coleman
Willis Jackson	Todd Bridges
Kimberly Drummond	Dana Plato
Mrs. Edna Garrett	Charlotte Rae
Adelaide Brubaker	Nedra Volz
Pearl Gallagher	Mary Jo Catlett
Aunt Sophia	Dody Goodman
Dudley Ramsey	Shavar Ross
Mr. Ted Ramsey	Le Tari
Miss Chung	Rosalind Chao
Charlene DuPrey	Janet Jackson
Robbie Jason	Steven Mond
Lisa Hayes	Nikki Swassy
Sam McKinney	Danny Cooksey
Maggie McKinney (1984–1985)	Dixie Carter
Maggie McKinney (1985–1986)	Mary Ann Mobley
Charlie	Jason Hervey

Dallas

First Broadcast: April 2, 1978
Last Broadcast: May 3, 1991

The opulent Southfork Ranch on the outskirts of Dallas was the setting for this prime time soap opera that took the nation by storm. The Ewing family were the players who kept viewers on the edge of their seats for an amazing 13 seasons.

Southfork was owned by wealthy patriarch Jock Ewing, a crusty oil wildcatter who, in his youth, struck it rich. He went into business for himself, and soon his business acumen as the president and CEO of Ewing Oil turned his newfound venture into a multimillion dollar company. Jock was married to Eleanor Southworth for more than 40 years when the series began. Miss Ellie was the daughter of a rich land baron and owner of Southfork Ranch. She and Jock have three grown sons, two of which are still living at home on the range. J.R., the eldest, is a chip off his father's block. He's ruthless, cunning and power hungry. J.R. is married to ex-beauty queen Sue Ellen, who throughout the series becomes increasingly unstable and excessively alcoholic due to J.R.'s philandering and mean spirit. She and J.R. have one son, John Ross III, born in the series's second season. Despite his infidelity and cruel behavior towards his wife, J.R. is a loyal son to Miss Ellie and Jock, and a devoted father to his son and heir, John Ross.

Gary, the middle brother, is a bit of a disappointment to his father. He never acquired the drive or the strong will of his siblings, and moved away from the ranch after marrying wife Valene, a lower-class lass that Jock and J.R. didn't approve of. Gary and Valene have one daughter, man-hungry temptress Lucy, who was left at Southfork for Jock and Miss Ellie to raise.

Bobby is the baby of the family. He not only has his father's strength and drive, but also his mother's conscience, which sets him apart from back-stabbing J.R. Early in the first season, Bobby brings home a wife, Pamela Barnes. Pamela is sweet, beautiful, smart, and the daughter of Digger Barnes, Jock's bitter ex-partner and the man he swindled out of both his share of the company and the hand of Miss Ellie. Pamela's brother, Cliff, is an assistant district attorney, who makes it his life's work to avenge his father's ruination by the Ewings by trying to expose Ewing Oil's illegal business practices.

Dealing with numerous acts of adultery, shady business practices, sibling rivalry and unhappy marriages, intrigue was just part of everyday life for the Ewings, but the revelation of Jock's illegitimate son, Ray Krebs, who worked as a hired hand on Southfork since he was a teenager, was one of the biggest blows the family had to face. Ray was floored to find out that Jock, a *father figure* to him, was actually his father. After getting over the betrayal, Miss Ellie embraced Ray as one of her own. Bobby and Gary also welcomed Ray with open arms, but J.R. saw Ray as a threat to his inheritance, and set out to make Ray's life miserable in the hopes he'd disinherit himself.

Throughout the show's run, infidelity, corruption, and revenge kept viewers coming back for more. Bobby and Pam's marriage succumbed to J.R.'s plots to pull them apart; Ray Krebs rose from hired hand to independent rancher; Sue Ellen fought alcoholism and was then critically injured in a car accident; J.R. and Sue Ellen divorced, then remarried;

Bobby was dead for an entire season, then came back out of nowhere, as if his demise was only a dream, but the cliffhanger episode that garnered the most ratings was "Who Shot J.R.?" at the end of the 1979–1980 season.

As we all know, only the good die young, and J.R. recovered to wreak havoc for many more years to come. Just when viewers thought he would never get his due, the show's finale has J.R. drunk and contemplating suicide. Suddenly, an angel named Adam appears, and, à la *It's A Wonderful Life*, shows J.R. how life for everyone around him would have been had he never been born. At the end of the revelation, Adam's eyes glow devilishly red. J.R. is seen picking up a pistol and viewers hear the gun go off. An alarmed Bobby bursts into the room. Shock registers on his face, and he alone learns the fate of his brother, because at that moment, the screen fades to black, leaving millions of frustrated viewers wondering what actually happened.

Broadcast History

CBS

April 1978	Sunday 10:00–11:00
September 1978–October 1978	Saturday 10:00–11:00
October 1978–January 1979	Sunday 10:00–11:00
January 1979–November 1981	Friday 10:00–11:00
December 1981–May 1985	Friday 9:00–10:00
September 1985–May 1986	Friday 9:00–10:00
September 1986–May 1988	Friday 9:00–10:00
October 1988–March 1990	Friday 9:00–10:00
March 1990–May 1990	Friday 10:00–11:00
November 1990–December 1990	Friday 10:00–11:00
January 1991–May 1991	Friday 9:00–10:00

Cast

John Ross (J.R.) Ewing, Jr	Larry Hagman
Eleanor Southworth (Miss Ellie) Ewing (1978–1984, 1985–1990)	Barbara Bel Geddes
Eleanor Southworth (Miss Ellie) Ewing (1984–1985)	Donna Reed
John Ross (Jock) Ewing (1978–1981)	Jim Davis
Bobby Ewing (1978–1985, 1986–1991)	Patrick Duffy
Pamela Barnes Ewing (1978–1987)	Victoria Principal

Lucy Ewing Cooper (1978–1985, 1988–1990)	Charlene Tilton
Sue Ellen Ewing (1978–1989)	Linda Gray
Ray Krebbs (1978–1988)	Steve Kanaly
Cliff Barnes	Ken Kercheval
Willard "Digger" Barnes (1978)	David Wayne
Willard "Digger" Barnes (1979–1980)	Keenan Wynn
Gary Ewing (1978–1979)	David Ackroyd
Gary Ewing (1979–1981)	Ted Shackelford
Valene Ewing (1978–1981)	Joan Van Ark
Kristin Shepard (1979–1981)	Mary Crosby
Dusty Farlow (1979–1982, 1985)	Jared Martin
Donna Culver Krebbs (1979–1987)	Susan Howard
Harve Smithfield	George O. Petrie
Vaughn Leland (1979–1984)	Dennis Patrick
Connie (1979–1981)	Jeanna Michaels
Louella (1979–1981)	Megan Gallagher
Jordan Lee (1979–1990)	Don Starr
Mitch Cooper (1979–1982)	Leigh McCloskey
John Ross Ewing III (1980–1983)	Tyler Banks
John Ross Ewing III (1983–1991)	Omri Katz
Punk Anderson (1980–1987)	Morgan Woodward
Afton Cooper (1981–1984, 1989)	Audrey Landers
Arliss Cooper (1981)	Anne Francis
Clint Ogden (1981)	Monte Markham
Leslie Stewart (1981)	Susan Flannery
Rebecca Wentworth (1981–1983)	Priscilla Pointer
Jeremy Wendell (1981, 1984–1988)	William Smithers
Clayton Farlow (1981–1991)	Howard Keel
Katherine Wentworth (1981–1984)	Morgan Brittany
Holly Harwood (1982–1984)	Lois Chiles
Mickey Trotter (1982–1983)	Timothy Patrick Murphy
Walt Driscoll (1982–1983)	Ben Piazza
Mark Graison (1983–1984, 1985–1986)	John Beck
Aunt Lil Trotter (1983–1984)	Kate Reid
Jenna Wade (1983–1988)	Priscilla Presley
Charlie Wade (1983–1988)	Shalane McCall
Jessica Montfort (1984, 1990)	Alexis Smith

Mandy Winger (1984–1987)	Deborah Shelton
Jamie Ewing Barnes (1984–1986)	Jenilee Harrison
Christopher Ewing (1984–1991)	Joshua Harris
Jack Ewing (1985–1987)	Dack Rambo
Angelico Nero (1985–1986)	Barbara Carrera
Dr. Jerry Kenderson (1985–1986)	Barry Jenner
Matt Cantrell (1986)	Marc Singer

The Dukes of Hazzard

First Broadcast: January 26, 1979
Last Broadcast: August 16, 1985

Cousins Luke, Bo and Daisy Mae Duke of Hazzard County lived on the farm that had been in the Duke family for five generations. While no state was ever mentioned, Hazzard county was located "east of the Mississippi and south of the Ohio." The cousins were raised by their Uncle Jesse, one of the best moonshine runners in all of Hazzard. Bo and Luke continued in Uncle Jesse's footsteps until they were caught while making a run. Uncle Jesse made a deal with the government that the Dukes would never make or run any moonshine again if Bo and Luke could stay out of jail, so the boys were put on probation. Terms of the probation said that they couldn't cross the state line without permission or use any firearms. Undaunted, the boys built a racing car called the General Lee, a 1969 Dodge Charger that was the fastest car in all of Hazzard. The General Lee may have been just a car to some, but to the Dukes, it was considered to be a member of the family. Surprisingly, the car actually got half of all the fan mail sent to the show.

Luke was the elder and more rational Duke boy. He is the one who usually came up with the ideas to get out of trouble. Bo was the younger, and drove the General Lee. A daredevil at heart, he was always willing to jump the General Lee no matter the distance, once jumping 32 cars. Bo was always friendly and outgoing but quite naive at times. Daisy Mae could shoot like Annie Oakley and drive like Richard Petty, and knew the words to every Dolly Parton song. She was always there to help the boys get out of trouble. Uncle Jesse ran the farm and offered sage advice to the boys, and everyone in Hazzard respected him. The Duke family's nemesis was the corrupt politician, Boss Hogg, whose equally corrupt and dimwitted brother-in-law, Sheriff Coltrane, was always trying to arrest a Duke.

The series, classified as a comedy/adventure, featured moonshine running, car chases and wrecks (nearly 300 look-alike General Lees were sacrificed during the filming of the series), and scantily dressed sexy, young women. The show went into the top ten in the second season, creating a merchandising franchise, and Waylon Jennings got a top 40 hit with the title theme. The show had product sales up to $200 million annually, which included more than 400 different products. Toy General Lees outsold Rubik's Cube as one of the most popular toys of the time.

In the spring of 1982, Tom Wopat and John Schneider left the show for most of the fifth season as the result of a contract dispute over salaries and shares of merchandising rights and royalties. Their absence on the show was explained by saying that Bo and Luke left the county to try their luck on the NASCAR racing circuit. Taking their place were Byron Cherry and Christopher Mayer as Coy and Vance Duke, long lost cousins returning to help Uncle Jesse run the farm. The show's ratings suffered and the following February, Tom Wopat and John Schneider came back to the show after their battle for more money and better story lines.

The show was canceled in 1985. At the time, Schneider says he couldn't believe the network canceled the popular show in 1985 after six years on the air. "When the show was canceled, we were a top 20 show," he says. "I didn't believe for a second that this show was gone. I didn't believe that anybody could be that inept."

Wopat put it another way. "You know, Warner Brothers was a great company, but I don't think they really ever understood [the show], and I know CBS didn't," he says. "I mean, William Paley was running the network then and he just said, 'I haven't a clue why this is a hit.'"

In 1996, the Nashville Network started running the Dukes with a huge success, and in 1997 CBS aired a brand new reunion movie. On April 26, 1981, with two *Dukes of Hazzard* reruns, the Dukes became number one and number two in the ratings for that week. CBS executives were perplexed that what they had considered the be the worst show on television could have gotten such great ratings.

Broadcast History

CBS

January 1979–November 1981	Friday 9:00–10:00
December 1981–February 1985	Friday 8:00–9:00
June 1985–August 1985	Friday 8:00–9:00

Cast

Beauregard "Bo" Duke (1979–1982, 1983–1985)	John Schneider
Lucas K. "Luke" Duke (1979–1982, 1983–1985)	Tom Wopat

Uncle Jesse Duke	Denver Pyle
Daisy Duke	Catherine Bach
Jefferson Davis "Boss" Hogg	Sorrell Booke
Lulu Coltrane Hogg	Peggy Rhea
Deputy Cletus Hogg (1980–1983)	Rick Hurst
Deputy Enos Strate (1979–1980, 1982–1985)	Sonny Schroyer
Sheriff Rosco P. Coltrane	James Best
Cooter Davenport	Ben Jones
Coy Duke (1982–1983)	Byron Cherry
Vance Duke (1982–1983)	Christopher Mayer
Sheriff Edward Thomas (1981–1984)	Don Pedro Colley
Little Miss Emma Tizdale (1981–1983)	Nedra Volz
Ace Parker	Jerry Rushing
Jamie Lee Hogg	Jonathan Frakes
Jeb Stuart Duke	Christopher Hensel
Hughie Hogg	Jeff Altman
Emery Potter	Charlie Dell
Sheriff Grady Byrd	Dick Sargent
Sheriff Buster Moon	James Hampton
Nancy Lou	Kim Richards
Benny "The Quill"	Boyd Bodwell
Mama Coltrane	Lucille Benson
Finchburg County Sheriff	Ross Elliott
The Balladeer	Waylon Jennings

5

The 1980s

The Energizer Bunny was banging his way across the screen, and in answer to the now-famous question, "Where's The Beef?" TV viewers were inundated with images of women's posteriors donning the Sassoon and Jordache logos of the oh-so-popular designer jeans that were a must for any well-dressed TV viewer.

Cable television networks were spreading across the country. Many viewers were defecting to the new "commercial-free offerings" and specialty channels offered. For the first time in history, television was competing against itself. The introduction of fiber optics and the near-incredible progress of cable technology led to the appearance of several new channels in 1984–85, including The Disney Channel, Lifetime, Playboy, Financial News Network, The Weather Channel, Discovery Channel, Home Shopping Network, Nashville Network, Arts & Entertainment, American Movie Classics, regional sports channels and pay-per-view. By 1985, 6,600 cable systems were serving nearly 42 million homes.

New trends in commercial television were emerging as well. Following in the footsteps of the highly acclaimed *Dallas*, nighttime soap operas were all the rage. *Dynasty, Falcon Crest* and *Dallas* spin-off *Knots Landing* were keeping viewers glued to their seats. People who used to laugh at those hooked on the daytime serials were now eating their words.

The other craze happening on the small screen was the advent of reality shows. Not quite as "real" as *Survivor* or *The Real World* would become in the new millennium, these were shows that set out to reflect the real world. It all started in 1979 with producer George Schlatter's *Real People,* a show that starred "real people" with offbeat professions, hobbies and interests. Among them were a man who ate soil, a man who went though life walking backwards and a sexy lady truck driver. That show was closely

The denizens of Falcon Crest, headed by matriarch Angela Channing (Jane Wyman), demonstrated to the power driven masses that the excesses of money and power don't necesarily buy happiness. Robert Foxworth and Susan Sullivan, Jamie Rose and William R. Moses portrayed Angela's relatives and rivals, the long suffering Gioberti family, while Abby Dalton and Margaret Ladd starred as the Channing daughters.

followed by such offerings as ABC's blatant imitation, *That's Incredible, Ripley's Believe It Or Not,* and *TV's Bloopers and Practical Jokes.* The most enduring show in the reality genre was the police documentary, *Cops. USA Today* described the show as being "real cops chasing real criminals down real streets." Between bodies being pulled out of the water and the scantily clad hookers, nothing was left to the imagination.

The all–American family was changing as well. Bill Cosby became television's super dad as Cliff Huxtable in *The Cosby Show.* The show remained in the top ten throughout its eight year run, five of those years being in the number one position. The denizens of *Full House* were an unlikely but loving family (of sorts), with three young males raising three young girls. *Roseanne*, a descendant of the blue-collar TV families of the past, really gave viewers a dose of "realism," and following in the footsteps of *The Flintstones* and *The Jetsons, The Simpsons* (a spin-off of *The Tracey Ullman Show*) brought about an updated cartoon family for the adults, as well as the kids, to chuckle over.

Too Close for Comfort

First Broadcast: November 11, 1980
Last Broadcast: September 15, 1983

Just when you gleefully think the kids are finally old enough to move away and get their own apartment, they move downstairs instead. Such was the fate of Henry and Muriel Rush.

Based on the British television series *Keep It in the Family*, the sitcom featured Henry as a conservative professional illustrator, most famous for his "Cosmic Cow" comic strip. Muriel had been a band singer in her single days and now worked as a free-lance photographer. The Rush family lived in San Francisco in the upstairs apartment of a two-story house. When their college-aged daughters wanted to be out on their own, they talked their dad into letting them move into the downstairs apartment. At first, Henry thought this was a good idea. The girls were technically out of the house, and out of his way, but not so far away that he couldn't keep a watchful eye on them. The downside to the plan was that Henry often didn't like what his watchful eye saw.

Jackie was the more sedate of the two girls, and worked as a bank teller, while bubbly sister Sara was a freshman in college. Sara's outrageous friend, Monroe Ficus, spent a lot of time at the Rush house, and was a constant irritant to Henry. Also responsible for raising Henry's blood pressure were Muriel's nagging mother, Iris, his publisher, Mr. Wainwright, and Mildred Rafkin, the caustic sister of the former downstairs tenant.

The Rush family experienced many of the same problems that all families with free-spirited daughters of the era went through. The size of the immediate family increased with the arrival of April, Henry's hippie niece from Delaware, who stayed with the family for a year. Muriel's pregnancy at age 42, resulting in the birth of a son, Andrew, also altered the family dynamic. Throughout all the turmoil, Henry's hand puppet, Cosmic Cow, lent a sympathetic ear.

The plot changed and so did the name of the series in April 1986. Henry had the opportunity to purchase 49 percent of a weekly newspaper, *The Marin Bugler*, and he, Muriel and Andrew moved to a new home in Mill Valley, north of San Francisco, to be close to his new place of employment. Monroe was still around attempting to help out at the *Bugler*, but Sara and Jackie were written out of the show in the guise of finally being out on their own.

The Ted Knight Show, as the new venture was aptly named, was scheduled to go into its second season of production when its star, Ted Knight, who had been sick with complications from cancer for several months, passed away during the summer of 1986.

Broadcast History

ABC

November 1980–September 1982	Tuesday 9:30–10:00
September 1982–June 1983	Thursday 9:00–9:30
August 1983–September 1983	Thursday 8:30–9:00
September 1983	Thursday 8:00–8:30

Cast

Henry Rush	Ted Knight
Muriel Rush	Nancy Dussault
Jackie Rush (1980–1985)	Deborah Van Valkenburgh
Sara Rush (1980–1985)	Lydia Cornell
Monroe Ficus	JM J. Bullock
Iris Martin	Audrey Meadows
Arthur Wainwright (1981)	Hamilton Camp
Mildred Rafkin (1980–1982)	Selma Diamond
April Rush (1981–1982)	Deena Freeman
Brad Turner (1982)	Jordan Suffin
Andrew Rush (1983–1984)	William & Michael Cannon
Andrew Rush (1984–1986)	Joshua Goodwin
Lisa Flores (1986)	Lisa Antille
Hope Stinson (1986)	Pat Carroll

Falcon Crest

First Broadcast: December 4, 1981
Last Broadcast: May 17, 1990

Catching the wave of other popular prime time soap operas, the denizens of Falcon Crest Winery in California's mythical Tuscany Valley were just as cunning and dysfunctional as the other rich and powerful television families of the day.

Angela Channing was the family matriarch, and owner of the business. She ran the Falcon Crest Winery with the precision of a drill sergeant, and ran her family in much the same way. Grown daughters Julia and Emma, along with Julia's playboy son, Lance, shared the palatial estate, as did Angela's trusted servant, Chao-Li. Angela was feared, loathed and respected by everyone in Tuscany. Her vast holdings and position were challenged when her late brother's son, Chase Gioberti, inherited fifty acres of the family vineyards from his father, who was accidentally killed by Angela's daughter, Emma. Chase, wife Maggie and their two children, Cole and Victoria, moved west from New York to Falcon Crest so he could properly manage his property. This did not set well with Angela, and she and Chase were constantly at odds, especially at the close of the first season when Chase gained control of Falcon Crest in a complicated legal maneuver. Additionally, Chase's good guy persona won him the position of county supervisor.

Rounding out the immediate family was Richard Channing. The son of Angela's ex-husband, Douglas, Richard came to San Francisco to run *The Globe* newspaper, 50 percent of which was left to him by his late father. The other 50 percent of the paper was owned by Angela's daughters. Richard was, for all intents and purposes, the ruthless male villain of the group, as power hungry as Angela and with fewer scruples. According to Richard, Angela told more lies than the devil himself, but that seemed to be the pot calling the kettle black.

The show encompassed all the necessary intrigue, fighting and contentious behavior to keep it a hit for nine seasons. People were murdered, swindled, spied upon and bombed. Power plays were the order of the day, both on and off screen, as many of Hollywood's biggest stars vied for a coveted guest appearance. Lana Turner, Rod Taylor, Cliff Robertson, Cesar Romero, Kim Novak, Eve Arden, Celeste Holm, Gina Lollobrigida and Robert Stack were but a handful of illustrious celebrities who won juicy roles on the series.

The final words of the series were uttered by iron-willed Angela Channing as she and Chase step outside to a porch overlooking Falcon Crest during Richard and Lauren's wedding. Waxing nostalgic about her years of manipulation and skullduggery to keep the Falcon Crest winery in her control, she raises her champagne glass and says, "A toast to you, Falcon Crest, and long may you live."

Broadcast History

CBS

December 1981–May 1985	Friday 10:00–11:00
September 1985–March 1990	Friday 10:00–11:00
April 1990–May 1990	Thursday 9:00–10:00

Cast

Angela Gioberti Channing	Jane Wyman
Chase Gioberti (1981–87)	Robert Foxworth
Maggie Gioberti Channing (1981–89)	Susan Sullivan
Lance Cumson	Lorenzo Lamas
Tony Cumson (1981–82, 1986–88)	John Saxon
Cole Gioberti (1981–86)	William R. Moses
Victoria Gioberti Hogan (1981–83)	Jamie Rose
Victoria Gioberti Hogan Stavros (1986–88)	Dana Sparks
Julia Cumson (1981–86)	Abby Dalton
Phillip Erikson (1981–84)	Mel Ferrer
Emma Channing (1981–89)	Margaret Ladd
Douglas Channing (1981–82)	Stephen Elliott
Chao-Li	Chao-Li Chi
Melissa Agretti Cumson Gioberti (1982–88)	Ana-Alicia
Richard Channing (1982–1990)	David Selby
Diana Hunter (1982–83)	Shannon Tweed
Nick Hogan (1982–83)	Roy Thinnes
Jacqueline Perrault (1982–83)	Lana Turner
Dr. Michael Ranson (1983–84)	Cliff Robertson
Terry Hartford Ranson (1983–86)	Laura Johnson
Francesca Gioberti (1984)	Gina Lollobrigida
Cassandra Wilder (1985)	Anne Archer
Jordan Roberts (1985–86)	Morgan Fairchild
Father Christopher (1985–86)	Ken Olin
Peter Stavros (1985–87)	Cesar Romero
Jeff Wainwright (1986)	Edward Albert
Kit Marlowe (1986–87)	Kim Novak
Dan Fixx (1986–88)	Brett Cullen

Roland Saunders (1987)	Robert Stack
John Remick (1987–88)	Ed Marinaro
Nicole Sauget (1987)	Leslie Caron
Madame Malec (1987–88)	Ursula Andress
Beth Everdene (1987–88)	Mary Ann Mobley
Carly Fixx (1988)	Mariska Hargitay
Frank Agretti (1988–90)	Rod Taylor
Pilar Ortega Cumson (1988–90)	Kristian Alfonso
Michael Sharpe (1989–90)	Gregory Harrison
Anne Bowen (1990)	Susan Blakely
Phillip Tindall (1987–1989)	Stanley Ralph Ross

Dynasty

First Broadcast: January 12, 1981
Last Broadcast: May 11, 1989

Even though *Dynasty* was originally going to be called *Oil*, the setting for this extremely popular nighttime soap opera was Denver and not Dallas. The show was known as a glorious television fairy tale, replete with beautiful people, fancy cars, opulent mansions, shoulder pads, big hair, and money to burn. Its primary focus was the emotional triangle involving Blake Carrington, a wealthy oil tycoon, his former wife Alexis and his present, much younger, wife, Krystle.

To outsiders, debonaire Blake Carrington had it made. He had a beautiful young wife and three grown children, Fallon, Adam and Steven. But behind closed doors, things were not exactly as they seemed. The Carrington children, relatives, friends, and business partners and business rivals, the Colbys, all caused their share of grief to Blake.

When the series began, Carrington's empire was on the verge of collapse, and his wife was unhappy because even though she was his former secretary and thought she knew him quite well, she was shocked to find out that he treated her as a mere possession. To make family matters even worse, Fallon was spoiled and mean spirited, and Steven was gay. The end of the first season found Blake on trial for the murder of his son Steven's male lover, and as if that wasn't bad enough, Blake's first wife and Steven's mother, the glamorous Alexis, made a memorable surprise entrance at the trial and stayed for the remainder of the series, making life miserable not only for Blake, but for Krystal as well.

The Carrington family faced the usual soap opera fare, of murder, treachery, kidnapping, amnesia, pregnancy, and infidelity. The show was criticized for having both weak and absurd plots, including the resurrection of both Fallon and Steven, who had been killed and were then brought back to life in the show's later seasons.

Dynasty, which emphasized beauty, wealth, and glamour to the extreme, had its ups and downs as far as ratings were concerned. It premiered as a three hour movie, and quickly rose to one of the top five rated programs. After being ranked number one in the 1984–85 season, *Dynasty* started to flail, and by its final season, *Dynasty* tied for fifty-seventh place, and was unceremoniously dumped by the network. Two years later, a TV movie tied up all the loose plot lines left dangling when the show was canceled.

From 1985 to 1987, *Dynasty* had a spin-off show called *Dynasty II—The Colbys*, which lasted for two seasons.

Broadcast History

ABC

January 1981–April 1981	Monday 9:00–10:00
July 1981–September 1983	Wednesday 10:00–11:00
September 1983–May 1984	Wednesday 9:00–10:00
August 1984–May 1986	Wednesday 9:00–10:00
September 1986–May 1987	Wednesday 9:00–10:00
September 1987–March 1988	Wednesday 10:00–11:00
November 1988–May 1989	Wednesday 10:00–11:00

Cast

Blake Carrington	John Forsythe
Krystle Jennings Carrington	Linda Evans
Alexis Carrington Colby	Joan Collins
Fallon Carrington Colby (1981–1984)	Pamela Sue Martin
Fallon Carrington Colby (1985, 1987–1989)	Emma Samms
Steven Carrington (1981–1982)	Al Corley
Steven Carrington (1982–1988)	Jack Coleman
Adam Carrington/ Michael Torrance (1982–1989)	Gordon Thomson
Cecil Colby (1981–1982)	Lloyd Bochner
Jeff Colby (1981–1985, 1987–1989)	John James
Claudia Blaisdel (1981–1986)	Pamela Bellwood
Matthew Blaisdel (1981)	Bo Hopkins
Lindsay Blaisdel (1981)	Katy Kurtzman

Walter Lankershim (1981)	Dale Robertson
Jeannette	Virginia Hawkins
Joseph Anders (1981–1983)	Lee Bergere
Kirby (1982–1984)	Kathleen Beller
Andrew Laird (1981–1984)	Peter Mark Richman
Sammy Jo Dean	Heather Locklear
Michael Culhane (1981, 1986–1987)	Wayne Northrop
Dr. Nick Toscanni (1981–1982)	James Farentino
Mark Jennings (1982–1984)	Geoffrey Scott
Congressman Neal McEane (1982–1984, 1987)	Paul Burke
Chris Deegan (1983)	Grant Goodeve
Tracy Kendall (1983–1984)	Deborah Adair
Farnsworth "Dex" Dexter (1983–1989)	Michael Nader
Peter de Vilbis (1983–1984)	Helmut Berger
Amanda Carrington (1984–1986)	Catherine Oxenberg
Amanda Carrington (1986–1987)	Karen Cellini
Dominique Deveraux (1984–1987)	Diahann Carroll
Gerard (1984–1989)	William Beckley
Gordon Wales (1984–1988)	James Sutorius
Luke Fuller (1984–1985)	William Campbell
Nicole Simpson (1984–1985)	Susan Scannell
Charles (1984–1985)	George DiCenzo
Daniel Reece (1984–1985)	Rock Hudson
Lady Ashley Mitchell (1985)	Ali MacGraw
Danny Carrington (1985–1988)	Jameson Sampley
Joel Abrigore (1985–1986)	George Hamilton
Garrett Boydston (1985–1986)	Ken Howard

Family Ties

First Broadcast: September 22, 1982
Last Broadcast: September 17, 1989

Family Ties followed the lives of the Keaton family of Columbus, Ohio. Patriarch Steven Keaton and wife Elyse were children of the '60s. One-time flower children, they are now staunch liberals in a staunchly conservative era. They try to raise their children with an open mind, an open heart and a great deal of idealism. Steven manages a public television station, WKS-TV, and Elyse is an architect and community activist. Eldest daughter Mallory, 15, is inarticulate and a bit shallow. She's unwilling to compete with her overachieving older brother Alex, and devotes herself to fashion and boyfriends. Preteen Jennifer is intelligent but prefers to play the role of observer, rather than that of instigator. Both girls blend right into the family values taught by their parents, but prodigal son Alex dipped a little too far back into the gene pool and grew up to be a suit wearing, briefcase-carrying ultraconservative, a lifetime subscriber to *The National Review*, with a picture of his idol, William F. Buckley, on his bedroom wall. They are a loving family, but the kids can't understand why their parents keep playing Bob Dylan records.

Family Ties' creator, Gary David Goldberg, an ex-hippie whose three earlier network shows had each been canceled within weeks, promised that *Family Ties* would be his last attempt at network television. He undertook the show as basically an autobiographical comedy which would explore the parents' adjustments to 1980s society and middle-aged family life. The *Family Ties* scripts covered a number of controversial topics of the day ranging from suicide to racism to drug dependancy.

At its inception, the show was to focus primarily on Steven and Elyse. But network surveys quickly revealed that audiences were more attracted by Michael J. Fox's skillful characterization of Alex. Goldberg and his collaborators decided to shift the emphasis to Alex. It was a change so fundamental that Goldberg told actors Michael Gross and Meredith Baxter-Birney that he would understand if they decided to quit.

During the 1984–1985 season another child was added to the cast when Elyse gave birth to baby Andrew. By the following fall, Alex had entered Leland College, espousing the virtues of the Reagan administration's supply-side economics. Back at home, Mallory, who was dating an aspiring sculptor named Nick Moore, barely graduated from high school and entered Grant Junior College with a career in fashion design in mind. When he was at home, Alex's chief sidekick was little brother Andrew, who idolized him. (Shortly after his birth, Andrew miraculously became 4 years old.) Every week they watched *Wall Street Week* together. In the show's last original episode, the nuclear family was finally dissolved when Alex graduated, accepted a plum job with a large Wall Street brokerage firm, and moved away.

The show was well received by viewers, including then president Ronald Reagan, who deemed *Family Ties* his favorite television show and offered to make an appearance on the show, which was politely declined by the producers.

Broadcast History

NBC

September 1982–March 1983	Wednesday 9:30–10:00
March 1983–August 1983	Monday 8:30–9:00
August 1983–December 1983	Wednesday 9:30–10:00
January 1984–August 1987	Thursday 8:30–9:00
August 1987–September 1987	Sunday 8:00–9:00
September 1987–September 1989	Sunday 8:00–8:30

Cast

Elyse Keaton	Meredith Baxter-Birney
Steve Keaton	Michael Gross
Alex P. Keaton	Michael J. Fox
Mallory Keaton	Justine Bateman
Jennifer Keaton	Tina Yothers
Andrew Keaton (1986–1989)	Brian Bonsall
Irwin "Skippy" Handelman	Marc Price
Ellen Reed (1985–1986)	Tracy Pollan
Nick Moore (1985–1989)	Scott Valentine
Lauren Miller (1987–1989)	Courteney Cox

Silver Spoons

First Broadcast: September 25, 1982
Last Broadcast: September 7, 1986

Military school didn't suit 12-year-old Ricky Stratton too well. He'd never known his father and his divorced mother, who had recently remarried, thought the school to be a good option at the time, to get Ricky out of the way. But when a bright child is fed lemons, he finds a way to make lemonade, and Ricky not only managed to figure out a way to meet his long lost dad, but to move in with him, as well. Little did he know that his father was just a big overgrown kid himself.

Edward Stratton III was a wealthy, charming, eligible bachelor happy to be living on his own. He'd been married to Ricky's mom for a mere week before they split up, and had no idea that he was a father. In many ways, he was a little boy living in a house filled with "big boy toys," like a rideable miniature train which he rode on from room to room, and an arcade of video games. Being the owner of a successful toy company helped feed his childlike nature. So what happens when you mix an irresponsible father who acts like a kid, and a sensible kid who acts older than his years? They teach each other to act their age. It might have been a daunting task, but the boys had some outside help.

Kate was Edward's gorgeous secretary, who would eventually become Ricky's stepmother. With the assistance of Leonard, Edward's lawyer, and his fussy business manger, Dexter, they did all they could to get manchild Edward Stratton through life, and child/man Ricky through his formative years relatively unscathed.

In the pilot episode, Edward's fortune has been siphoned off through outside computer hacking from a scheming business manager while Edward was blissfully playing with his trains. Ricky comes along and spots the scam and ultimately restores his dad's big bucks.

There were life lessons to be learned throughout the show for both Strattons. Once Ricky came into Edward's life, Edward, in turn, attempted to make peace with his estranged father, Edward II, a stuffy tycoon. Eventually, Ed also matured enough to fall in love with Kate. Once wed, he was able to settle down as a functioning adult, and a true family unit was formed. Ricky learned how to be a kid again and went through the requisite growing pains of a normal teenage boy, which involved dealing with bullies, girls, cars, getting into trouble, and trying to establish his independence.

Many famous guest stars made appearances on the show. Fran Drescher appeared as Kate's maid of honor, Barbara Billingsley was Rick's teacher, Christina Applegate was his date, Matthew Perry was a friend, and Gary Coleman appeared as Arnold Jackson in a crossover episode from *Diff'rent Strokes.* Celebrities like Whitney Houston, Mr. T., Menudo, Ed McMahon and Thomas "Tip" O'Neill appeared as themselves.

The series moved from NBC to first-run syndication in its final season.

Broadcast History

NBC

September 1982–September 1984	Saturday 8:30–9:00
September 1984–May 1985	Sunday 7:00–7:30
June 1985–March 1986	Sunday 7:30–8:00
May 1986–September 1986	Sunday 7:00–7:30

Cast

Ricky Stratton	Ricky Schroder
Edward Stratton III	Joel Higgins
Kate Summers Stratton	Erin Gray
Leonard Rollins	Leonard Lightfoot

Dexter Stuffins	Franklyn Seales
Derek Taylor	Jason Bateman
Freddy Lippincottleman	Corky Pigeon
Alfonso Spears	Alfonso Ribeiro
J.T. Martin	Bobby Fite
Grandfather Edward Stratton II	John Houseman
Uncle Harry Summers	Ray Walston
Brad	Billy Jacoby

Mama's Family

First Broadcast: January 22, 1983
Last Broadcast: August 17, 1985

The series began as a popular sketch on *The Carol Burnett Show* called *The Family.* The show was eventually syndicated into thirty-minute segments and retitled *Carol Burnett and Friends.* Vicki Lawrence played Mama, Carol Burnett was daughter Eunice, and Harvey Korman played Eunice's good for nothing husband, Ed. Tim Conway would occasionally be put into a family sketch playing Ed's looney employee Mickey Hart, and guest stars of the Burnett show often appeared as members of *The Family.* Actress Betty White made several appearances as Mama's successful daughter Ellen, and was the object of envy for hapless Eunice. The characters were so popular that getting their own show was inevitable, although initially, it was Carol Burnett who was slated to play Mama, and with Vickie Lawrence portraying her daughter, Eunice. The show's original title was going to be *The Family*, but apparently Mama wanted top billing. Harvey Korman, Carol Burnett, and Betty White would guest star occasionally and become a part of *Mama's Family.*

Mama and her clan lived in the fictional hamlet of Raytown, a city based on Raytown, Missouri, a suburb of Kansas City. Mama was a widow who shared the family home with her sister, Fran, who wrote for the local paper; Mama's adult son Vint, a locksmith by trade but lazy by nature; his wife, Naomi, who was the town sexpot and a cashier at the local market; and their two teenage children, Sonia and Buzz.

Mama was an opinionated church lady who rarely had a nice to say about anyone, and was particularly critical of her family. When a stranger once asked, "Aren't you going to introduce your family?" Mama's quick retort was, "Not if I can help it."

The show always opened with Harvey Korman in the role of Alistair Quince, sitting in an armchair with his weekly introductory comments.

Story lines were based on the constant family squabbles often brought on by Thelma's sharp tongue. When reading the headlines of a tabloid, "Psychic predicts world to explode by Christmas," Mama's immediate thought was, "Then why the hell am I dusting?

Thirty-five episodes were produced for NBC, and the show was canceled by the network in the spring of 1985. In 1986, it returned in syndication with all-new episodes and a few cast changes: Buzz, Sonja, Fran, Ellen, Eunice, and Ed were taken out of the show and new characters, Iola Boyland and Bubba Higgins, were introduced.

BROADCAST HISTORY

NBC

January 1983–June 1983	Saturday 9:00–9:30
August 1983–December 1983	Thursday 8:30–9:00
January 1984–May 1984	Saturday 9:30–10:00
June 1984–July 1984	Saturday 9:00–9:30
July 1984–September 1984	Saturday 9:30–10:00
June 1985–August 1985	Saturday 9:30–10:00
September 1986–September 1990	In syndication

CAST

Thelma (Mama) Harper	Vicki Lawrence
Aunt Fran Crowley	Rue McClanahan
Vinton Harper	Ken Berry
Naomi Oates Harper	Dorothy Lyman
Buzz Harper	Eric Brown
Sonja Harper	Karin Argoud
Bubba Higgins	Allan Kayser
Iola Boylen:	Beverly Archer
Ellen Jackson	Betty White
Eunice Higgins	Carol Burnett
Ed Higgins	Harvey Korman
Alistair Quince	Harvey Korman

Webster

First Broadcast: September 16, 1983
Last Broadcast: September 11, 1987

In a life imitates art scenario, former NFL football star Alex Karras stars as former NFL football player George Papadapolis in this ABC sitcom that puts him in the unlikely position as surrogate father to a precocious 7-year-old child.

George and his wife Katherine, a consumer advocate, had a whirlwind romance. They met on a Greek cruise, fell madly in love and were married before the vacation, which became their honeymoon, was over. Knowing that it would take a while to get to know each other better, they returned home to begin their lives together and undergo the normal adjustments of married life. After all, they came from two different worlds, but had the feeling that love, and a little time living as husband and wife, would conquer all. They had no sooner returned home to Chicago than they found George's godson, a 7-year-old black child, on their doorstep. Webster was the son of one of George's old teammates and best friends, Travis. Travis and his wife had recently been killed in an automobile accident, and since there was no next of kin, George and Katherine became instant parents.

For Katherine, who was pretty inept at domestic skills, this newfound parenthood came naturally, but it was a bit more difficult for George. In the show's second season, Ben Vereen appeared as Webster's uncle, Philip Long, who unsuccessfully tried to win custody of his diminutive nephew.

Before comedian Jerry Seinfeld found fame on his own highly successful weekly sitcom, he worked as a writer for *Webster*. Unfortunately, he was fired after only a few episodes. Seinfeld has said that getting sacked from the show was one of his most humiliating experiences.

Broadcast History

ABC

September 1983–March 1985	Friday 8:30–9:00
March 1985–March 1987	Friday 8:00–8:30
March 1987–April 1987	Friday 8:30–9:30
May 1987	Friday 8:00–8:30
June 1987–August 1987	Friday 8:00–8:30
August 1987–September 1987	Friday 9:30–10:00

Cast

Webster Long	Emmanuel Lewis
George Papadapolis	Alex Karras
Katherine Calder-Young Papadapolis	Susan Clark
Jerry Silver	Henry Polic II
Bill Parker	Eugene Roche
Cassie Parker	Cathryn Damon
Uncle Phillip Long	Ben Vereen

Papa Papadapolis	Jack Kruschen
Rob Whitaker/Joiner	Chad Allen
Tommy	Gabe Witcher
Roger	Carl Steven
Andy	Danny McMurphy
Benny	Nick DeMauro
Nicky Papadapolis	Corin "Corky" Nemec

The Cosby Show

First Broadcast: September 20, 1984
Last Broadcast: September 17, 1992

American families fell in love with the Huxtable clan, but the show had an incarnation or two before it finally hit the airwaves. First proposed as the story of a blue-collar worker and his family, it was turned down by both ABC and NBC. When the show was rewritten so that the lead characters were upscale professionals, ABC again decided to pass. Fortunately, NBC had the foresight to see it through, despite Cosby's conditions that the show be filmed in New York, not Hollywood, and that he have total creative control of the show's contents.

The Huxtables challenged viewers' perceptions of the black family experience they had been exposed to in the past with such offerings as *Good Times* and *Sanford and Son*. The Huxtables were a rich, classy, strong nuclear family. Grandparents were revered, not shunned or made fun of, education was vitally important, and ethnic pride was embraced but not preached. Both the children and their parents managed to lead their own lives outside the house and still remain a close-knit group. The show easily managed to cross the color barrier and was lovingly embraced by all races.

Jazz aficionado and head-of-household Cliff Huxtable was an obstetrician, with an office located in the downstairs portion of the spacious brownstone in which the family lived at 10 Stigwood Avenue in Brooklyn. Wife Clair was a savvy, strong-willed, successful legal aid attorney. She handled her job, her children and her sometimes eccentric husband lovingly and efficiently. The Huxtables had five children. Sondra was the eldest, and her parents had the highest hopes for her. She was smart, mature and attended Princeton. Denise was next in line, and the closest thing to a rebel in the family. She wore zany outfits, didn't do too well in school, and while she made her parents happy by enrolling in Cliff's alma mater, Hilman College, she dropped out after only two years. Theo was the only son and was doted on by his father. Overall, he was a good kid, but his parents worried a lot about his future, since his main priorities were food, girls and sports. Vanessa was the classic middle child. Outspoken, smart and also a bit rebellious as she got older, she caused her share of problems trying to keep up with her older sisters while simultaneously hanging onto her childhood. The baby of the family was five year old Rudy. Always in a hurry to grow up, she sometimes suffered from the youngest child syndrome, where she felt ignored and unloved, but she was the apple of her father's eye.

With a house full of rambunctious children, Cliff and Clair's parenting skills were constantly being put to the test, and Cliff regularly longed for the day the children would grow up and get out of the house. Cliff's interactions with his kids as they went through life was the show's main focus. The Huxtables were strict but fair parents who used patience, logic, warmth and humor rather than screaming and yelling to solve the weekly dilemma. The story lines taught life lessons, sometimes in the humorous vein. During one episode where Cliff's patience was tried to the limit, he wearily turns to Clair after having a minor epiphany and states, "The problem is, we had the children too close together. We should have had them 20 years apart."

The show received three Emmys, three NAACP Image Awards, a Peabody, the Humanitas Prize, numerous People's Choice Awards and various critics awards. The show is touted as having been watched by more people than any other situation comedy in the history of television.

Broadcast History

NBC

September 1984–June 1992	Thursday 8:00–8:30
July 1992–September 1992	Thursday 8:30–9:00

Cast

Dr. Heathcliff (Cliff) Huxtable	Bill Cosby
Clair Huxtable	Phylicia Rashad
Sondra Huxtable Tibideaux	Sabrina Le Beauf
Denise Huxtable Kendall	Lisa Bonet
Theodore Huxtable	Malcolm-Jamal Warner
Vanessa Huxtable	Tempestt Bledsoe
Rudy Huxtable	Keshia Knight Pulliam
Anna Huxtable	Clarice Taylor
Russel Huxtable	Earl Hyman
Peter Chiara (1985–1989)	Peter Costa

Elvin Tibideaux (1986–1992)	Geoffrey Owens
Kenny ("Bud") (1986–1992)	Deon Richmond
Cockroach (1986–1987)	Carl Anthony Payne II
Denny (1987–1991)	Troy Winbush
Lt. Martin Kendall (1989–1992)	Joseph C. Phillips
Olivia Kendall (1989–1992)	Raven-Symone
Pam Tucker (1990–1992)	Erika Alexander
Dabnis Brickey (1991–1992)	William Thomas, Jr

Kate and Allie

First Broadcast: March 16, 1984
Last Broadcast: September 11, 1989

By the 1980s, nuclear families were becoming as rare as the dodo bird, and *Kate and Allie* ushered in the trend of single parent households to television.

Kate McArdle and Allie Lowell might not have been the original odd couple, but there was enough dissimilarity in their personalities to cause a great deal of turmoil when the two recently divorced mothers decided to move into a Greenwich Village apartment together, kids in tow. It was both a financial and emotional move, allowing each woman coming out of a similar situation to support each other. Kate had always been a bit of a rebel, participating in protest marches and fighting for a cause. Allie was always the retiring wallflower. When she sees Kate out in the world still doing her thing, Allie slowly begins to realize that she may have missed out on life.

They'd been friends since high school, and their opposite personalities had not changed a bit. Kate, a travel agent, had one teenage daughter, Emma. Old-fashioned Allie had always been a housewife and was mother to teenager Jennie and preteen son Chip. During her marriage, Allie had somehow lost her identity. She had always thought of herself as a mere extension of her husband and her children. Now out on her own, she struggled to become a person in her own right. Kate struggled in a different way. She was always her own person, but found that being a single female lacked the equality and respect that she constantly fought for.

The show revolved around with the problems of single parenthood, adjusting to a new lifestyle, financial and children's issues, dating after divorce, getting along with ex-spouses, and, in Allie's case, finding herself. It also touched on some sensitive issues of the day. Teenage sex was addressed when Allie found a condom in son Chip's pocket, the homeless problem was touched on when Allie left her purse in a cab and found herself stranded in Manhattan without a nickel to her name and began to understand the hardships of being poor. A landmark episode dealing with homosexuality had Kate and Allie's lesbian landlady assuming that they were a lesbian couple and them debating whether or not to pretend that she's right.

In the show's second season, the women faced the arduous task of welcoming the opposite sex back into their lives when Kate started dating again. A year later, when Kate didn't get the job promotion she'd been hoping for, she talked Allie into joining her in their own catering business. That same year, both of their daughters enrolled in Columbia University. Emma moved into a dormitory, which allowed her more freedom than Jennie. Allie was forced to stop being such an overprotective mother and to give Jennie some of the same freedom at home.

In December of 1988, Allie married and moves into a new, high-rise apartment. When new husband Bob got a job as a sportscaster on a Washington, D.C., TV station and decided to commute to work from New York, Kate moved in to keep Allie and Chip company during the week while he was away. By then, Jenny was a sophomore at Columbia and Emma had transferred to UCLA to be close to her dad.

Broadcast History

CBS

March 1984–May 1984	Monday 9:30–10:00
August 1984–September 1986	Monday 9:30–10:00
September 1986–September 1987	Monday 8:00–8:30
September 1987–November 1987	Monday 8:30–9:00
December 1987–June 1988	Monday 8:00–8:30
July 1988–August 1988	Saturday 8:00–8:30
August 1988–September 1988	Monday 9:00–9:30
December 1988–March 1989	Monday 8:30–9:00
March 1989–June 1989	Monday 10:30–11:00
June 1989–September 1989	Monday 8:00–8:30

Cast

Kate McArdle	Susan Saint James
Allie Lowell	Jane Curtin
Emma McArdle (1984–1988)	Ari Meyers
Chip Lowell	Frederick Koehler
Jennie Lowell	Allison Smith
Charles Lowell (1984–1986)	Paul Hecht

Ted Bartelo (1984–1985, 1987–1988)	Gregory Salata
Bob Barsky (1987–1989)	Sam Freed
Lou Carello (1988–1989)	Peter Onorati

The Colbys

First Broadcast: November 20, 1985
Last Broadcast: March 26, 1987

The 1980s were touted as the era of exceedingly wealthy, dysfunctional television families and the Colbys were no exception. An early ABC press release described the show as "The Authority of Wealth, the Passions of Love and the Intrigues of Willful Sensuality Ignite the Interrelationships of the Dynamic, Strong-willed Colby Family…." Just so *Dynasty* fans didn't somehow manage to overlook the spinoff, it was called *Dynasty II— The Colbys* during its first two months on the air.

While the parent show centered on the sometimes sordid life of Blake Carrington, his family, and empire, his biggest rival in business was the ruthless Jason Colby, who was even more wealthy and more powerful than Blake. Jason owned Colby Enterprises, an international conglomerate dealing in real estate, oil, shipping and the aerospace industry.

The two shows were tied together in the series' opener, when Jeff Colby (son-in-law of the Carrington family from *Dynasty*) relocates to California to reconnect with his own family and claim his share of the family fortune. Jeff also hopes to reconnect with his ex-wife Fallon, who was believed to have perished the previous year, but who was not only very much alive, but suffering from amnesia and newly married to Jeff's cousin, Miles.

The setting was Belvedere, the opulent Colby estate set high above Los Angeles. Charlton Heston starred as magnate Jason, who was married to the devious Sabella Scott-Colby, and supposedly was the father of their three children. Unbeknownst to Jason, twins Miles and Monica were the result of a rape by an uncontrolled admirer that Sable conveniently forgot to tell him about. There was no doubt about daughter Bliss's paternity. Sable always fought for her beloved children, but turned against Jason when she found out that he was in love with her sister, Francesca, aka Frankie.

The similarities between the two shows and the frequent crossovers from *Dynasty* cast members did little to help *The Colbys* establish its own identity during its initial season. During the show's second season, efforts were made to improve the show, such as adding a handful of new characters and curtailing the crossovers with the original series. In March 1987, the show made its boldest move ever, when, in the season-ending cliffhanger, the show's heroine, Fallon, was abducted by a UFO! And while that particular episode scored the highest ratings for the series, it was not enough to save the show.

BROADCAST HISTORY

ABC

November 1985	Wednesday 10:00–11:00
November 1985–March 1987	Thursday 9:00–10:00

CAST

Jason Colby	Charlton Heston
Constance Colby Patterson	Barbara Stanwyck
Sable Scott Colby	Stephanie Beacham
Francesca Scott Colby Hamilton Langdon	Katharine Ross
Jeff Colby	John James
Fallon Carrington Colby	Emma Samms
Monica Colby	Tracy Scoggins
Miles Colby	Maxwell Caulfield
Bliss Colby	Claire Yarlett
Zachary Powers	Ricardo Montalban
Lord Roger Langdon	David Hedison

Mr. Belvedere

First Broadcast: March 15, 1985
Last Broadcast: July 8, 1990

The character of Mr. Belvedere was originally created by Gwen Davenport in her 1947 novel, *Belvedere.* Clifton Webb played the character in three popular movies, *Sitting Pretty* in 1948, *Mr. Belvedere Goes to College* in 1949, and *Mr. Belvedere Rings the Bell* in 1951. At least three unsuccessful attempts were made to produce a television series based on the character during the 1950s and 1960s. Pilots were made in 1956 starring Reginald Gardiner, in 1959 with Hans Conried, and in 1965 with Victor Buono. *Mr. Belvedere* made it to the small screen under the guidance of executive producers Frank Dungan and Jeff Stein, Emmy-Award winners for *Barney Miller*. Following the conclusion of *Barney Miller,* they were asked by ABC to develop the *Mr. Belvedere* pilot.

The series centered around the Owens family, who lived in a suburb of Pittsburgh. George Owens was a sports writer and his wife, Marsha, was a homemaker/law-student. They had three children, sixteen-year-old Kevin, fourteen-year-old Heather and eight-year-old Wesley. Marsha couldn't handle the household and her schoolwork, so she placed an ad for a housekeeper. A sarcastic, wisecracking Englishman in the guise of Lynn Belvedere answers the ad and takes on his new role as housekeeper for the dysfunctional Owens family. He becomes the family butler, nursemaid, baby sitter, cleaner, cook, confidant, and conscience — a far cry from the service he had previously given to Winston Churchill and other notable royals.

George Owens is certainly no Winston Churchill and is not thrilled with Mr. Belvedere or his influence on the family, but everyone else loves the prim and proper manservant. He becomes a Dutch uncle to the kids, offering advice when they need it, and often puts George in his place when needed as well. Each episode ended with Belvedere writing the lessons of the day in his diary.

Lynn Belvedere followed in the footsteps of many other notable outspoken fictional housekeepers. "The notion of a servant with a sharp tongue has been around for about 3,000 years, all the way back to Roman comedy; as old as the drama itself," says Daniel Davis, who portrayed the outspoken, irreverent butler, Niles, on *The Nanny*. "They are instantly likable characters because they get to say what everybody else is thinking, what everybody else wishes they had the nerve to say."

While the show is classified as a sitcom, they did air a few very special and more serious episodes regarding such topical matters as AIDS, molestation, and rape.

Broadcast History

ABC

March 1985–April 1985	Friday 8:30–9:00
August 1985–March 1987	Friday 8:30–9:00
May 1987–September 1987	Friday 8:30–9:00
October 1987–January 1988	Friday 9:00–9:30
January 1988–February 1988	Friday 8:30–9:00
March 1988–July 1989	Friday 9:00–9:30
August 1989–September 1989	Friday 8:30–9:00
September 1989–December 1989	Saturday 8:00–8:30
July 1990	Sunday 8:30–9:00

Cast

Mr. Lynn Belvedere	Christopher Hewett
George Owens	Bob Uecker
Marsha Owens	Ilene Graff
Kevin Owens	Rob Stone

Heather Owens	Tracy Wells
Wesley Owens	Brice Beckham
Angela	Michele Matheson

227

First Broadcast: September 14, 1985
Last Broadcast: July 28, 1990

227 had its origins in a play written by Christine Houston of Chicago, and performed by lead character Marla Gibbs' own Cross Roads Academy, a local community theater troupe in Los Angeles. (It was at the Academy that Gibbs struck up a friendship with the young actress, Regina King. That friendship translated to King being hired for the role of Gibbs' daughter Brenda in the series.) The play was so well received that Gibbs sold NBC on the concept for a series, and Lorimar adapted it for television. In the beginning, *227* was criticized as being too much like *The Cosby Show*, but the show soon proved to be successful in its own right, because viewers pointed out that while the Huxtables were an upper-middle class family, *227* depicted a more working-class environment. Episodes dealt with the everyday lives of the tenants of apartment building 227.

The sentiment of the show's theme song translated perfectly into this sitcom depicting the everyday life of a close-knit and loving working-class family: "There's no place like home. With your family around you, you're never alone. When you know that your loved, you don't need to roam. Cause there's no place like home."

Marla Gibbs, whom viewers know well as Florence, the wisecracking maid on *The Jeffersons*, portrayed Mary Jenkins. While not quite as sharp-tongued as her alter ego, Mary was still a strong-willed woman in her own right, a loving wife to husband Lester, and devoted mother to fourteen-year-old Brenda.

The Jenkins family lived in an apartment building, number 227, in a racially mixed neighborhood in Washington, D.C. Mary's best friend, Rose Lee Holloway, was the landlady, and the two friends loved to gossip. They spent a great deal of time on the front stoop talking about all the neighbors. Their busybody elderly neighbor, Pearl, always had her head poking out of her first floor apartment to join them. Much of the talk centered around Sandra Clark, the building's sexy vamp.

Lester was a contractor, smart and down to earth. While the Jenkins clan wasn't rich, they always had enough to make do. Brenda was a good student and good child in general. She rarely caused her family any grief, except when it came to her boyfriend, Calvin, who was Brenda's first love and Pearl's grandson.

As is popular on many television sitcoms, the principals often appeared on current game shows of the time. During the run of *227*, Mary and Sandra competed on *Wheel of Fortune* and headed opposing teams on TV's *Family Feud*, and Sandra appeared on *The Love Connection.*

BROADCAST HISTORY

NBC

September 1985–March 1986	Saturday 9:30–10:00
April 1986–June 1986	Saturday 9:30–10:00
June 1986–May 1987	Saturday 8:30–9:00
June 1987–July 1987	Saturday 8:00–8:30
July 1987–September 1988	Saturday 8:30–9:00
October 1988–July 1989	Saturday 8:00–8:30
September 1989–February 1990	Saturday 8:30–9:00
April 1990–May 1990	Sunday 8:30–9:00
June 1990–July 1990	Saturday 8:00–8:30

CAST

Mary Jenkins	Marla Gibbs
Lester Jenkins	Hal Williams
Rose Lee Holloway	Alaina Reed-Hall
Sandra Clark	Jackee (Harry)
Brenda Jenkins	Regina King
Tiffany Holloway (1985–1986)	Kia Goodwin
Pearl Shay	Helen Martin
Calvin Dobbs	Curtis Baldwin
Alexandria DeWitt (1988–1989)	Countess Vaughn
Eva Rawley (1989–1990)	Toukie A. Smith
Julian C. Barlow (1989–1990)	Paul Winfield
Dylan McMillan (1989–1990)	Barry Sobel
Travis Filmore (1989–1990)	Stoney Jackson
Warren Merriwether (1989–1990)	Kevin Peter Hall

Growing Pains

First Broadcast: September 24, 1985
Last Broadcast: August 27, 1992

The upper-middle class Seaver family of 15 Robin Hood Lane in suburban Long Island, New York, did a great deal of growing during the show's seven year run. Two working parents raising four children is never easy, and life lessons abound. Especially with two working parents. The responsibility of who was going to stay home with the kids was often juggled, even fought over between the two, but eventually settled. Father Jason was a psychiatrist who practiced out of a home office. Maggie, his wife, was a journalist who worked for the Long Island newspaper in the first three seasons of the sitcom. Then she got a job as the news anchor for Channel 19 News and worked there through the middle of the fifth season, when she decided to stay at home. Jason moved his practice out of the house to an office. During the last seasons, Maggie worked at home writing a consumer awareness column for the local newspaper.

One might assume that a psychiatrist as head of household would produce sensible, well-adjusted children, but like all kids, they went through their own stages of growing pains. The oldest child, Mike, called "a hormone with feet" by his mother, was a little irresponsible and lived to party. Sister Carol was brainy, nerdy and shy. The littlest Seaver, Ben, was a typical 9-year-old, a clever con artist who had inherited his brother Mike's penchant for getting into trouble and chasing girls. Another child, Chrissy, was born during the show's fourth season. She was cute, precocious and had an imaginary friend named Ike. While the other children had ample time to grow, Chrissy had an incredible growth spurt from toddler to five year old between the fifth and sixth seasons.

During the fourth season, Mike moved out of the house … to the loft above the garage. Sixteen-year-old Leonardo DiCaprio joined the cast during the final season when the Seavers, reluctantly at first, took in a homeless boy, Luke Brower. Luke was one of Mike's students at the Community Health Clinic and quickly became one of the Seavers.

In the final season, Maggie got a job in Washington, D.C., which required the family to move. In the last episode, the Seaver family gathered around a picnic blanket on the floor of their empty living room, reminiscing. Mike is now a savvy ad executive married to Kate McDonald (with three adopted kids to raise); Carol is a ruthless corporate attorney; Chrissie is a high school student; and Ben is a failed dot-com entrepreneur who is now cleaning pools in Beverly Hills. Maggie becomes the new senator for Washington, D.C.

One of the supporting characters in *Growing Pains* was high school phys-ed teacher Graham Lubbock, played by Bill Kirchenbauer. Despite strong support from many of the students, including Mike and Carol Seaver, he was fired from Dewey High. He eventually found a new job at a school in the northern California coast town of Eureka. These events, unfolding during two *Growing Pains* episodes, was actually a pilot of sorts for a spin-off series. Called *Just the Ten of Us*, it was a sitcom centered around Lubbock and his large family.

Many of today's biggest stars made guest appearances during the show's seven year run, including the aforementioned Leonardo DiCaprio, Brad Pitt, Hank Azaria, and Matthew Perry.

BROADCAST HISTORY

ABC

September 1985–March 1986,	Tuesday 8:30–9:00
May 1986–March 1988	Tuesday 8:30–9:00
March 1988–August 1990	Wednesday 8:00–8:30
August 1990–August 1991	Wednesday 8:00–8:30
August 1991–September 1991	Friday 9:30–10:00
September 1991–January 1992	Saturday 8:30–9:00
February 1992–April 1992	Saturday 9:30–10:00
May 1992–July 1992	Wednesday 8:30–9:00
July 1992–August 1992	Thursday 8:30–9:00

CAST

Dr. Jason Seaver	Alan Thicke
Maggie Seaver	Joanna Kerns
Mike Seaver	Kirk Cameron
Carol Seaver	Tracey Gold
Ben Seaver	Jeremy Miller
Chrissy Seaver (1988–1990)	Kelsey and Kirsten Dohring
Chrissy Seaver (1990–1992)	Ashley Johnson
Richard Stabone ("Boner")	Josh Andrew Koenig
Kate MacDonald	Chelsea Noble
Luke Bower (1991–1992)	Leonardo DiCaprio

The Golden Girls

First Broadcast: September 14, 1985
Last Broadcast: September 14, 1992

Families come in all shapes, sizes and forms. One of Webster's definitions of family is: *a group of individuals living under one roof.* Such is the case with *The Golden Girls*, a group of vintage, single roomies functioning as a family while sharing their golden years together in Miami.

Atlanta native Blanche DuBois, a steamy, self centered, man-hungry

Southern belle, was a widow who needed a couple of new roommates to share the cost of living in her very nice home, so she tacked up an ad on a supermarket message board and hoped for the best. Widow Rose Nyland, a grief counselor originally from the Minnesota hamlet of St. Olaf, was the first to answer the ad. Rose was naive, sweet, and just a wee bit muddled. She and Blanche hit it off right away. Shortly thereafter came Dorothy Zbornak, an outspoken divorcee who worked as a substitute schoolteacher. Dorothy was a tough cookie with a short temper and lots of repressed anger. Her no-good ex-husband, Stan, had recently dumped her for a young bimbette. Just as the improbably matched threesome were settling in and getting to know each other, there was a knock on the door, and *picture it*: in walks Sophia Petrillo, Dorothy's outspoken and irreverent elderly Sicilian mother. Sophia had been living at the Shady Pines Retirement Home but it had just burned to the ground, leaving her homeless. Of course, she was invited to share the home, and it didn't take long for the girls to expect the unexpected from Sophia. This tiny, purse-clutching mighty mite had a tongue as loose as an old girdle with impromptu revelations as, "You know something? When I turn my hearing aid up to ten, I can hear a canary break wind in Lauderdale!"

While at first it looked as though the frisky foursome might not be able to live in perfect harmony, they began to bond, despite the squabbles and disagreements. The girls would often congregate late at night around the kitchen table with a cheesecake to sort out their problems. It wasn't unusual for Rose to tell a rather long and pointless St. Olaf-based story, like "The Great Herring War" that she thought would relate to the current problem of the evening. Unfortunately, her stories rambled on and on, often prompting Dorothy to explode, "The point, Rose. Get to the point!" Sophia would often chime in with her own wisdom with a subject-related Sicilian yarn, always beginning the story with, "Picture it…."

Many important issues facing senior citizens were addressed each week, like sex after sixty, menopause, health issues, the job market, dealing with ex-spouses and grown children, elderly parents, and even death. *The Golden Girls* was a hit in over 60 countries.

With all the emphasis on youth for viewing audiences, how did such a show become an instant success? "I think a lot of it has to do with the fact that there were these old, post menopausal ladies who looked good, wore fabulous earrings, dressed well and had very active sex lives," said series star Bea Arthur. "It showed people that old people don't have to look and smell funny and hide in the corner."

BROADCAST HISTORY

NBC

September 1985–July 1991	Saturday 9:00–9:30
August 1991–September 1991	Saturday 8:00–8:30
September 1991–September 1992	Saturday 8:30–9:00

CAST

Dorothy Zbornak	Bea Arthur
Rose Nylund	Betty White
Blanche Devereaux	Rue McClanahan
Sophia Petrillo	Estelle Getty
Stan Zbornak	Herb Edelman
Miles Webber	Harold Gould

The Hogan Family

First Broadcast: March 1, 1986
Last Broadcast: July 20, 1991

The Hogan Family was produced by Thomas L. Miller and Robert L. Boyett who also brought *Perfect Strangers, Full House, Step by Step* and *Family Matters* to television. They had been previously partnered with Edward Milkis at Paramount Studios where they produced such top-rated series such as *Happy Days, Laverne & Shirley* and *Mork and Mindy.*

The Hogan Family went through several name changes during its run. The original name for the pilot was *Close to Home.* That was changed to *Valerie* during its first two seasons, but when star Valerie Harper left the show, it was renamed *Valerie's Family* for the 1987–1988 season. Finally, during the final three seasons, it became *The Hogan Family.*

Valerie Hogan was married to Michael, an airline pilot who was frequently flying the friendly skies, leaving her to raise their three rowdy boys pretty much on her own. The family lived in the Chicago suburb of Oak Park, Illinois. Between juggling a career and a household, life was hardly a laugh a minute for the harried wife and mother. David, the oldest son, was a girl crazy teenager. Mark and Willie were twelve year old fraternal twins. While Mark was the brain and perfectionist of the duo, Willie, the carefree clown, seemed to always be in trouble. Story lines focused on a quasi-single mother's struggle.

Valerie Harper starred for the first 32 episodes, then Sandy Duncan took over the lead in the show's third season when Valerie was written out of the series due to a well publicized dispute between Valerie Harper and the producers. Her departure was explained by having her character suddenly die. At that point Michael's recently divorced sister, Sandy, moved in to help raise the boys. Story lines changed over to focus more on the boys growing up and dating as well as Michael and Sandy each getting out in the dating scene. In 1988, the title was changed again, this time to *The Hogan Family.* At the end of the 5th season, NBC dropped the show, but CBS picked it up for another season, adding John Hillerman as the character of Lloyd Hogan, Michael and Sandy's father.

On the February 1987 episode entitled "Bad Timing," *The Hogan Family* made television history when the word "condom" was used for the first time in a sitcom script.

Broadcast History

March 1986	NBC Saturday 8:30–9:00
March 1986–June 1986	NBC Monday 8:30–9:00
June 1986–September 1986	NBC Monday 8:00–8:30
September 1986–November 1986	NBC Sunday 8:30–9:00
November 1986–January 1987	NBC Sunday 8:00–8:30
January 1987–March 1987	NBC Sunday 8:30–9:00
March 1987–June 1990	NBC Monday 8:30–9:00
September 1990–December 1990	CBS Saturday 8:30–9:00
July 1991	CBS Wednesday 8:00–8:30
July 1991	CBS Saturday 8:00–9:00

Cast

Valerie Hogan	Valerie Harper
David Hogan	Jason Bateman
Willie Hogan	Danny Ponce
Mark Hogan	Jeremy Licht
Michael Hogan	Josh Taylor
Barbara Goodwin	Christine Ebersole
Annie Steck	Judith Kahan
Mrs. Patty Poole	Edie McClurg
Peter Poole	Willard Scott
Sandy Hogan	Sandy Duncan
Rich	Tom Hodges
Burt	Steve Witting
Lloyd Hogan	John Hillerman

Our House

First Broadcast: September 11, 1986
Last Broadcast: June 26, 1988

Crusty Wilford Brimley played the role of cantankerous widower and ex–Marine Gus Witherspoon, a 65-year-old grandfather who enjoys rambling around by himself in his old Victorian house. An engineer by trade, Gus is self-sufficient, has a core group of friends, keeps himself busy with his hobby of HO scale trains, and thinks he has a pretty good life. When Gus's son suddenly dies and leaves a wife and three children penniless, the only option is for them to move in with Gus, forcing three generations to try and live in harmony.

Fifteen-year-old Kris is as strong willed and stubborn as her grandfather. David is the middle child, a 12-year-old who puts on a good front of being comfortable in his own skin, but is actually quite unsure of himself. Molly, the youngest of the clan at 8, is cute, sweet, and impressionable. She doesn't understand why everyone is having such a hard time adjusting to the new family unit, and decides to try and say something about it, so she talks to David, and the two of them unsuccessfully try to make their home come up to the standards of television households.

After the initial awkward stage, the family begins to come to grips with the fact that they have to leave their old lives in the past and begin face the problems of a new, everyday life. They grow to become fiercely protective of each other, as when stubborn Gus thinks he's dying and stalls on getting treatment for his recently diagnosed diabetes. The family rallies together and strongly urges him to take care of the problem, rather than give up on life, or them. Kris, being the oldest, seems to have the lion's share of conflict. Her lifelong ambition is to join the Air Force Academy, and is crushed to find out that her local school doesn't offer the classes she needs. When she befriends a girl with a drinking problem, she learns a life lesson about teenage alcoholism. When baby-sitting for a teacher, she ends up being accused of child abuse, and the family comes to her aid to help disprove the allegations.

Mother Jessie worked at a variety of jobs to help contribute to the household, including that of a freelance photographer. Eventually, she attempts to get her personal life back on track and goes on her first date despite David's strong disapproval.

While Gus has to give up his solitary life and adjust to raising a whole new family, he's always got his best friend, Joe Kaplan, around to help ease the way.

BROADCAST HISTORY

NBC

September 1986	Thursday 8:30–9:00
September 1986–May 1987	Sunday 7:00–8:00
May 1987–June 1987	Sunday 8:00–9:00
June 1987–June 1988	Sunday 7:00–8:00

CAST

Gus Witherspoon	Wilford Brimley
Jesse Witherspoon	Diedre Hall
Kris Witherspoon	Shannen Doherty
David Witherspoon	Chad Allen
Molly Witherspoon	Keri Houlihan
Joe Kaplan	Gerald S. O'Loughlin

ALF

First Broadcast: September 22, 1986
Last Broadcast: June 18, 1990

So what's a family to do when an alien spaceship crashes into their garage? Invite the alien to move in and become a member of the family, of course.

Gordon Shumway, aka ALF (for "Alien Life Form"), was born October 28, 1756, on the planet Melmac. Back home, ALF was an orbit guard, a professional Bouillabaseball player, a model for a short time, and ran his own Phlegm dealership. One night, while ALF was out in his orbit guard patrol ship, Melmac exploded in a freak boating accident. The explosion sent ALF's patrol ship hurtling into deep space. He flew for months looking for a new home. One night, ALF zigged when he should have zagged and got caught in Earth's gravitational pull. He plummeted to Earth and crashed-landed into the Tanners' garage. After head-of-household Willie Tanner realized that ALF's ship couldn't be fixed, ALF was told that he could stay with the family as long as he behaved. Famous last words.

As one might expect, ALF didn't know how to behave according to Earth standards, and his presence in the house became a bit disruptive, to say the least. He was outspoken, sarcastic, and had an insatiable appetite, especially where cats were concerned. That didn't bode well for either the Tanners or their pet cat, Lucky. ALF learned quickly that on Earth, people don't eat cats, but that didn't stop him from salivating every time he saw one. ALF's table manners were atrocious, and his idea of a balanced meal was, "As much food as I can carry in both hands without dropping it."

Willie and wife, Kate, often had second thoughts about ALF staying on, especially when he would comment sarcastically on the foibles of earthlings. Because it was necessary to hide ALF from other human beings, he had to be kept hidden in the kitchen when the Tanners had guests. Teenage daughter Lynn had mixed feelings about an alien living in their home, but son Benji loved having ALF around. A new baby named Eric was born to the Tanner clan in 1989, giving ALF new human customs to wisecrack about.

In a final episode cliffhanger in March 1990, ALF was contacted by Melmacians who invited him to leave with them and colonize a new planet—just as the U.S. government's Alien Task Force closed in to capture him. An animated version of ALF, recounting Gordon Shumway's exploits of the planet Melmac, ran on NBC's Saturday morning lineup from September 1987 to August 1990.

BROADCAST HISTORY

NBC

September 1986–February 1990	Monday 8:00–8:30
March 1990	Saturday 8:00–8:30
April 1990–May 1990	Sunday 8:00–8:30
May 1990–June 1990	Monday 8:00–8:30

CAST

ALF (Gordon Shumway)	Paul Fusco (voice only)
Willie Tanner	Max Wright
Kate Tanner	Anne Schedeen
Lynn Tanner	Andrea Elson
Brian Tanner	Benji Gregory
Dorothy Halligan	Anne Meara
Raquel Ochmonek	Liz Sheridan
Trevor Ochmonek	John LaMotta
Jake Ochmonek	Josh Blake
Neal Tanner	JM J. Bullock

Thirtysomething

First Broadcast: September 29, 1987
Last Broadcast: September 3, 1991

TV Guide pretty much summed it up by saying, "Trials and tribulations abound in this series that follows a group of 'yuppie' friends through marriages, divorce, relationship struggles, death and birth."

Elliot Weston and Michael Steadman were best buddies in college, and continued that friendship after graduation. They once worked together in a large Philadelphia advertising agency, then left to open a smaller agency of their own. Michael always wanted to be a writer but somehow ended up in advertising. He was married to Hope, an overachiever and Princeton graduate who opted to become a stay at home mother to newborn baby Janey. Elliot had always been the funny one, the life of the party, until his marriage, kids and job responsibilities offered him up a hard dose of reality. Wife Nancy was an artist, a free spirit and ex-hippie staying at home raising young Ethan and Brittany. The Westons' marriage is a bit rocky at best.

The show focused on both the personal and professional lives of the two young, urban professional families, but also included three unmarried friends from college who were considered "extended family." Ellyn was a career executive in city government, Gary an English teacher at a liberal arts college, and Melissa, a freelance photographer, who also happened to be Michael's cousin.

The series hit home with a younger viewing audience who could identify with the everyday lives portrayed in the series, and dealt with not only the mundane routine of life, but also such weighty topics as infidelity, sexual relations, disease and death.

According to Marshall Herskovitz and Edward Zwick, co-creators of *thirtysomething*, it was a show about people, not ages. "It was all about growing up — no matter how old you are. And it's a show about creating your own family. All these people live apart from where they grew up, and so they're trying to fashion a new sense of home — one made up of friends, where holidays, job triumphs, birthdays, illnesses, and gossip all take on a kind of bittersweet significance. Though each episode will be a complete story, it's the deeper currents among these friends that will be revealed over time."

Broadcast History

ABC

September 1987–September 1988	Tuesday 10:00–11:00
December 1988–May 1991	Tuesday 10:00–11:00
July 1991–September 1991	Tuesday 10:00–11:00

Cast

Michael Steadman	Ken Olin
Hope Murdoch Steadman	Mel Harris

Janey Steadman	Brittany & Lacey Craven
Elliot Weston	Timothy Busfield
Nancy Weston	Patricia Wettig
Ethan Weston	Luke Rossi
Brittany Weston	Jordana "Bink" Shapiro
Melissa Steadman	Melanie Mayron
Ellyn	Polly Draper
Prof. Gary Shepherd	Peter Horton
Miles Drentell (1989–1991)	David Clennon
Susannah Hart (1989–1991)	Patricia Kalember
Billy Sidel (1990–1991)	Erich Anderson

Full House

First Broadcast: September 22, 1987
Last Broadcast: August 29, 1995

There are television shows depicting motherless families and those depicting fatherless families, and then came the Tanner household headed by sportscaster Danny Tanner, who was a young widower left with three young daughters to raise. After his wife died suddenly, Danny needed help at home to be able to continue to hold down his job as well as the household so his brother-in-law, Jesse, and old friend Joey moved in to help ease the financial and emotional burdeon.

The newly formed Tanner household closely resembled a three ring circus at times, with Danny as the ringmaster; Joey, an aspiring stand up comic, as the clown; and Uncle Jesse, a professional rock musician, as the cool, hip daredevil. One would think that three grown men could easily handle three little girls, but it seemed to be the other way around. D.J., the oldest child, was a 10-year-old charmer. Five year old Stephanie was very outspoken and demanding. Baby Michelle was the apple of everyone's eye, and as she got older, could easily wrap her Dad, Joey and Jesse around her little pinky.

When Danny eventually turned in his sportscasting blazer to become the co-host of a local morning television show, the dynamics of the Tanner household changed. His partner on the show, Rebecca, became involved with Jesse, and they eventually married. Instead of moving out on their own, Rebecca just moved in. They soon became parents of twin boys, expanding the household by three.

Neither Danny nor Joey was as lucky in the romance department. Try as they might, they never had an enduring relationship during the show's run.

While none of the stars hit the skids after the show's cancellation, surprisingly, it is the Olsen twins, who took turns playing baby Michelle, that benefitted most from the series. Five years after ABC canceled the sitcom that made them famous, the girls, at 13 years of age, ran a multifaceted business worth about $60 million, and their combined personal fortune at that time was reported to be at least $17 million. At the age of seventeen, as of this writing, Mary-Kate and Ashley Olsen are the celebrities behind the most successful girls' brand in the world. *The Hollywood Reporter* named them "the most powerful young women in Hollywood." Mary-Kate and Ashley are the youngest celebrities in history to be awarded stars on Hollywood's Walk of Fame. Mary-Kate and Ashley were named to *People* magazine's 50 Most Beautiful People, as well as being named to The World's Richest Kids in a *People* magazine cover feature story. As little Michelle used to say, "You got it, Dude."

BROADCAST HISTORY

ABC

September 1987	Tuesday 8:30–9:00
September 1987–February 1988	Friday 8:00–8:30
March 1988–June 1989	Friday 8:30–9:00
July 1988–September 1988	Tuesday 8:30–9:00
August 1989–August 1991	Friday 8:00–8:30
August 1991–August 1995	Tuesday 8:00–8:30

CAST

Danny Tanner	Bob Saget
Joey Gladstone	Dave Coulier
Jesse Katsopolis	John Stamos
D.J. Tanner	Candace Cameron
Stephanie Tanner	Jodie Sweetin
Michelle Tanner	Mary-Kate Olsen / Ashley Olsen
Rebecca Donaldson	Lori Loughlin
Kimmy Gibler	Andrea Barber

My Two Dads

First Broadcast: September 20, 1987
Last Broadcast: June 16, 1990

The serious question of paternity was the basis for this situation comedy about a mismatched pair of single men brought together to raise a 13-

year-old child which might be either's daughter. Factor in that neither man knows a thing about each other or child rearing, and that the two have totally opposite lifestyles, and you've got the makings of a potential disaster.

Each week, the show began with a picture of daughter Nicole and her "parents," with the following explanation: "This is me, Nicole Bradford. Cute, huh? This is my dad and this is my dad. How did I get two dads? They inherited me. One dad who's down to earth and one dad with his head in the clouds."

The saga began when 13 years before, when stuffy financial advisor Michael Taylor and free spirit artist Joey Harris had been in love with the same woman. Both had ugly breakups with her, but unbeknownst to either, one of them had fathered a child before the split. When the young woman died prematurely, she left a will giving Michael and Joey joint custody of her 12-year-old daughter, Nicole. She wasn't sure who the father was, either.

The two men met at the reading of the woman's will, and the best possible solution to this unlikely joint custody was for the men and Nicole to set up housekeeping and move in together.

The fact that neither man knows whether or not he is the father lends some funny moments as they each believe in their own hearts that they are Nicole's dad, and constantly bicker about where Nicole got her genetic traits, both good and bad. Wise beyond her years, Nicole keeps reminding her dads that whether or not one or the other shares her genes, both men share the job of raising and enjoying time with her. By the time the two dads got around to actually doing a paternity test, they decided against completing it. Neither could bear the idea of finding out he was not Nicole's dad. The unlikely trio underwent the same problems as any normal family: grades, dating, both Nicole's and the dads, the difficulties experienced by the two guys in being both father and "mother" to the girl, and the disputes arising from their different personalities. As Nicole got older, the two dads worried less about her education and spiritual upbringing and more about her romantic life, especially in her relationships with boyfriends Cory and Zach.

While Nicole had an overabundance of Dad and no mother figure, outspoken Judge Wilbur, who had awarded them custody in the first place, happened to own the building in which they lived, so she was there to play surrogate mom from a short distance away. It's interesting to note that Judge Wilbur started as a minor recurring character on *Night Court* before she became a full time character on *My Two Dads.* Although this coincidence could possibly be seen as a spin-off, it really wasn't.

The show's theme song was composed and performed by series star Greg Evigan.

Broadcast History

NBC

September 1987–February 1988	Sunday 8:30–9:00
June 1988–September 1988	Sunday 8:30–9:00
January 1989–June 1989	Wednesday 9:30–10:00
July 1989	Saturday 8:00–8:30
August 1989–November 1989	Sunday 8:30–9:00
November 1989–January 1990	Wednesday 9:30–10:00
March 1990–April 1990	Monday 8:00–8:30
June 1990	Saturday 8:00–8:30

Cast

Michael Taylor	Paul Reiser
Joey Harris	Greg Evigan
Nicole Bradford	Staci Keanan
Judge Margaret Wilbur	Florence Stanley
Ed Klowicki	Dick Butkus
Cory Kupjus	Vonni Rabisi
Zach Nichols	Chad Allen
Shelby Haskell	Amy Hathaway
Julian	Don Yesso

Married ... with Children

First Broadcast: April 5, 1987
Last Broadcast: July 7, 1997

Viewers either loved the show or hated it, but it was never overlooked. Some might argue that the chaotic Bundy household was as atypical of the classic American family as one could find, but in truth, they were probably more like the norm than anyone would like to admit. They were just a lot bigger than life. The show was conceived as a a parody on American family sitcoms of the mid-eighties, and therefore, the working title of the show was *Not the Cosbys*. While most viewers loved the show's irreverence, others just didn't get it at all. In 1989, Terry Rakolta of Bloomfield Hills, Michigan, started a campaign against the series because she objected to it as "negative for families." She wrote to all the sponsors of the series and took part in several talk shows to stop *Married ... with Children*. The show lost a few sponsors for a short time, but Rakolta's fight had the opposite effect of that she desired. It made viewers curious about this series, and all the ruckus she created improved the ratings so greatly that the producers sent a fruit basket to Rakolta every Christmas.

Al and Peg Bundy had been married for 15 years, lived in Chicago and were the parents of two children, Kelly and Bud. The family didn't really like each other, but were pretty much stuck with each other. According to Al, "Love, hate, look, we're a family, what's the difference?" The Bundys might have been losers, but they weren't quitters.

Al was a male chauvinist from the word "go." He made his minimum wage living working as a shoe salesman at "Gary's Shoes & Accessories for Today's Woman." Beer, bowling and TV sports were his main priorities. He hated nothing more than fat women, having sex with his wife, and showering.

Peg was an inept, lazy housewife who never cooked or cleaned. She spent her days watching TV talk shows and eating bonbons. Tight pants, stiletto heels and "big hair" were her trademarks. Unlike Al, she'd have very much loved to have sex with her husband on occasion, but channeled her unanswered desires by looking at young, hunky guys.

Kelly was the apple of her daddy's eye even though her IQ was substandard and she lived the life of a trashy sex kitten. She and her brother Bud, the only one in the family with half a brain, were constantly battling. Buck, the family dog, was known to verbalize his thoughts to the audience. Buck must've had exceedingly bad karma, because when he died, he was immediately reincarnated into the Bundys' new puppy, Lucky, rather than the eagle he'd so desperately hoped to become.

Al's credo was, "Anytime I can embarrass my spouse, it makes me feel better." A modified version of this not so honorable motto is "When one Bundy is embarrassed, the rest of us feel good about ourselves."

One never seen character on the show was Peggy's hillbilly mother from Wanker County, who occasionally visited the Bundy household. Al ran for cover when she arrived and prayed that he could afford to pay the grocery bills for his unwanted, overweight mother-in-law, whom he referred to as "Free Willy." The audience only heard her voice coming from the upstairs bedroom. She was apparently so big she could hardly move, and when she did, chips of plaster flaked from the ceiling, or the camera lens would sway with the tremors of her movements. On the 1995 season opener, Peggy's mom threatened to move in forever when she left her husband. The episode was titled "Something Humongous This Way Comes!"

Broadcast History

FOX

April 1987–October 1987	Sunday 8:00–9:00
October 1987–July 1989	Sunday 8:30–9:00

July 1989–August 1996	Sunday 9:00–9:30
September 1996–June 1997	Saturday 9:00–9:30

CAST

Al Bundy	Ed O'Neill
Peggy Bundy	Katey Sagal
Kelly Bundy	Christina Applegate
Bud Bundy	David Faustino
Steve Rhoades (1987–1990)	David Garrison
Marcy Rhoades D'Arcy	Amanda Bearse
Jefferson D'Arcy (1991–1997)	Ted McGinley

The Wonder Years

First Broadcast: March 15, 1988
Last Broadcast: September 1, 1993

In the 1960s, people were yearning to relive their youth in the '40s. In 1988, we were nostalgic for the '60s. Every era yearns for the good old days, and in every decade there are programs that help take us back. Such is the case with *The Wonder Years*, a show that gave audiences a whimsical view of growing up in the suburbs through the eyes of a 12-year-old.

Fred Savage starred as Kevin Arnold, a prepubescent boy in his first year of junior high school. The show was an innovative mix of drama, comedy and situation comedy. It was presented entirely from the point of view of the show's main character. Daniel Stern did the voice-over narration, portraying an adult Kevin, commenting on the events of his youth with the near perfect 20/20 hindsight only adulthood can bring. The program often opened with TV news clips from the era—depicting a war protest, President Nixon waving goodbye at the White House, or other instantly recognizable events, always accompanied by a classic bit of rock music.

It was an era of Vietnam protest, Beatles music and the space program. And for a boy caught between childhood and the teenage years, fitting in wasn't as easy as it seemed. The transition from elementary school to junior high was tough enough, but life at home was even more of a challenge. Kevin's older teenage brother, Wayne, was a typical wise guy whose main pleasure in life was to tease and humiliate him. Older sister Karen lived in her own little hippie world and had little interaction with the rest of the family. By the fall of 1990, Karen had moved out of the house and in with her boyfriend, Michael (David Schwimmer.) At the end of the 1991–1992 season, Karen and Michael married in an outdoor "hippie" ceremony that upset her family, and moved to Alaska.

Mom Norma was not the typical doting mother. She appeared to be emotionally distant, as did Kevin's sometimes argumentative and intimidating dad, Jack, who was always wrung out from a hard day at work. They seemed to be a couple of put-upon parents who probably married too young and were suffering from burnout in trying to cope with life in general, and the care and feeding of three rambunctious teenagers in particular. So what's a guy to do?

The series' theme song, "With a Little Help from My Friends" by Joe Cocker, says it all. You hang out with your bespectacled best friend Paul and your hoped-for girlfriend, Winnie, and try to make the best of it.

The Wonder Years never garnered the spectacular ratings of a show such as *Cosby*, but it did wind up in the Nielsen Top Ten for two of its five seasons. And as with most programs where "the kid eventually grows up," there comes a time when all good things must come to an end. Creative differences between producers and ABC began to spring up, and economic pressures, including rising actor salaries and the need for more location shooting after Kevin acquired a driver's license both helped to unravel those wonderful years. In the final episode, which aired on May 12, 1993, Kevin quit his job working in his dad's furniture store and struck out on his own — without his beloved Winnie.

Among the awards *The Wonder Years* earned during its run were an Emmy for best comedy series in 1988 — after only six episodes had aired — and the George Foster Peabody Award in 1990. *TV Guide* named the show one of the 1980s' 20 best.

Broadcast History

ABC

March 1988–April 1988	Tuesday 8:30–9:00
October 1988–February 1989	Wednesday 9:00–9:30
February 1989–August 1990	Tuesday 8:30–9:00
August 1990–August 1991	Wednesday 8:00–8:30
August 1991–February	Wednesday 8:30–9:00
March 1992–September 1993	Wednesday 8:00–8:30

Cast

Kevin Arnold (age 12)	Fred Savage
Kevin (as adult; voice only)	Daniel Stern
Wayne Arnold	Jason Hervey

Karen Arnold	Olivia d'Abo
Norma Arnold	Alley Mills
Jack Arnold	Dan Lauria
Paul Pfeiffer	Josh Saviano
Winnie (Gwendolyn) Cooper	Danica McKellar
Coach Cutlip	Robert Picardo
Becky Slater	Crystal McKellar
Mrs. Ritvo (1988–1989)	Linda Hoy
Kirk McCray (1988–1989)	Michael Landes
Carla Healy (1988–1990)	Krista Murphy
Mr. DiPerna (1988–1991)	Raye Birk
Mr. Cantwell (1988–1991)	Ben Stein
Doug Porter (1989–1991)	Brandon Crane
Randy Mitchell (1989–1993)	Michael Tricario
Craig Hobson (1989–1990)	Sean Baca
Ricky Halsenback (1991–1993)	Scott Nemes
Jeff Billings (1992–1993)	Giovanni Ribisi
Michael (1992)	David Schwimmer

Roseanne

First Broadcast: October 18, 1988
Last Broadcast: August 26, 1997

Roseanne was one of the most successful series of the late '80s and early '90s. It always received great ratings and was awarded with four Emmys, three Golden Globes and four American Comedy Awards.

Comedienne Roseanne Arnold created the "domestic goddess" character Roseanne Conner, based on her own comic persona — an outspoken, loudmouthed, working class mother and wife who jokes and mocks the unfairness of her situation, men and sexism. Her humor aggressively attacks whomever and whatever would denigrate fat poor women — husbands, family and friends, the media, or government welfare policies.

Roseanne and Dan Connor were not the picture perfect couple. They didn't have a perfect life, perfect children or perfect looks, but the Connors were a loving, struggling, blue collar family, living in Lanford, Illinois. Dan Connor was a frequently unemployed small time contractor, who eventually opened up his own motorcycle shop. Roseanne worked at a plastics plant when the series began, then had a stint as a waitress, and finally went into the restaurant business for herself. At home, she loudly ruled the roost — whose decor was not shabby-chic, but just shabby. According to Roseanne, they were white trash, and proud of it. When, in the show's last season, the Connors won $108 million in the Illinois State Lottery, Roseanne gleefully proclaimed, "We're everyone's worst nightmare: White trash with money."

Daughter Becky was the oldest of three. When the series began, she was a typical, boy-crazy 13-year-old who was often embarrassed by her parents' unabashed behavior, especially when they were out in public or in front of her friends. Middle child Darlene was a bit of a tomboy who loved to torment both her siblings as well as Roseanne. She was the loner of the clan, preferring her own company to that of the rest of the world. D.J. was the six year old baby of the family, impressionable, gullible and the only child who truly idolized his dad.

Roseanne's sister Jackie was a frequent guest in the Connor household. Jackie was single and dated a lot of men, always looking for Mr. Right. She worked with Roseanne at the plastics plant, then quit to become a Lanford police officer, and finally ended up as the co-owner of a diner, the Lanford Lunchbox, where pulled meat sandwiches were their specialty. Roseanne and Jackie's mother gave them each a lump sum of money, and the three women pooled it to open the restaurant.

Roseanne and Dan's parenting skills were not politically correct, but they were effective. With all the yelling, threatening, and punishment doled out, the kids knew right from wrong. They just didn't always apply it.

Broadcast History

ABC

October 1988–February 1989	Tuesday 8:30–9:00
February 1989–September 1994	Tuesday 9:00–9:30
September 1994–March 1995	Wednesday 9:00–9:30
March 1995–May 1995	Wednesday 8:00–8:30
May 1995–September 1995	Wednesday 9:30–10:00
September 1995–May 1997	Wednesday 8:00–8:30

Cast

Roseanne Connor	Roseanne
Dan Connor	John Goodman
Jackie Harris	Laurie Metcalf
Darlene Connor	Sara Gilbert
Becky Connor (1988–1992, 1995–1996)	Lecy Goranson
Becky Connor (1993–1997)	Sarah Chalke

D.J. Connor	Michael Fischman
Ed Connor	Ned Beatty
Bev Connor	Estelle Parsons
Crystal Anderson	Natalie West
Mark Healy	Glenn Quinn
David Healy	Johnny Galecki
Leon Carp	Martin Mull

Empty Nest

First Broadcast: October 8, 1988
Last Broadcast: July 8, 1995

The Golden Girls creator Susan Harris decided to develop a companion show, set just down the street from the girls, centering around the empty nest syndrome, an idea never touched on before in the plot of a weekly series. Harris stated that she herself was experiencing the empty nest syndrome in her own life at the time she wrote the script. The show's title was a bit of a misnomer, in that Dr. Harry Weston's happy "nest" was rarely empty.

Empty Nest originally aired as an episode of *The Golden Girls* on May 16, 1987. It starred Rita Moreno, Paul Dooley, Geoffrey Lewis, David Leisure, and Jane Harnick and centered around the girls' neighbor Renee Corliss and her doctor husband, George. Moreno played Renee, who was coping with the empty nest syndrome and was tired of George (Dooley) always being busy with his medical practice. But Harris was fearful that the show would become stagnant with a married couple complaining of being lonely week after week, despite the help that would no doubt come with a strong lead-in like *The Golden Girls*. So producers scrapped the idea of the Corliss clan, "killed off the wife" (in Harris' words), and retooled the series around a widowed pediatrician, his adult daughters who lived on their own, a wacky neighbor, countrified nurse, and lovable dog. The new and improved version of *Empty Nest* debuted in the fall of 1988 and the rest, as they say, is history.

Dr. Weston was a successful pediatrician, father of three daughters, a recent widower, and one of the most eligible bachelors in town. Eldest daughter Carol and middle child Barbara shared his Miami home. A third daughter, Emily, was away at college, and rarely seen during the series' run. Harry had his hands full with a hectic workload, a wisecracking secretary, Laverne, and two grown daughters with their own myriad of problems. There were days when the only sane being in Harry's life was his huge, faithful dog, Dreyfuss.

Carol was a lonely, needy, nagging, meddlesome divorcee on a constant quest for the perfect mate. But according to sister Barbara, "When Carol drives down the highway of men, she always gets off at the idiot exit." In addition to going from man to man, she also went from job to job and nervous breakdown to nervous breakdown. At the start of the show's fifth season, an eccentric artist, Patrick Arcola, went from the Westons' sprinkler man to Carol's live-in lover, much to Harry's chagrin.

Barbara was a financially troubled police officer, but always upbeat and carefree. Her job didn't necessarily worry her father, except on those occasions when she trotted out the door dressed like a hooker for her latest undercover assignment. A frequent guest in the Weston house was next door neighbor Charlie Dietz. Charlie would make a good used car salesman if he weren't already gainfully employed as a skirt-chasing cruise ship worker. He dropped in all the time to "borrow" food and get on everyone's nerves.

In the series' last season, *Empty Nest* made room for yet another tenant when *Golden Girl* Sophia Petrillo moved in with the Westons. She had moved back to the Shady Pines Retirement Home when *The Golden Girls* ended its run, but the strict rules of the Shady Pines manager become too much for her to handle, so she took off and landed on Harry Weston's doorstep. Sophia eventually became too much for Harry to handle and nearly drove him to the verge of insanity.

Broadcast History

NBC

October 1988–July 1991	Saturday 9:30–10:00
August 1991–July 1994	Saturday 9:00–9:30
August–October 1994	Saturday 8:30–9:00
October 1994–March 1995	Saturday 8:00–8:30
June–July 1995	Saturday 8:00–8:30

Cast

Dr. Harry Weston	Richard Mulligan
Barbara Weston (1988–1992)	Kristy McNichol
Carol Weston	Dinah Manoff
Charley Dietz	David Leisure
Nurse Laverne Todd	Park Overall
Patrick Arcola (1992–1993)	Paul Provenza
Emily Weston (1993)	Lisa Rieffel
Dr. Maxine Douglas (1993–1995)	Marsha Warfield
Sophia Petrillo (1993–1995)	Estelle Getty

The Simpsons

First Broadcast: December 17, 1989
Last Broadcast:

Ever since they made their television debut as a series of short vignettes on the *Tracy Ullman Show* in 1987, the animated Simpson family of Evergreen Terrace, the nicest upper-lower-middle class section of the fictional town of Springfield, have become cultural icons. *The Simpsons* often parodies the hypocrisy and contradictions found in social institutions such as the nuclear family (and nuclear power), the mass media, and religion. Two of the show's most striking characteristics are its social criticism and satire. It's also been touted as one of the most culturally literate entertainment programs on prime time, strongly proving the point that cartoons are not just for children.

If one were to choose the absolute worst role model for a father, it would be Homer Simpson. He's a beer guzzling lazy slob with a voracious appetite. While he tries to be a good parent, his habit of venting his frustration on son Bart by choking him will not win Homer any Father of the Year awards. Despite the fact that Homer is as dumb as dirt, he earns his living as an ineffectual safety inspector at the Springfield Nuclear Plant. His favorite hangout is Moe's Tavern, and his beverage of choice is Duff Beer, which he guzzles like water. Wife Marge, Homer's high school sweetheart, is the patient, gentle, family peacemaker with an enormous blue beehive hairdo. She's a happy homemaker and mother of their three children, Bart (her "special little guy"), Lisa and Maggie. She's a strong, savvy, fairly intelligent woman (so why is she married to a buffoon?) who loves her "Homie" unconditionally, even though he tests her patience on a daily basis.

Of their three children, fourth-grader Bart could easily be considered every parent's worst nightmare. He's the consummate wise guy, always gleefully getting into trouble and loving every minute of it. The two most important things in Bart's life are grossing people out and being cool. Middle sister Lisa is 8 years old, going on 30. For some reason, she managed to elude Homer's gene pool and is quite the brainiac. A straight-A student and saxophone prodigy, she can't wait for college. A strict vegetarian, she stands up for her convictions and longs for world peace ... and a pony. Baby sister Maggie spends most of her time crawling around the floor sucking on a pacifier. Although she can't speak, she did learn how to write her name with an Etch-a-Sketch.

There are dozens of recurring characters, such as Homer's father, Abe, who lives in a retirement home; Marge's chain-smoking twin sisters, Selma and Patty Bouvier; Homer's boss, Mr. Burns; school principal Seymour Skinner; Bart's favorite TV show host, Krusty the Klown; neighbor Ned Flanders, and Kwik-E-Mart clerk, Apu Nahasapeemapetilon.

The show is now seen in more than 70 countries worldwide. Its popularity has celebrities clamoring for a guest-starring role. Bob Hope, Paul McCartney, Meryl Streep, Jay Leno, Tom Jones, Elizabeth Taylor, Larry King, and Britney Spears have lent their dulcet tones to characters on the series.

Broadcast History

FOX

December 1989–August 1990	Sunday 8:30–9:00
August 1990–April 1994	Thursday 8:00–8:30
April 1994–May 1994	Thursday 8:00–9:00
May 1994–July 1994	Thursday 8:00–8:30
August 1994	Sunday 8:00–9:00
September 1994–October 1994	Sunday 8:00–8:30
October 1994–December 1994	Sunday 8:00–9:00
December 1994–April 1996	Sunday 8:00–8:30
January 1995–February 1995	Sunday 7:00–7:30
April 1996–May 1996	Sunday 8:00–9:00
May 1996–July 1998	Sunday 8:00–8:30
August 1998	Sunday 8:00–9:00
August 1998–	Sunday 8:00–8:30

Cast (voices)

Homer Simpson (Also Barney Gumble, Grandpa Simpson, Mayor Quimby, Krusty the Clown and others)	Dan Castellaneta
Marge Simpson (Also Selma and Patty Bouvier, Grandma Jackie Bouvier)	Julie Kavner
Bartholomew J. "Bart" Simpson	Nancy Cartwright
Lisa Simpson	Yeardley Smith
Mrs. Krabappel	Marcia Wallace
Moe Szyslak (Also Apu, Chief Wiggum, Dr. Nick Riviera, and others)	Hank Azaria

Family Matters

First Broadcast: September 22, 1989
Last Broadcast: July 17, 1998

Apparently family did matter to the Winslows of suburban Chicago, because their home was packed floor to ceiling with relatives. The show focused on the lives of the middle-class black family and their extended clan. A spin-off of the hit series *Perfect Strangers* (where Harriette Winslow was the elevator operator), this show introduced America to what Harriette had to put up with when she came home from work: all the trials and tribulations that go into making one big, happy family. Her role on *Perfect Strangers* was supposed to be a small one, but good things do come in small packages.

Carl Winslow was a tough Chicago cop by day, but a big, lovable teddy bear at home. Like many television dads, he was the put-upon, taken for granted head of household, who frequently suffered the slings and arrows of fatherhood. He and wife Harriette had three children when the series began, but at the end of the show's fourth season, Judy, the youngest of the three Winslow children, walked upstairs to her room ... and was never seen again, the result of "a budget consideration." Of the two remaining children, Eddie, 19, was a typical, hormonal college guy whose interests included hanging out with his buddy Waldo Faldo and girls. Laura was a bright 18-year-old who clearly inherited her mother's take-charge personality and clever wit. Much of her time was spent trying to get away from nerdy neighbor Steve Urkel, who has a major crush on her.

You might say that Harriet wears the pants in the family. She has her hands full with not only working full-time at the department store but also in tending to the needs of her family. Between working out of the house and taking care of home and hearth, both Carl and Harriette, like most working parents, get frazzled at times. Carl's outspoken and opinionated mother also lives at home, having moved in during the show's first episode. Harriette's recently widowed sister, Rachel, and her toddler son, Ritchie, are also living under the same roof. No matter how large the family got or how many problems were needed to be solved, the show was all about sending out the message that family matters.

In the second season, the Winslows' neighbor Steve Urkel became a regular on the show. The character was intended to be a one-time guest role, but his popularity turned into a nine-year run. Urkel's presence infuriated everyone, but Carl was particularly chagrined by the nerdy, precocious child with oversized glasses, hiked up trousers and a nasal voice. Steve Urkel was so popular, story lines changed quite a bit, and many of the cast members felt pushed off to the side. When JoMarie Payton's character of Harriette was upstaged, she felt there should be more stories about the mom and dad and their relationship with the children, but the studio had a different point of view. In 1997 she left the series and producers filled her role with another actress, Judyann Elder.

Broadcast History

September 1989–April 1991	ABC Friday 8:30–9:00
August 1990–September 1990	ABC Tuesday 8:00–8:30
April 1991–May 1991	ABC Friday 9:00–9:30
May 1991–August 1991	ABC Friday 8:30–9:00
August 1991–May 1997	ABC Friday 8:00–8:30
June 1997–August 1997	ABC Saturday 8:00–8:30
September 1997–October 1997	CBS Friday 8:00–8:30
November 1997–June 1998	CBS Friday 9:00–9:30
June 1998–July 1998	CBS Friday 9:00–10:00

Cast

Carl Winslow	Reginald VelJohnson
Harriette Winslow	JoMarie Payton
Grandma Winslow	Rosetta LeNoire
Eddie Winslow	Darius McCrary
Laura Winslow	Kellie Shanygne Williams
Judy Winslow	Jaimee Foxworth
Rachel Crawford	Telma Hopkins
Ritchie Crawford	Bryton McClure
Steve Urkel	Jaleel White
Waldo Faldo	Shawn Harrison
Myra Monkhouse	Michelle Thomas
Maxine Johnson	Cherie Johnson

Major Dad

First Broadcast: September 17, 1989
Last Broadcast: September 13, 1993

In the show's pilot, Polly Cooper, a widow with three daughters and liberal reporter for *The Oceanside Chronicle*, is given an assignment to interview the conservative Maj. J.D. "Mac" MacGillis, a career Marine and lifelong bachelor. She ends up writing a rather disparaging article on the Marines, and the Major sets out to prove her wrong. As he tries to do so, romantic sparks begin to fly. While it would seem unlikely that the twosome have anything at all in common, they fall in love. When Mac proposes to Polly, with the approval of her daughters, the couple are married. Once the clan moves in together, their settling in turns out to be a domestic boot camp for them all.

At first, both Mac and Polly have trouble finding time for each other because of their busy schedules, and because Mac is such a staunch disciplinarian, it's difficult for him to adjust to being the father of three young daughters, thirteen-year-old Elizabeth, eleven-year-old tomboy Robin and six-year-old Casey. Elizabeth attends Keefer High School. Robin likes to play baseball and basketball and ran for president of her student council. Casey is still into dolls. Mac makes mistakes left and right in his newly appointed role of father, as when the family ends up having to see a counselor after the Major unceremoniously tosses out the girls' dead pet bird.

In the show's second season, the family adjusts to the move to Mac's new post at Camp Hollister, and Polly gets a new job at a newspaper on the base, writing human interest stories for *The Bulldog*. John's new position is staff secretary to Gen. Marcus Craig. The series incorporated real-life events of the day, such as government cuts and the Gulf War, into its story lines, and then Vice President Dan Quayle appeared in an episode that marked the Marine Corps' 215th anniversary.

Throughout the series, both Polly and Mac learned to make allowances, as when the Persian Gulf War interrupted the family's routine and John prepared to leave for overseas. The major got to realize a lifelong dream when he performed in the Marine Corps silent drill team. He also posed as a "hunk" for a Camp Hollister "Ideal Serviceman" calendar.

Polly, in an attempt to fit in with the other camp spouses, endured a survival-training day of Marine wives. Eventually, John adopted Polly's children, at which time they dropped their Cooper surname in favor of MacGillis. The moral of the show seemed to be that with love and family on your side, most differences can be ironed out.

Broadcast History

CBS

September 1989	Sunday 8:30–9:00
September 1989–September 1990	Monday 8:00–8:30
September 1990–June 1991	Monday 8:30–9:00
June 1991–July 1991	Monday 8:00–8:30
July 1991–September 1992	Monday 8:30–9:00
August 1992–April 1993	Friday 8:30–9:00
May 93–September 1993	Monday 8:30–9:00

Cast

Major John MacGillis	Gerald McRaney
Polly Cooper MacGillis	Shanna Reed
Elizabeth Cooper	Marisa Ryan
Robin Cooper	Nicole Dubuc
Casey Cooper	Chelsea Hertford
2nd Lt. Gene Holowachuk	Matt Mulhern
Sgt. Byron James	Marlon Archey
Merilee Gunderson	Whitney Kershaw
Chip Russell	Rod Brogan
Gunnery Sgt. Alva Bricker	Beverly Archer
Maj. Gen. Marcus Craig	Jon Cypher

6

The 1990s

This was the decade to show the former top three networks that they weren't the only kids on the block. Besides the growing popularity of cable television, which by the early '90s was pulling in a revenue of $22 billion a year, satellite was starting to become more accessible to the mainstream audience. The regular networks also had to compete with the new mavericks of the WB, UPN and FOX. FOX came up with many new and controversial shows which created a niche for a younger generation, and advertisers played to the younger viewers in a variety of ways, including commercials for condoms.

Cable didn't have as many censorship restrictions as the major networks, but there were still limitations that varied among channels. Stations like Comedy Central really pushed the envelope of good taste and created a niche for those who want television without restriction. *South Park* and *The Man Show* have been both praised and criticized for the same reasons: they have gone far beyond what was considered appropriate. With 60 percent of homes subscribing to cable, there was something for everyone.

By 1995 came WebTV, allowing viewers to combine their regular TV with the internet. That same year, the FCC approved a digital HDTV standard, and in 1998 the first digital TV programs were broadcast.

As with every TV generation before it, another nostalgic TV family was introduced. This time it was the combined Silver/Berger family in *Brooklyn Bridge*. Another African-American family entered the picture with *The Hughleys*, everybody was loving Ray Romano's fictionalized family and *The Golden Girls* was as close-knit a clan as any other conventional television family ever was.

While Peg Bundy and Roseanne still ruled the roost in sitcom-land,

Everybody loves Raymond Barone (Ray Romano) because he's the beleaguered father that most people can relate to. Patricia Heaton stars as his patient and understanding wife, Debra.

well into the decade, HBO introduced a dynamic new dramatic series in 1998, *The Sopranos*, that introduced viewers to another strong woman in the character of Carmela Soprano, wife of mob boss Tony Soprano. Carmela was a different breed of TV wife, and in a strange way, a lot more realistic (despite the fact that she was married to the mob) than many before her.

With the success of such animated shows as *The Simpsons, Beavis and Butt-Head* and the aforementioned *South Park*, another cartoon family joined the roster. They were the redneck Hills of Arlen, Texas, in *King of the Hill.* As in the past, there was plenty of family diversity on the small screen.

Fresh Prince of Bel Air

First Broadcast: September 10, 1990
Last Broadcast: September 9, 1996

You can take the kid out of West Philly, but you can't take West Philly out of the kid.

Now this is a story about how his life got flipped, turned upside down, and how he became the prince of a town called Bel Air.

It all began when things got a little too dicey in black rapper Will Smith's neighborhood and his mother sent him off to live with his wealthy aunt and uncle, who lived in an ornate and posh mansion in Bel Air, California. The culture clash was deafening. The series was co-executive produced by music legend Quincy Jones, and Grammy Award winning singer and actor Will Smith portrayed the kid from a tough West Philadelphia neighborhood.

Will's uncle, Philip Banks, was a snooty, successful judge. Will immediately clashed with Uncle Phillip, even though Phillip was raised in a tough neighborhood much like Will's, and understood the young rapper to a tee. Philip and wife Vivian, who spent a lot of time trying to mediate between Will and her husband, shared their palatial mansion with three children and the requisite butler. Carlton was their eldest child and only son. While he and Will were about the same age, Carlton was as preppy as Will was hip-hop. Carlton loved Tom Jones and his idol was Macaulay Culkin. Teenage daughter Hilary was as spoiled as she could possibly be, and as obsessed with clothing as she was with herself. Then there was Ashley, the sweet, unaffected baby of the family. Ashley and Will became instant allies. Will adapted easily to the indulgent lifestyle and became a constant reminder to the family that the simplest pleasures of family life can't be bought at any price.

Throughout the series' run, many guest stars made appearances on the show, including Naomi Campbell, Isiah Thomas, Queen Latifa, boxing champ Evander Holyfield, Vivica A. Fox, Vanessa Williams, Tom Jones, Boyz II Men, Donald Trump, Marla Maples, Dick Clark and Chris Rock.

In the show's final episode, Uncle Phil has the family's Bel Air home up for sale. Many prospective buyers stop by to check out the house including George and "Weezie" Jefferson and Arnold and Mr. Drummond from *Diff'rent Strokes.*

Broadcast History

NBC

September 1990–June 1995	Monday 8:00–8:30
June 1995–July 1995	Monday 8:00–9:00

July 1995–May 1996	Monday 8:00–8:30
May 1996–September 1996	Monday 8:00–9:00

CAST

Will Smith	Will Smith
Phillip Banks	James Avery
Vivian Banks (1990–1993)	Janet Hubert–Whitten
Vivian Banks (1993–1996)	Daphne Maxwell Reid
Carlton Banks	Alfonso Ribeiro
Hilary Banks	Karyn Parsons
Ashley Banks	Tatyana Ali
Geoffrey	Joseph Marcell
Nicky Banks (1994–1996)	Ross Bagley
Jazz (1990–1994)	Jeff Townes (D.J. Jazzy Jeff)
Vy Smith	Vernee Watson Johnson

Brooklyn Bridge

First Broadcast: September 20, 1991
Last Broadcast: August 6, 1993

The creator/producer of *Brooklyn Bridge* was Gary David Goldberg of *Family Ties* fame, and the show, set in 1956 Brooklyn, was a semi-autographical labor of love. Goldberg notified CBS that he'd do this "comedy, with drama" only on his own terms. "It's an eccentric show. It has a specific voice and a specific point of view. And I am not going to be involved in the homogenization of that point of view," Goldberg told TV critics.

His recollections were rosy. The women played mah-jongg, and the boys obsessed about the Dodgers. From her nearby apartment, Grandma Sophie Berger (Marion Ross), based directly on Goldberg's grandmother, was always looking out for her brood, not to mention defrosting the dinner before she's even put out the breakfast.

"There was a simplicity of life then," said Goldberg in an interview shortly after the show debuted. "The bedrock feeling was that the world was getting better and that kids would have what their parents didn't have. In that neighborhood, you could come home from school, you could go into any apartment, and they'd know just what to do. Milk and cookies, change your clothes, send you back out to the school yard again. That sense of security and safety is gone, everywhere."

Brooklyn Bridge focused on the young life of 14-year-old Alan Silver, the product of an extended middle-class Jewish family. At 14, Alan's main aspiration was to be a Brooklyn Dodger. He lived in a lower-middle class apartment with his parents, Phyllis and George, and younger brother, Nathaniel. Unlike most brothers, there was very little sibling rivalry between the two. For the most part, Nathaniel idolized Alan. A bit unusual for the 1950s, both of Alan's parents worked — Dad at night at the post office, and Mom in an insurance office during the day — so in some ways, Alan took on the role of Nathaniel's surrogate dad. His maternal grandparents, Jules and Sophie, lived in the same building, and because of conflicting working schedules, the boys would go down and have breakfast with their grandparents and go there after school as well. Grandma Sophie was indeed the overprotective matriarch of the clan. She was strong willed and always had the last word. Grandpa Jules had more of a "live and let live" attitude. Both Polish immigrants, they contributed to an "old world/new world" clash on the show. Because the two boys spent as much time with their grandparents as at home, the two families were a close-knit extension of each other.

Outside the home, Alan and his multiethnic collection of friends including Nicholas, Benny and Warren were either found in the senior Berger's apartment looking for Alan, or sitting at the counter of the neighborhood candy store, run by wisecracking, cigar smoking Sid Elgart. Alan also had a girlfriend, Katie Monahan, and the fact that she was as Catholic as could be drove Sophie nuts.

When the show debuted, the only recognizable face was that of Marion Ross. After playing the white bread "Mrs. C" on *Happy Days* for many years, some thought it was a stretch that Marion Ross could portray the head of a Jewish immigrant family from Poland. But she did, very capably.

Because of her convincing performance, many have mistaken her for being Jewish, "but I'm not," she admitted in an interview. "I'm really a Scots Irish Presbyterian who grew up in the Midwest." Still, playing ethnic roles is something she's done throughout her career.

While Ross went from mother on *Happy Days* to grandmother on *Brooklyn Bridge*, Louis Zorich (who is married to Oscar winner Olympia Dukakis), who portrayed Jules Berger, did just the opposite when he subsequently went from grandfather to father as Paul Reiser's TV dad on *Mad About You*.

Even though the show had a relatively short run, it was well received by audiences and won several awards including a Golden Globe, a Humanitas Prize and eight Emmy nominations. "That program was too good for television," Ross said of the CBS series, which was yanked in 1995 after a year and a half on the air.

Broadcast History

CBS

September 1991–October 1991	Friday, 8:30–9:00
October 1991	Friday 8:00–8:30
November 1991–December 1991	Wednesday 8:00–8:30
December 1991–June 1992	Wednesday 8:30–9:00
September 1992–October 1992	Saturday 8:30–9:00
October 1992–November 1992	Saturday 8:30–9:00
April 1993	Saturday 9:30–10:00
July 1993–August 1993	Friday 8:30–9:00

Cast

Alan Silver	Danny Gerard
Sophie Berger	Marion Ross
Jules Berger	Louis Zorich
Phyllis Berger Silver	Amy Aquino
George Silver	Peter Friedman
Nathaniel Silver	Matthew Louis Siegel
Nicholas Scamperelli	Adam Lavorgna
Katie Monahan	Jenny Lewis
Benny Belinsky	Jake Jondeff
Warren Butcher	Aeryk Egan
Sid Elgart	David Wohl
Uncle Willie	Alan Blumenfeld
Aunt Sylvia (1991–1992)	Carol Kane
Aunt Miriam (1991–1992)	Natalia Nogulich
Uncle Buddy (1991–1992)	Murray Rubin
Cousin Bernie (1991–1992)	Armin Shimerman

The Torkelsons

First Broadcast: September 21, 1991
Last Broadcast: July 3, 1993

Millicent Torkelson's fate in life is to be an abandoned mother of five, scrimping and saving to make ends meet. But despite hard times, Millicent is usually upbeat and keeps a positive attitude. Along with her children Dorothy Jane, Steven Floyd, Ruth Ann, Chuckie Lee, and Mary Sue, the Torkelsons live in a huge, old home in Pyramids Corner, Oklahoma, and because they are financially strapped, Millicent rents out a room to a border, Wesley Hodges. Fourteen-year-old Dorothy Jane is totally embarrassed by her family's financial situation, but keeps it to herself. Like all teenagers, she just wants to fit in with her peers, but her impoverished lifestyle makes that a bit difficult. The school snobs often verbally tear her apart because of her handmade or thrift shop clothing. Each night, Dorothy Jean pours her heart out to "the man in the moon," an imaginary god-like figure that she confides in. One topic she and "the man" discuss on a regular basis is Riley Roberts, the boy next door. Dorothy Jean has a big crush on him, but her prince charming seems oblivious.

In the show's first season, plot lines revolved around Dorothy Jean's life, both within the family and at school. When she's not pining over Riley, she deals with sibling rivalry, trying to rectify her mother's single status, trying to become an exchange student so she can leave barren Oklahoma and move to Paris, and her dad popping in and out of her life on an irregular basis. One theme that runs throughout the show is homespun family values. Even though they don't have a whole lot of money, they have each other, and a whole lot of love.

Millicent sets a great example for her children. She uses her homespun Yankee ingenuity to make ends meet, is always smiling and goes out of her way to find family bonding activities. She makes homemade preserves to supplement the family income, haggles over prices while shopping, and is fiercely protective of her brood.

After *The Torkelsons* was canceled after only 20 episodes, the show was resurrected and renamed *Almost Home.* The premise for the updated version of the series was that Millicent was financially forced to move out of their house, so she packed up most of the kids and moved to Seattle, Washington, where Millicent became a nanny for widower/businessman Brian Morgan's two spoiled, mean children, Molly and Greg. Children Steven Floyd, Ruth Ann, and Border Hodges did not make the trip West.

Broadcast History

NBC

September 1991–November 1991	Saturday 8:30–9:00
November 1991–March 1002	Sunday 7:30–8:00
May 1992–June 1992	Saturday 8:30–9:00
February 1993–July 1993	Saturday 8:00–8:30

Cast

Millicent Torkelson	Connie Ray
Dorothy Jane Torkelson	Olivia Burnette
Mary Sue Torkelson	Rachel Duncan
Bootsie	Ronnie Claire Edwards

Kirby Scroggins	Paige Gosney
Riley Roberts	Michael Landes
Steven Floyd Torkelson	Aaron Michael Metchik
Chuckie Lee Torkelson	Lee Norris
Ruth Ann Torkelson	Anna Slotky
Wesley Hodges	Willaim Schallert
Brain Morgan	Perry King
Molly Morgan	Brittany Murphy
Greg Morgan	Jason Marsden

Blossom

First Broadcast: January 3, 1991
Last Broadcast: June 5, 1995

The Russos were yet another divorced family of the '90s, but in their case, it was the father who got custody of the kids while Mom moved to Paris to start a new life.

Blossom was the middle child and only girl in the clan. Older brother Anthony, a paramedic, also happened to be a recovering substance abuser. Younger brother Joey was intellectually clueless, but a teeny bopper's dream guy, whose catch phrase was "Whoa!" While not a raving beauty, Blossom had "chutzpah." When life handed her lemons, she made lemonade. With a little help from her best friend, Six, and her rough around the edges boyfriend, Vinnie, Blossom tackled life with gusto.

In the process, she took on all the usual teenage dilemmas like school, teenage crushes, burgeoning sexuality, and passing her driver's test, but her world was even more complicated than that. Blossom had to assume the role of mother hen, having to deal with problems such as Anthony's struggle to stay sober and her slightly irresponsible father's new girlfriends when she should have been able to be a carefree teenager. Her coping mechanisms included recording her thoughts in a video diary and a little bit of day dreaming. Blossom often fantasized about getting advice from the likes of Phil Donahue and Sonny Bono. While most kids snuggled up to teddy bears at night, Blossom slept with an ALF doll.

By the show's fourth season, Blossom longs to spend time with her mother, so off she flies to Paris. By the fourth episode of the season, Blossom must make a difficult decision and decide whether to stay in Paris with her mother. Of course, she returns home.

The last season of the show saw many changes which Blossom was reluctant to accept. A now-married Anthony moves out of the house and is about to become a father, Nick marries girlfriend Carol, Blossom enrolls in UCLA then gets her first real job, Joey proposes to his girlfriend, and Nick and Carol are expecting a baby. Through it all, Blossom dealt with a lot of frank issues that she worked through while remaining true to her values.

BROADCAST HISTORY

NBC

January 1991	Thursday 8:30–9:00
January 1991–June 1991	Monday 8:30–9:00
August 1991–March 1995	Monday 8:30–9:00
May 1995–June 1995	Monday 8:30–9:00

CAST

Blossom Russo	Mayim Bialik
Anthony Russo	Michael Stoyanov
Joey Russo	Joey Lawrence
Six LeMuere	Jenna Von Oy
Carol Russo	Finola Hughes
Vinnie Bonitardi	David Lascher
Nick Russo	Ted Wass
Buzz Richman	Barnard Hughes
Shelly Russo	Samaria Graham

Dinosaurs

First Broadcast: April 26, 1991
Last Broadcast: July 20, 1994

The Sinclair family lived in in the year 60,000,003 B.C., on the continent of Pangaea. Head of the cave was Earl Sinclair, a blue collar worker, employed for the past 25 years by the Wesayso Development Corporation as a tree pusher. His job description was to level trees to make way for new tract housing. Earl smoked cigars, was blustery and a bit henpecked. Sensible Fran, Earl's wife, stayed at home and took care of her husband and the children, teenagers Robbie and Charlene, and an adorable toddler, Baby. Charlene's a typical teenager who has only one hobby: shopping. Robbie is the good guy of the family. He works hard at school and has a great interest in the environment. Baby is in a constant state of the terrible twos. Aside from food, his favorite thing in life is to hit his father over the head with a frying pan. Rounding out the family is Grandma Ethyl, Fran's eccentric yet devoted mother, who lives with the Sinclairs and loves to antagonize Earl. Earl gleefully awaits "Hurling Day" when he'll have the ritual honor of heaving his mother-in-law into the tar pits.

The family dynamics resemble that of *The Simpsons* and *The Flintstones*: a loving but bumbling Dad, a mother who holds the family together and solves most of the problems, and kids who are normal kids, going through the normal phases of growing up. Much like his modern counterparts, Earl had problems at work with his mean, triceratops boss, B.P. Richfield, and had difficulty keeping up with the Jonesasauruses, and his kids. Like the characters in *The Flintstones*, the Sinclairs enjoyed all the modern conveniences, like television and supermarkets. The main difference between the Sinclair family and those in modern times is twofold. In the first place, everything in the family's refrigerator was alive, and often talked back. But more to the point, what made this series unique was that the Sinclairs were dinosaurs. Earl was a megalosaurus and Fran an allosaurus.

Because *Dinosaurs* depicted everyday prehistoric dinosaur life as being very close to human life, the show was able to tackle relevant social concerns in their stories and allowed itself a unique opportunity to comment on our foibles as human beings. In fact, the few human beings depicted in the series were either portrayed as pets or as wild savages, busily scrambling around to try and invent the wheel.

The original idea for the series came from the late Jim Henson, who envisioned using the animatronic technology of his Creature Shop to bring to life a family of dinosaurs in an otherwise normal situation comedy. He enjoyed creating new worlds where none existed before, and this idea seemed to be one whose time had come. The Creature Shop developed huge, lifelike puppets that could be operated from inside by puppeteers, and Brian Henson, Jim's son, devised a process called audio animatronics to bring the facial expressions of these puppets to life.

Gary Owens narrated the series, and in addition to a stellar cast supplying the voices of the show's main characters, folks like Jason Alexander, Christopher Meloni, Buddy Hackett, Michael McKean, Julia Louis Dreyfuss, Tim Curry and Dan Castellaneta (the voice of Homer Simpson) all lent their dulcet tones to the show.

Broadcast History

ABC

April 1991–May 1991	Friday 8:30–9:00
August 1991–February 1992	Wednesday 8:00–8:30
March 1992–February 1993	Friday 9:00–9:30
April 1993–May 1993	Sunday 7:30–8:00

June 1993–September 1993	Friday 9:00–9:30
June 1994–July 1994	Wednesday 8:00–8:30

CAST

Earl Sinclair	Stuart Pankin
Fran Sinclair	Jessica Walter
Charlene Sinclair	Sally Struthers
Robbie Sinclair	Jason Willinger
Baby	Kevin Clash
Grandma Ethel	Florence Stanley
B.P. Richfield	Sherman Hemsley
Spike	Christopher Meloni
Roy Hess	Sam McMurray

Home Improvement

First Broadcast: September 17, 1991
Last Broadcast: May 25, 1999

Home Improvement was conceived from comic Tim Allen's standup act, which had a "Men Are Pigs" theme. The universal themes of the sitcom were family, parenting, the battle of the sexes, and man's need for "more power."

The Taylor family was a throwback to the nuclear family of the 1950s. They live at 510 Glenview Road in suburban Detroit. Father Tim Taylor is an accident-prone bumbler who makes his living as the unlikely host of a local cable television show called "Tool Time." Tim approaches every project as an opportunity to reaffirm his masculinity. His answer to every household repair job was to give it "more power!" but he has a tough time exerting any power around his own home. Wife Jill is the sensible one, and after 11 years of marriage, is often forced to treat Tim like one of their three kids, because a lot of the time, he acts as irresponsibly as their sons, Brad, Randy and Mark. Tim and Jill love each other very much, but they seem to have one basic problem: She has trouble understanding his thought processes and he doesn't understand women at all. Much to Jill's chagrin, Tim tries hard to teach his sons the joys and requirements of manhood, and it's ultimately up to Jill to clean up after Tim's goof ups and gaffes.

Tim Taylor is nothing if not a consistent bumbler. He's got Jill to pick up the pieces at home, and Tim's friend and *Tool Time* costar, Al Borland, saves face for Tim on the show, because Al knows a great deal more about tools and construction. Tim picks on Al mercilessly nonetheless, especially when it comes to Al's mother, who apparently is quite obese. Al's trademark outfit is a flannel shirt.

When lost soul Tim becomes completely befuddled over something, he opts for a backyard over-the-fence chat with his obscure neighbor, Wilson, whose infinite wisdom Tim can never quite grasp. Wilson's face is never fully seen, obscured by a fence or other object, but he's a scholar and often shares quotations of famous people while talking to Tim as they stand on their respective sides of the backyard fence. Wilson's catch phrase is "Hi-dee-ho" and "Howdy, good neighbor" and "Hi ho, neighborette," to Jill.

Despite his foibles on the show, Tim Allen was rated top TV dad by 40 percent of participants in MCI's Friends & Family Father's Day survey. He placed second in Mobil Oil's Father's Day poll in 1996.

Even with a sitcom format, the show's plots weren't always a laugh a minute, as evidenced by the episode "The Longest Day," which aired on April 2, 1996. It dealt with every parent's nightmare: The pain of finding out that one of their children could potentially have cancer.

BROADCAST HISTORY

ABC

September 1991–August 1992	Tuesday 8:30–9:00
August 1992–September 1994	Wednesday 9:00–9:30
March 1994–May 1994	Wednesday 8:00–8:30
September 1994–May 1999	Tuesday 9:00–9:30

CAST

Tim Taylor	Tim Allen
Jill Taylot	Patricia Richardson
Mark Taylor	Taran Smith
Randy Taylor	Jonathan Taylor Thomas
Brad	Zachary Ty Bryan
Wilson	Earl Hindman
Al	Richard Karn
Tool Time Girl Lisa (1991–1993)	Pamela Anderson
Tool Time Girl Heidi (1993–1999)	Debbie Dunning

Step by Step

First Broadcast: September 20, 1991
Last Broadcast: July 17, 1998

Starring former *Dallas* lead Patrick Duffy and *Three's Company* alum Suzanne Somers, a modern day *Brady Bunch* was created when divorced contractor Frank Lambert married widowed beautician Carol Foster. Frank and Carol met while both were on vacations in Jamaica. It was love at first sight, and by the time the vacation ended, they were husband and wife; but any similarity to the Brady clan stops there. This was the '90s, not the saccharine '70s, and the insults and putdowns from the kids flew fast and furious. What a difference two decades made.

Returning to the reality of their lives in Port Washington, Wisconsin, the newlyweds had to break the news of their nuptials to their three respective children, and set up housekeeping together. Their plan was to make the children think they were just dating, but early on, Frank accidentally let the truth slip. Since the secret was out, the Lambert men packed up and moved into the Fosters' house. While Frank and Carol could not have been happier in their marriage, their children could not get along.

Carol's children, teenage Dana, middle child Karen and young Mark, are as neat, tidy and well organized as their mother. The Lambert brood, comprised of teenage son J.T., preteen tomboy Alicia, "Al" and young Brendan, are just the opposite. While the kids are dissimilar in most areas, they all agree on one thing. Neither group feels the need for a new mother or father, and sparks fly early on when Carol sets about creating order by instituting a few rules. Frank gets the chance to get away from the insanity while he's at work, but Carol runs a beauty shop next door to the house along with her sister and mother, so she's always in the thick of things.

The kids attended different schools and were involved in a number of activities. Karen was a cheerleader for the Wildcats football team, and J.T. was on the track team. To earn money Dana worked at the 50's Cafe as the assistant manager and J.T. worked there as a waiter, a shampoo boy in his mother's home salon and later as a car salesman. Karen was a teen model at Peterson's Department Store and Alicia worked at Mr. Chips. For fun, Dana studied; Karen shopped; Alicia played Beavers little league baseball and studied to become an actress; and J.T. chased the young ladies, hung out at the Burger Palace and had his own cable access program called "J.T. and Cody's World." Because all the kids lived very independent lives, Carol was always trying to think of ways to bring the two families closer, which rarely worked out.

In the show's fourth episode, Frank's spacy nephew, Cody, shows up and becomes a permanent fixture, living in his van in the family's driveway. By season two, Carol's mother and sister were written out of the show, and stories dealt more with the children's conflicts than anything else. By season three, Cody was the main focus of the show. During the fourth season, Carol and Frank surprised the family with the news that Carol was expecting a child. She was named Lilly Foster-Lambert.

Lilly would appear irregularly during season five, but in season six, Lilly was more involved in the plot, because she was now miraculously five years old.

BROADCAST HISTORY

ABC

September 1991–August 1993	Friday 8:30–9:00
August 1992–September 1992	Tuesday 8:30–9:00
August 1993–March 1997	Friday 9:00–9:30
March 1996	Friday 9:30–10:00
April 1996–September 1996	Friday 9:00–9:30
March 1997–May 1997	Friday 9:30–10:00
June 1997–August 1997	Friday 8:00–8:30
September 1997–March 1998	Friday 9:30–10:00
June 1998–July 1998	Friday 9:30–10:00

CAST

Frank Lambert	Patrick Duffy
Carol Lambert	Suzanne Somers
J.T. Lambert	Brandon Call
Alicia "Al" Lambert	Christine Lakin
Brendan Lambert	Josh Byrne
Dana Foster	Staci Keanan
Karen Foster	Angela Watson
Mark Foster	Christopher Castile
Lilly Lambert (1995–1996)	Lauren/Kristina Mayering
Lilly Lambert (1997–1998)	Emily Mae Young
Cody	Sasha Mitchell
Ivy Baker	Peggy Rea
Penny Baker	Patrika Darbo

Grace Under Fire

First Broadcast: September 29, 1993
Last Broadcast: September 17, 1998

Grace Under Fire was a blue collar comedy centered around the life of a Victory, Missouri, single mom, struggling to raise her three children as best she can. Interestingly enough, *Grace Under Fire* became the first American sitcom to be broadcast regularly in Russia. The show's star, comedienne Brett Butler, began her career as cocktail waitress and then as a writer for the Dolly Parton TV series *Dolly* in 1987. Eventually, her standup routine that poked fun of her southern heritage and her relationships with men became the inspiration for the ABC series.

Grace Kelly is a smart-talking, wisecracking, no-nonsense, 36-year-old survivor. After spending eight years as her alcoholic husband Jimmy's punching bag, she opts to set off and raise their three children by herself. Out on her own, Grace is one tough cookie. To support her family she has worked as a waitress at Stevie Ray's Bar and at the CBD Oil Refinery. Being a recovering alcoholic herself, she has many demons to conquer while trying to raise her kids the best way she can. Son Quentin is an eight-year-old troublemaker, just like his dad. He idolizes his father and not knowing the whole story, often blames Grace for the breakup. Five-year-old Libby is a sweetie, and compared to Quentin, an easy child to raise. Baby Patrick spends most of his time in his crib. Despite disruptive visits from her ex-husband and her meddlesome former mother-in-law, Jean, her financial instability and trying to be "one of the boys" at work, Grace forges on.

In what little spare time Grace can muster, she volunteers her time at the local Crisis Center where she gives counsel to other women who suffer some of the same indignities that she herself has gone through: drug addiction, physical abuse and other traumas.

Her contempt for men and authority figures is quite obvious, as is her angst about having to juggle the tasks of raising a family and working full time. Grace's opinionated mother-in-law Jean Kelly later moved in to take care of the kids while Grace worked. Ex-husband Jimmy is a constant source of irritation, and there are times she's helpless to resolve certain issues between them, especially when it comes to keeping the delicate balance between her hatred of him and trying not to pass that hatred down to her children. When the kids aren't listening, Grace refers to Jimmy as a "knuckle-dragging, cousin-loving, beer-sucking redneck husband."

Grace suffers the same problems as many financially strapped single mothers, such as back child support, latchkey kids, co-workers' wives and girlfriends who perceive her as a rival and a threat, and sexual harassment. Trying to improve her social life, Grace soon learns that single mothers with children have it rough in the dating arena as when her new boyfriend, Ryan, comes to dinner and learns that Grace's kids are more than he'd bargained for. Fortunately, Grace has a great support group nearby. Her best friend is Nadine Swoboda, Grace's pal from high school who lives next door with her fourth husband, Wade Swoboda. Russell Norton, a recently divorced pharmacist who used to date Grace, has remained a good friend and is always around to help Grace maintain her sanity. Through it all,

Grace loves her children, tries to forgive Jimmy for his past abuses, and tries to set a good example for her family.

BROADCAST HISTORY

ABC

September 1993–March 1994	Wednesday 9:30–10:00
May 1994–September 1994	Wednesday 9:30–10:00
September 1994–March 1995	Tuesday 9:30–10:00
March 1995–November 1996	Wednesday 9:00–9:30
August 1995–September 1995	Wednesday 8:00–8:30
December 1996–July 1997	Wednesday 8:00–8:30
August 1997–September 1997	Tuesday 8:30–9:00
November 1997–December 1997	Tuesday 8:00–8:30
January 1998–February 1998	Tuesday 9:30–10:00

CAST

Grace Kelly	Brett Butler
Quentin Kelly (1993–1996)	Jon Paul Steuer
Quentin Kelly (1996–1998)	Sam Horrigan
Libby Kelly	Kaitlin Cullum
Patrick Kelly	Cole/Dylan Sprouse
Emmett Kelly	Matt Clark
Russell Norton	Dave Thomas
Nadine Swoboda	Julie White
Wade Swoboda	Casey Sander
Jimmy Kelly	Geoff Pierson
Faith Burdette	Valri Bromfield
Dougie	Walter Olkewicz
Rick Bradshaw	Alan Autry
Jean Kelly	Peggy Rea
Floyd Norton	Tom Poston
Matthew	Tom Everett Scott
Bev Henderson	Julia Duffy

Frasier

First Broadcast: September 16, 1993

Last Broadcast: May 13, 2004

In 1992, Kelsey Grammer decided that he'd had enough of playing the character Frasier Crane on *Cheers* and would leave at the end of the season. He asked *Cheers* writers and producers David Angell, Peter Casey and David Lee if they wanted to work with him on developing a new alter ego for him, and they said yes. Their first idea was to develop a series where Kelsey would play a bedridden millionaire. John Pike, head of Paramount Television, however, wanted Kelsey to continue playing Frasier on his own spinoff. Pike persuaded Kelsey to carry on with *Frasier* by saying he would have a guaranteed hit if he did. So when recently divorced psychiatrist Dr. Frasier Crane left *cheery* Boston and moved back to his hometown of Seattle, little did he realize that life with father would be such a challenge.

Settling into what he hoped would be a new, less stressful life, the pompous and neurotic Frasier sets himself up in a luxurious-high-rise apartment, ready to begin his new job as a radio psychiatrist with a call-in advice show. At first the entire show was to be set at KACL, the radio station where Frasier worked. But producer David Lee had an idea. In addition to the stresses of a new job, the doctor's peaceful home life is also shattered by the arrival of his gruff, ex-cop father, Martin. As his own father had recently had a stroke, this gave David the idea of Frasier having to look after a disabled father. Ignoring the fact that on *Cheers*, Frasier had said his father was dead, they created the character of Martin Crane.

As the story goes, Martin had been injured in the line of duty and forced to move in with one of his two sons, and Frasier won the coin toss. Martin is the complete opposite of his two sons, preferring a beer rather than a glass of sherry and a baseball game to *La Boheme*.

Martin brought with him his live-in home-care provider, Daphne Moon, his pesky Jack Russell terrier, Eddie, and a duct-taped recliner that stands out like a sore thumb amid Frasier's more aesthetically pleasing decor. Their home is frequently visited by Frasier's snobbish, equally neurotic and competitive brother, Niles. One big happy family? Not really. The conflict caused by Martin's blue collar notions and Frasier's uppity convictions is never ending. The two men could not be farther apart in personality. It's obvious that Frasier and Niles take after their late mother's side of the family, but despite their differences, Martin cares deeply for both his sons.

Niles and Frasier spend a great deal of time at their favorite coffee house, Café Nervosa, to try and hash out the day's current dilemma. It is at Café Nervosa that Frasier first meets Niles upon his return to Seattle. It is there in the show's first episode that Frasier and Niles decide that Martin should live with Frasier.

As the show entered its 11th and final season, Kelsey Grammer explained to *Entertainment Tonight* why it would be their last. "Actually when we started the show, I thought we would do 11 seasons. That was my goal, and as we closed in on it, and somewhere toward the end of the tenth season last year, the producers and I sat down and thought, 'Let's call it after this year.'"

Lots of loose ends were tied up in the end. Frasier's issue with co-worker Roz was resolved, Niles' ex-wife, the never-seen Maris, re-enters Niles' life as an off-screen presence and stirs up a little trouble, Frasier's ex-wife Lilith and son will visit, and newlyweds Daphne and Niles will struggle to have a baby. Much of the show's focus that season was on Frasier's continuing search for love, which has caused him an extra dose of angst in the face of Niles' and Daphne's announcement that they're having a child, and father Martin's engagement to Frasier's old baby-sitter, Ronee (Wendie Malick). The finale's guest stars include *Harry Potter* giant Robbie Coltrane and *Without a Trace*'s Anthony LaPaglia, who nabbed an Emmy for his guest turn as the brother of Frasier's sister-in-law, Daphne. And in the end, Frasier also finally found love, so in essence, they all lived happily ever after.

Frasier has earned a total of 30 Emmys , more than any other series in history, including three for Outstanding Lead Actor in a Comedy Series (Kelsey Grammer) and two for Outstanding Supporting Actor in a Comedy Series (David Hyde Pierce). Grammer is also the only actor to ever receive Emmy nominations for playing the same character on three different shows. In addition to *Cheers* and *Frasier*, Dr. Crane also appeared in a 1992 episode of *Wings* that earned Grammer an Outstanding Guest Star nomination.

Broadcast History

NBC

September 1993–May 1994	Thursday 9:30–10:00
September 1994–May 1998	Tuesday 9:00–9:30
September 1998–May 2000	Thursday 9:00–9:30
September 2000–Present	Tuesday 9:00–9:30

Cast

Dr. Frasier Crane	Kelsey Grammer
Dr. Niles Crane	David Hyde Pierce
Martin Crane	John Mahoney
Daphne Moon	Jane Leeves
Roz Doyle	Peri Gilpin
Bob "Bulldog" Briscoe	Dan Butler
Frederick Crane	Trevor Einhorn
Bebe Glazer	Harriet Sansom Harris

Gil Chesterson	Edward Hibbert
Noel Shempsky	Patrick Kerr
Sherry Dempsey	Marsha Mason
Kenny Daly	Tom McGowan
Donny Douglas	Saul Rubinek
Kate Costas	Mercedes Ruehl
Nikos Crane	Joseph Will
Dr. Melinda 'Mel' Karnofsky	Jane Adams
Nanette Stewart	Karen Ann Genaro
Simon Moon	Anthony LaPaglia
Mrs. Gertrude Moon	Millicent Martin
Dr. Lilith Sternin-Crane	Bebe Neuwirth
Lorna Lenley/Lana Gardner	Jean Smart
Eddie (the dog)	Moose

Party of Five

First Broadcast: September 12, 1994
Last Broadcast: May 3, 2000

Party of Five refers to five brothers and sisters determined to stay together and make it on their own after the sudden death of their parents in a car crash. Oldest brother Charlie is appointed legal guardian. At 24, he works as a carpenter during the day and as a bartender at Salinger's, his father's San Francisco restaurant that he took over, at night. Trying to preserve the meaning of family, the Salingers gather together once a week for dinner at the restaurant.

The siblings were as different as night and day. Bailey was a very precocious 16 when his parents died. He originally took over the financial responsibilities of the household, but during the third season suffered from the alcoholism he had inherited from his father. Julia was a year younger than Bailey. She was always a good student in school, but without a parental figure to guide her, she fell prey to the temptations of peer pressure. Having suffered a miscarriage during high school, she married just after graduation and decided to go against everyone's expectations and not attend college. Claudia is a violin prodigy, a talent inherited from her mother. She was the hardest hit by the loss of her parents at the age of 11, and has been trying desperately to fit in as a normal kid ever since. Owen is the youngest of the clan and was just under a year old when his parents died. Charlie is the only parent he knows.

Together, they go through all sorts of problems, from running the family business to disastrous relationships and school problems. Soon they realize that in order to survive, no one can be selfish and they all have to help each other. They're a family and have to stick together.

While *Party of Five* is a show about survival, one of its most appealing characteristics is that it depicts the relationships, traumas, emotions, and struggles faced by teenagers and young adults around the world, and it does so realistically. It also emphasizes the way the family uses all the lessons taught to them by their parents to handle everyday life.

BROADCAST HISTORY

FOX

September 1994–December 1994	Monday 9:00–10:00
December 1994–March 1995	Wednesday 9:00–10:00
June 1995–April 1997	Wednesday 9:00–10:00
August 1997–May 1999	Wednesday 9:00–10:00

CAST

Charlie Salinger	Matthew Fox
Bailey Salinger	Scott Wolf
Julia Salinger	Neve Campbell
Claudia Salinger	Lacey Chabert
Kirsten Salinger	Paula Devicq
Sarah	Jennifer Love Hewitt

The Nanny

First Broadcast: November 3, 1993
Last Broadcast: June 23, 1999

The Nanny was created by actress Fran Drescher and then-husband Peter Marc Jacobson. The series told the story of two unwittingly blended families; the rich Sheffield clan of Manhattan, and the Fines, a lower middle-class Jewish "mishpocheh" from Queens.

Fran Fine was fresh out of her job as a bridal consultant in her boyfriend's shop when she first appeared on the doorstep of British broadway producer, Maxwell Sheffield, peddling cosmetics door to door. She was immediately mistaken for an applicant for the Sheffields' vacant nanny position, and quickly stumbled upon the opportunity to become the nanny for the widower's three children, Maggie, Brighton and Grace. Fran was like a gefilte fish out of water when she moved into the Sheffield mansion. She'd been used to the modest Queens apartment she shared with her parents, Morty and Sylvia. And little did the Sheffields know they were going to get more than just a nanny. They got Sylvia, Fran's pushy, nosy, compulsive-eating mother; Fran's not too bright best friend, Val; and Yetta, Fran's senile grandmother, as well. While Fran's family didn't exactly move into the Sheffield mansion, they seemed to always be there.

Fran brought new life into the house. The Sheffields had been in mourning ever since Mrs. Sheffield passed away. Much to Maxwell's chagrin, the trashy-dressing sexpot with a heart of gold quickly became an unlikely role model for shy teenager Maggie, a formidable opponent for mischievous ten-year-old Brighton, and a ray of sunshine to neurotic six-year-old Grace. She also became a quick ally to nosy butler Niles, who was always aware of everything going on in the house thanks to a convenient intercom in every room, and a threat to Maxwell's business partner, C.C. Babcock, who had dreams of becoming the next Mrs. Sheffield.

Even though Maxwell has dated sexy supermodels, savvy businesswomen and even Marla Maples, the attraction to Fran became evident as the years went by. On an airplane back from a trip to Paris, the plane goes through heavy turbulence, and upon the threat of a disaster, Maxwell opens his heart and tells Fran he loves her. Just as they are about to arrive safely at home, Mr. Sheffield takes back saying "I love you" to Fran, and she is devastated. They play cat and mouse over the next few seasons, but in season five, Maxwell asks Fran out on their first official date. The relationship progresses quickly from there, and five years after their first encounter, the couple wed. Fran finds herself pregnant shortly thereafter and gives birth to twins, Jonah and Eve. Maxwell receives an offer to turn one of his failed plays into a movie, and they move to California to live happily ever after.

Broadcast History

CBS

November 1993	Wednesday 8:00–8:30
December 1993	Monday 8:30–9:00
December 1993–April 1994	Wednesday 8:00–8:30
May 1994–November 1994	Monday 8:00–8:30
November 1994	Monday 8:30–9:00
November 1994–February 1995	Monday 8:00–8:30
May 1995	Wednesday 8:00–8:30
May 1995–May 1996	Monday 8:00–8:30
September 1996	Wednesday 8:00–8:30
September 1996	Wednesday 8:30–9:00
October 1996–March 1999	Wednesday 8:00–8:30

March 1999	Wednesday 8:30–9:00
May 1999–June 1999	Wednesday 8:00–8:30
June 1999	Wednesdays 8:30–9:00

CAST

Fran Fine	Fran Drescher
Maxwell Sheffield	Charles Shaughnessy
Niles	Daniel Davis
C.C. Babcock	Lauren Lane
Maggie Sheffield	Nicholle Tom
Brighton Sheffield	Benjamin Salisbury
Grace Sheffield	Madeline Zima
Sylvia Fine	Renee Taylor
Val Toriello	Rachel Chagall
Grandma Yetta	Ann Guilbert

The Parent 'Hood

First Broadcast: January 18, 1995
Last Broadcast: July 25, 1999

Robert and Jerri Peterson are very much in love. They live in a New York City brownstone with their outspoken housekeeper and four children, aged 15, 14, 7 and 3. The two eldest, Michael and Zaria, are at an age where they're eager to spread their wings and avoid being seen with their not-quite-cool parents at all costs. Meanwhile, 7-year-old Nicholas is quickly discovering the joys of mischief, while toddler Cece is the darling of the family.

Robert is a professor of communications at NYU, and Jerri's in law school. Robert is a big kid at heart who continually dreams up untraditional solutions to traditional family problems. Both parents do their best to share responsibilities, but often have very different ideas about how to get things done. Their lives revolve around trying to balance their lives, their work, and their children at the same time.

Raising a family in the '90s was much more complicated than in previous eras, and sometimes the available tools used to teach could backfire, as when Robert tried to avoid a sex chat with Michael and sent him online to a health program website. Michael used the site to access a computer sex line catering to swingers.

Kids with credit cards was another issue that was not heard of in decades past. Upset when her parents refused to front her the cash for a pair of expensive running shoes, Zaria took a second job at a clothing store where she discovered the wonderful world of buying on credit.

In season four, another cast member was added when the family met with a down-and-out 16-year-old street kid, T.K., who's "broken every law except gravity." Jerri decides to save him before he's "swallowed up by the system" and take him into the Peterson home which at first affects the younger kids quite negatively, but as usual with sitcom fare, all's well that ends well.

Broadcast History

WB

January 1995–July 1996	Wednesday 8:30–9:00
July 1995–August 1995	Wednesday 8:00–8:30
March 1996–July 1996	Sunday 7:30–8:00
July 1996	Wednesday 8:00–8:30
August 1996	Wednesday 8:30–9:00
August 1996–June 1997	Sunday 8:00–8:30
June 1997–July 1997	Wednesday 8:30–9:00
July 1997–December 1997	Sunday 7:30–8:00
January 1998–March 1998	Sunday 8:00–8:30
March 1998–May 1998	Sunday 7:30–8:00
May 1998–June 1998	Sunday 7:00–7:30
June 1998–July 1998	Sunday 7:30–8:00
July 1998–August 1998	Sunday 7:00–8:00
May 1999–July 1999	Sunday 7:00–8:00
July 1999	Sunday 7:00–7:30

Cast

Robert Peterson	Robert Townsend
Jerri Peterson	Suzzanne Douglas
Michael Peterson	Kenny Blank
Zaria Peterson	Reagan Gomez-Preston
Nicholas Peterson	Curtis Williams
CeCe Peterson	Ashli Adams
Wendall Wilcox	Faizon Love

King of the Hill

First Broadcast: January 12, 1997

Mike Judge, creator of *Beavis and Butt-head*, and Greg Daniels, a former writer for *The Simpsons*, are responsible for bringing the animated Hill family of Arlen, Texas, to the small screen. As this and some of the other aforementioned cartoon shows demonstrated, animated offerings of the '90s weren't just for kids anymore.

Patriarch Hank Hill sells propane and propane accessories for Strickland Propane when not spending time in the back alley chewing the fat and having a beer with his motley boyhood friends, Dale, Boomhauer and Bill. An exterminator by trade, Dale is obsessed with conspiracy theories and is the only person in town who doesn't realize that his wife is cheating on him with Native American John Redcorn. Army sergeant Bill has been unshaven and beer-bellied since his wife divorced him, and Boomhauer is an unintelligible ladies' man who works in a barbed-wire factory.

Hank is a staunch conservative who lives and breathes propane, is a devoted family man and proud of his country and of the state of Texas. He's a robust, healthy man, whose only physical shortcoming is his narrow urethra. An old-fashioned guy, Hank's life's ambitions are to turn his chubby, 12 year old son, Bobby, into a "real man" and have the lushest lawn in the neighborhood. Liberals in general and his Laotian next door neighbor, Kahn Souphanousinphone, in particular, are the bane of his existence.

Wife Peggy is a housewife, mother and substitute Spanish teacher. Her proudest achievement to date is winning the Texas State Boggle Tournament. She is a strong-willed Texan woman with a mind of her own who demands and often gets total respect. She reapplies her lipstick 30 times a day, is recognized by family and neighbors as one of the smartest people in Arlen, and has exceptionally big feet. She manages to keep up with the current fashion trends by making special furtive trips to Lubbock's Very Large Shoes.

Bobby's a student at Tom Landry Middle School. He has many life ambitions, including becoming a ladies' man, runway model, proctologist, comic (stand-up or prop), shaman, or following in his father's footsteps and trying his hand as a salesman of propane and propane accessories.

Rounding out the family is Hank's vapid niece, Luanne Platter. She's been sleeping on the fold-out couch in Hank's den ever since her mom went to jail for stabbing her dad with a fork during a nasty brawl over who drank the last beer. Luanne's a C student at the local beauty academy.

The show follows the day-to-day activities of Hank Hill, his family and their neighbors. Hank's home life, a portrait of the "average" American family, is examined, as are the dynamics of a small town whose residents make it their business to know everybody else's business.

BROADCAST HISTORY

FOX

January 1997–July 1998	Sunday 8:30–9:00
July 1998–September 1998	Tuesday 8:00–9:00
September 1998–October 1998	Tuesday 8:00–8:30
October 1998–November 1998	Tuesday 8:00–9:00
November 1998–January 1999	Tuesday 8:00–8:30
June 1999–	Sunday 7:30–8:00

CAST

(Voices)

Hank Hill / Boomhauer	Mike Judge
Peggy Hill	Kathy Najimy
Bobby Hill	Pamela Segall
Luanne Platter	Brittany Murphy
Dale Gribble	Johnny Hardwick
Joseph Gribble	Breckin Meyer
Bill Dauterive	Stephen Root
Cotton Hill/ Kahn Souphanousinphone	Toby Huss
Nancy Gribble	Ashley Gardner
Buckley / Eustis	David Herman
John Redcorn	Jonathan Joss
Minh Souphanousinphone, Connie Souphanousinphone	Lauren Tom

7th Heaven

First Broadcast: August 26, 1996
Last Broadcast:

Eric Camden is a minister in the suburban town of Glen Oak and his wife, Annie is a stay-at-home mom to their seven children, who range in age from early 20s to toddlers. Eric and Annie face the daunting challenge of raising a family during less than God-fearing times. They want what's best for their children and watch out for them, no matter how old they get. Despite his minister status, Eric comes from the progressive school of child rearing, and in spite of their differences, the family is functional. Through all the trials and tribulations of family, the love and support this family has for one another is quite evident. And even with the hectic lives they lead, Eric and Annie manage to keep their romance alive and their family together.

Oldest son Matt has picked up a habit of smoking and not being able to keep a job. Oldest daughter Mary is wanting to kiss a boy. Middle child Lucy is hoping to become a woman and looking forward to getting her period very soon. Belligerent Simon, the youngest son, is hoping for a dog, even though his parents tell him that he is too young. Ruthie, the youngest daughter, is just a cute five-year-old, and toddler twins David and Samuel prove to be a challenge at times. In addition to the usual child rearing issues, Annie is devastated to find out that not only is she going through the change of life, but her mother has just been diagnosed with leukemia, and the family has to deal with the issue of death when her mother does not recover.

Because story lines touched on such topics as the Holocaust, hate crimes, violence in schools, drug use, vandalism, drinking and driving, teen pregnancy, gang violence and homelessness, the series has received numerous awards for chronicling the many complex problems of growing up in the world today.

Broadcast History

WB

August 1996–	Monday 8:00–9:00
May 1998–June 1998	Monday 9:00–10:00
August 1998–November 1999	Sunday 7:00–8:00
November 1999–December 1999	Monday 9:00–10:00
January 2000–September 2000	Sunday 7:00–8:00
September 2001–Present	Monday 8:00–9:00

Cast

Eric Camden	Stephen Collins
Annie Camden	Catherine Hicks
Matt Camden	Barry Watson
Simon Camden	David Gallagher
Mary Camden	Jessica Biel
Lucy Camden	Beverly Mitchell
Ruthie Camden	Mackenzie Rosman
David and Samuel Camden	Nikolas and Lorenzo Brino
Roxanne	Rachel Blanchard
Cecilia	Jessica Simpson
Kevin Kinkirk	George Stults
Ben Kinkirk	Geoff Stults
Roxanne Richardson	Rachel Blanchard
Chandler Hampton	Jeremy London

Everybody Loves Raymond

First Broadcast: September 13, 1996
Last Broadcast: May 16, 2005

Ray Romano never really gave stand-up comedy any serious thought until one fateful open-mike night at a New York comedy club in 1984. He did well. After several odd jobs, including futon mattress delivery boy by day and journeyman comedian by night, he decided to pursue comedy full time. His regular appearances at comedy clubs throughout the country led to guest spots on *The Tonight Show* and finally in 1995, Ray performed a five-minute routine on *The Late Show with David Letterman.* A few days later, Letterman called and offered Romano his own show and a development deal with his production company, Worldwide Pants Inc. From that association, *Everybody Loves Raymond* was born.

Romano took a page from his off-screen life when he created the fictional Barone clan for television. His parents, Lucy and Al, still live in the Forest Hills house where Romano grew up, and his divorced older brother Richard (the city cop upon whom the show's brother Robert is based) resides with them. Ray lived in his parents' house until he was 29. When he got married, he only moved a mile away, to Middle Village. The show's charm springs from its perceptive portrayal of family life. It's not primarily focused on the kids, but on the trifles of adult interactions.

Romano's alter ego, sportswriter Ray Barone, is the married father of three, living in suburban New York. Life on Long Island is hectic at best, what with working full-time to provide for his family, which includes an 11-year-old daughter and seven-year-old twin boys. To everyone's amazement, the fact that Ray Barone writes for a living is nothing short of a miracle. "When I was a teenager," says Ray, "I wanted to write the Great American novel. But then I realized that I didn't even want to *read* the Great American Novel."

Ray's life is made considerably more complicated than it should be because of his squabbling parents, Marie and Frank, and his single brother, Robert, who live just across the street. They feel the need to pop in and out of the Barone house at will, leaving the Barones with no privacy at all. There's no love lost between Ray's wife Debra and overbearing, meddling Marie, a typical mother-in-law. Marie truly believes it is her duty to criticize, criticize, criticize, especially when it comes to Debra's cooking. Dutiful son Ray will never put his foot down where his parents are concerned, lest he upset them; never mind that this lack of support upsets Debra. Ray's only retort is, "I was born with this family, and I'm stuck with them."

The moral of this story is that love and a sense of humor will conquer all.

BROADCAST HISTORY

CBS

September 1996–February 1997	Friday 8:30–9:00
March 1997–June 1998	Monday 8:30–9:00
June 1996–August 1998	Monday 8:30–9:30
August 1998–September 1998	Monday 9:00–10:00
September 1998	Monday 9:00–9:30
April 1999–May 1999	Wednesday 8:00–8:30
September 1999–	Monday 9:00–9:30

CAST

Ray Barone	Ray Romano
Debra Barone	Patricia Heaton
Marie Barone	Doris Roberts
Frank Barone	Peter Boyle
Robert Barone	Brad Garrett
Ally Barone	Madylin Sweeten
Jeffrey Barone	Sawyer Sweeten
Michael Barone	Sullivan Sweeten
Nemo	Joseph V. Perry
Garvin	Len Lesser
Stan	Victor Raider-Wexler
Andy	Andy Kindler
Amy	Monica Horan
Gianni	Jon Manfrellotti
Father Hubley	Charles Durning

3rd Rock from the Sun

First Broadcast: January 9, 1996
Last Broadcast: May 22, 2001

Described by the show's producers as "Carl Sagan meets The Marx Brothers," *3rd Rock from the Sun* was a clever, funny show about a friendly alien invasion, of sorts.

The Solomon clan are comprised of a small group of space aliens who were sent down to the third rock from the sun (Earth) to study the planet and its so-called advanced species known as humans. In order to blend in, they assume human forms. Being trapped in these alien bodies constantly amazes them with little surprises such as puberty, emotions, and even passion, as when the High Commander becomes hopelessly infatuated with his Earthling co-worker. The extraterrestrial team's only worldly power is truthfulness.

Dick Solomon is the High Commander. He goes through life on planet Earth trying to figure everything out and usually getting it all wrong, because he's quite gullible and usually takes everything literally. Sally Solomon, in her original form, is a decorated male military officer. As Security Officer, the second-in-command, she is frustratingly reduced to an inferior role as a woman. Although Tommy Solomon has taken on an adolescent human form, he is actually older than Dick. Harry Solomon is along for the ride because they happened to have an extra seat on the spaceship, but makes himself useful as the transmitter through which the aliens communicate with their leader, the Big Giant Head. This mysterious galactic overlord is both respected and feared by the visiting aliens, but never seen on camera.

The Solomons landed in the college town of Rutherford, Ohio, and live in an apartment owned by eccentric Mrs. Dubcek. The aliens got their last name, Solomon, off the side of a truck. They had discussed whether to become Italian or African American, but chose a Jewish identity without realizing the significance of the choice. It wasn't until later that they discovered their "Jewishness" when Mrs. Dubcek pointed out that their name was obviously Jewish. This observation gave the Solomons a comforting feeling knowing that they were part of an identifiable culture and were in someway starting to fit in with the earthlings. When Sally reported she met a nice guy, the first thing out of Harry's mouth was "Is he Jewish?"

Dick lands himself a job teaching physics at a nearby university, where he finds himself strangely attracted to his office mate, Dr. Mary Albright. Dick gives Tommy an assignment to check out high school, an institution that in four short years can "take a bright, inquisitive child and spit out a burger-flipping automaton." Sally concludes that if she has to be a woman, she's at the ideal age and has the body to prove it. After all, she concludes, they are on an anthropological mission and intend to experience all the emotions and activities life on earth has to offer. Their faith in human nature is shaken at times, but during the course of their journey, they learn, they grow, they fall in love, and while they never completely blend in, their insight is keen enough to allow viewers the chance to see ourselves for what we are, only human.

After six seasons, as a result of the manner in which Dick settled a dispute with another alien, the group is ordered home, and the series concludes with the Solomons ending their mission on Earth. At their farewell party, the clan decides to charge everything and not worry about being around to pay the bill. They even hire Elvis Costello to sing (what else?) "Fly Me to the Moon."

BROADCAST HISTORY

NBC

January 1996–April 1996	Tuesday 8:30–9:00
April 1996–July 1996	Tuesday 8:00–8:30
July 1996–August 1996	Thursday 9:30–10:00
August 1996–September 1997	Sunday 8:00–8:30
August 1997–September 1997	Thursday 9:30–10:00
September 1997–May 1998	Wednesday 9:00–9:30
December 1997–February 1998	Wednesday 8:00–8:30
May 1998–June 1998	Wednesday 8:00–8:30
June 1998–December 1998	Wednesday 9:00–9:30
June 1998–August 1998	Tuesday 9:30–10:00
December 1998–July 1999	Tuesday 8:00–8:30
May 1999–June 1999	Tuesday 9:30–10:00
July 1999–May 2000	Tuesday 8:30–9:00
January 2001–May 2001	Tuesday 8:30–9:00

CAST

Dick Solomon	John Lithgow
Sally Solomon	Kristen Johnson
Tommy Solomon	Joseph Gordon-Levitt
Harry Solomon	French Stewart
Mary Albright	Jane Curtin
Mamie Dubcek	Elmarie Wendel
Vicki Dubcek	Jan Hooks
Larisa Oleynik	Alissa Strudwick
Officer Don	Wayne Knight
Simbi Khali	Nina Campbell

The Hughleys

First Broadcast: September 22, 1998
Last Broadcast: August 6, 2002

The Hughleys is another series that comes from the real-life experiences of its star. D.L. Hughley began his career as a comedian working in small clubs. He claims his appearance on HBO's "Def Comedy Jam" was one of his earliest breaks.

With Chris Rock as *The Hughleys'* producer, Hughley created a family sitcom about a man who has it all, but doesn't know what to do with it.

Hughley plays a man who has become successful and lives in a middle class neighborhood, but cannot forget that he grew up poor in a bad neighborhood. The comedy unfolds as Darryl struggles to try and fit into his new environment, worrying all the while that he needs to keep his African American roots and teach his kids their heritage.

In the series premiere, "Vending Machine King," Darryl Hughley and his family are getting settled into their new home in the L.A. suburbs, having moved from the inner city. It's a bit of a culture shock for the totally devoted husband and father of three, trying to raise his headstrong kids in an upwardly mobile world that he fears will spoil them. Although his wife and children have assimilated just fine, he is not convinced that buying into a swank white suburb was the best move for his family. Now a prosperous businessman and a fun dad, he can also be tough to live with. Wife Yvonne strives to bring Darryl back down to earth and convince him that enjoying his hard-earned lifestyle will not make him lose touch with his roots. Unfortunately, this is contrary to what his best friend and employee, Milsap, believes.

Of the show, which moved to UPN beginning with its third season, Hughley commented, "I think there's a lot of material in my act that is positive and real, which is what my show is all about. I just want to be great at making people laugh."

Broadcast History

September 1998–July 1999	ABC Tuesday 8:30–9:00
July 1999–September 1999	ABCFriday 8:30–9:00
September 1999–October 1999	ABC Friday 8:00–8:30
October 1999–March 2000	ABC Friday 9:30–10:00
April 2000	ABC Friday 8:30–9:00
September 2000–February 2001	UPN Tuesday 9:00–9:30
March 2001–August 2001	UPN Tuesday 8:30–9:00
September 2001–July 2002	UPN Monday 8:00–8:30
June 2002	UPN Tuesday 9:30–10:00
July 2002–August 2002	UPN tuesday 9:00–9:30

Cast

Darryl Hughley	D.L. Hughley
Yvonne Hughley	Elise Neal
Dave Rogers	Eric Allan Kramer
Sally Rogers	Marietta DePrima

Seth Milsap	John Henton
Sydney Hughley	Ashley Monique Clark
Michael Hughley	Dee Jay Daniels
Mrs. Fitch	Frances Bay

The Sopranos

First Broadcast: January 10, 1999

The New York Times called it "the greatest work of American popular culture of the last quarter century." But before landing at HBO, *The Sopranos* was rejected in turn by each of the four major broadcast networks. The show's creator, David Chase, an Italian American (the family name, before his paternal grandmother changed it, was DeCesare), has been interested in the mob since childhood. Growing up in New Jersey, he was fascinated not only by films such as *The Public Enemy* with James Cagney, but by local newspaper articles written about mob stories and bodies found in trunks of cars. The fascinations of youth and the colorful characters he saw every day became the role models for *The Sopranos*.

Anthony Soprano leads a very complicated life. He tries to be a good family man because in his mind, family comes before everything else. But in Tony's case, the family he's most devoted to is not necessarily the one he goes home to each night. When asked, he tells people he works in Waste Management, but what he *wastes* is human beings, and what he manages is a very, very large extended family as capo in the New Jersey mob. Leading a double life, the pressures of work and family cause Tony to develop anxiety attacks, so he starts seeing a female psychiatrist, Dr. Melfi, which is not the kind of thing a man in his position openly discusses. In his circle, it could get him killed.

At home, his marriage is shaky, his kids are unruly, and his overbearing and bitter widowed mother once tries to whack Tony for putting her in a nursing home. Tony's ever-suffering wife Carmela, the mother of their children Meadow and Anthony Jr., puts up with Tony's illegal activities and extramarital dalliances because she enjoys the material gains; but since money doesn't buy happiness, Carmela suffers in silence quite a lot of the time.

Meadow is smart, and because she is well aware of what's going on with the family, she wants to get as far away from it as possible. Three years into the show, she is able to distance herself when she enters college and moves away to the dorms. A.J. is a naive 13-year-old kid when the series began, but a chip off the old block, and is starting to get in a little bit of trouble. By season three, he learns what his father does for a living and enters into a rebellious stage. Rounding out the immediate family is Tony's uncle Corrado "Junior" Soprano, his father's brother and the head of the family business, and Janice Soprano, Tony's troublesome big sister.

When David Chase was asked about Tony's parenting skills, his comment was, "I think he's a loving father, I think he really loves his kids. I don't think he does what's right by them very often. A good father would probably get out of that. Take them all to Utah and go into the program, I suppose. Right?"

BROADCAST HISTORY

HBO

January 10, 1999–Present	Sunday 8:00–9:00

CAST

Anthony Soprano	James Gandolfini
Dr. Jennifer Melfi	Lorraine Bracco
Carmela Soprano	Edie Falco
Christopher Moltisanti	Michael Imperioli
Livia Soprano	Nancy Marchand
Adriana La Cerva	Drea de Matteo
Meadow Soprano	Jamie-Lynn DiScala
Anthony Soprano Jr	Robert Iler
Salvatore "Big Pussy" Bonpensa	Vincent Pastore
Corrado "Uncle Junior" Errico	Dominic Chianese
Silvio Dante	Steve Van Zandt
Arthur "Artie" Bucco	John Ventimiglia
Paulie Walnuts	Tony Sirico

Judging Amy

First Broadcast: September 19, 1999
Last Broadcast:

Based on the real-life story of series star Amy Brenneman's own mother, *Judging Amy* is the story of three generations of women living together as they confront the personal and professional dilemmas in their changing lives.

Amy Gray is a 35-year-old former New York City attorney. She is recently divorced from her husband, and is raising a young daughter by herself. When she is selected as a juvenile court judge in Hartford, Connecticut, Amy moves in with her opinionated mother, Maxine, a retired social worker, and takes a stab at making a fresh start in life. Amy finds her life becoming increasingly complicated. She needs to figure out how to juggle a new job where she is treated like a novice by many of her colleagues, a young daughter striving to understand why mommy and daddy don't live together anymore, and a no-nonsense mother who is not always thrilled to have house guests. It's a life changing experience for them all. Amy is often stressed to the breaking point and how she balances the various elements in her life forms the foundation of the series. Moving back to Hartford, she also re-establishes relationships with her troubled cousin, Kyle, her older brother, Peter, and his wife, Gillian, and is making a concerned effort to make a better life for herself and Lauren.

In the pilot, Brenneman's character was a scattered nervous Nellie, the least authoritative of judges. But over the course of the show's run, Amy has toughened up considerably. By the 2003 season, Amy switches to criminal court, ponders a wedding to her boyfriend, Stu, and considers kicking mother Maxine out of her house. There is never a dull moment, and many of the situations this single, working mother faces seem to be more than overwhelming; but Amy continually manages to tackle each problem as it comes.

Broadcast History

CBS

September 19, 1999–Present	Tuesday 10:00–11:00

Cast

Judge Amy Madison Gray	Amy Brenneman
Maxine Gray	Tyne Daly
Vincent Gray	Dan Futterman
Bruce Van Exel	Richard T. Jones
Gillian Gray	Jessica Tuck
Peter Gray	Marcus Giamatti
Lauren Cassidy	Karle Warren
Donna Kozlowski-Pant	Jillian Armenante

7

The New Millennium

The expectations of today's savvy viewing audiences lend themselves to a new kind of programming. All stereotypes have been broken as far as the media's depiction of the all–American television family is concerned, and there seems to be no turning back.

Words that were nonexistent on the airwaves in the late '60s to mid '70s pepper the lingo of today's television families. Seeing couples, married or unmarried, in bed together is nothing unusual, either. Even cartoons have drastically changed, in that they are not just for kids anymore. Adults love (and can even relate to) the antics of Homer Simpson, and the potty-mouth kids of *South Park* are now cultural icons. Violence is at an all-time high, and risqué is a screenwriter's new mantra. Arguably, we have evolved as a society, and what we watch on television supposedly reflects that evolution.

They say there are only seven basic plots in fiction, and all things written are offshoots of that. You have man vs. nature, man vs. man, man vs. the environment, man vs. machines/technology, man vs. the supernatural, man vs. self and man vs. God/religion. The scripts written for most television families followed those guidelines to a tee, but use love and togetherness as the underlying theme. Then came reality television, and all bets were off. While many people think reality television is new and innovative, the concept of documenting the lives of families has been around for at least 20 years.

The first family to submit to the reality format were the Louds, who opened up their home and lives for seven months, in 1973. When PBS debuted *An American Family*, critics called the documentary series unsettling, yet fascinating. Three hundred hours of footage were shot, but only 12 hours made it to television. Ten million viewers sat glued to their tele-

While Joan of Arcadia (Amber Tamblyn) is one who actually speaks to God, it is left to her parents (Joe Mantegna and Mary Steenburgen) and siblings (Jason Ritter and Michael Welch), to decipher her quirky behavior resulting from his enigmatic directives.

vision sets and watched the marriage of Bill and Pat Loud come to an end, and saw their son Lance blatantly declaring himself a homosexual.

An American Family was undoubtedly an inspiration for MTV's *The Real World* in the 1990s. The show depicts seven strangers living in a house, trying to get along, with cameras rolling day and night. Somewhere down the line, it was inevitable that a celebrity family would have their daily lives taped for all the world to see. Then came *The Osbournes*, a show that really challenged people's perception of reality.

Providence

First Broadcast: January 8, 1999
Last Broadcast: December 20, 2002

An idealistic doctor in a small town who talks to her dead mother? Every episode opens with a tongue-in-cheek fairy tale skit, usually involving Dr. Syd Hansen and her recently deceased mother, Lynda. Syd talks to her mother in her dreams, and Lynda offers Syd motherly advice, usually about Syd's troubled love life. The character of Sydney's mother was only supposed to appear in the first episode, but the chemistry between stars Concetta Tomei and Melina Kanakaredes was so good that the producers decided to have Mom stick around for regular visits in Sydney's dreams.

Dr. Sydney Hansen is an altruistic plastic surgeon who abandons her career specialty and unfulfilling lifestyle to return to her colorful family and hometown in Providence, Rhode Island. Her disenchantment with her career, a relationship breakup and the sudden death of her mother prompt her to move back to the safe haven of Providence, where she finds fulfillment working in a low-income medical clinic.

Sydney arrives as her family struggles to recover from Lynda's death. She soon feels that the collective weight of the close-knit Hansen clan has become her responsibility, especially where her father, Jim, is concerned. Jim seems to relate better to the cuddly animals in his veterinary practice than he does with his family, but has the strong moral fiber that taught his children well. Sydney's younger sister, Joanie, is a new, unwed mother who divides her time between her infant daughter and assisting her dad in his cozy vet office in the basement of their home. Joanie was jilted on her wedding day, which coincidentally was the same day her mother died. Twenty-something Robbie is Sydney's scheming, bad-boy baby brother. He's always getting into trouble, and is a bit of a drifter. They all live in the house where the kids grew up, and form a seemingly perfect unit, just flawed enough to cause a little tension.

On every episode of *Providence*, Syd was presented with either a sickness to cure or a potential new love interest, and often the two complications in her life coincided. In the second season, Syd romanced a high school basketball coach, who just happened to suffer from a degenerative heart condition. They fell in love and he died, all in one episode.

BROADCAST HISTORY

NBC

January 1999–December 2002	Friday 8:00–9:00

CAST

Dr. Sydney Hansen	Melina Kanakaredes
Robbie Hansen	Seth Peterson
Dr. Helen Reynolds	Leslie Silva
Lynda Hansen	Concetta Tomei
Dr. Jim Hansen	Mike Farrell
Elizabeth "Izzy" Nunez	Samaria Graham
Joanie Hansen	Paula Cale

The Gilmore Girls

First Broadcast: October 5, 2000
Last Broadcast:

The Gilmore Girls is a humorous, heartfelt, multigenerational "dramedy" about friendship, family and the ties that bind, set in the storybook Connecticut town of Stars Hollow. The "girls" are 32-year-old Lorelai Gilmore and her 16-year-old daughter, Rory. Lorelai has made her share of mistakes in life, and she's been doing her best to see that her teenage daughter, and best friend in the world, doesn't follow in her footsteps. That may be easier said than done considering that the two share the same interests and same intellect. Rory is more serious than Lorelai, but there are tendencies, especially in the love department, that clearly show she is her mother's daughter.

From day one, the mother-daughter team has been growing up together. Lorelai was just Rory's age when she became pregnant and made the tough decision to raise her baby alone. This defiant move caused a rift between her and her extremely wealthy, proper, and patrician parents, Emily and Richard. Lorelai was forced to reconcile with them when she found herself in desperate need of money for Rory's tuition. The weekly Friday night dinners at the elder Gilmores' elegant and oppressive house are filled with witty repartee and simmering resentment.

Single parenthood seems to agree with Lorelai. She has a successful career managing an inn and lives in a charming old house with plenty of room. She really does seem happy. Rory's not angry or resentful with her life, either. She's a straight-A student at the Chilton School in Hartford, is smart, hardworking, and reads literature like *Madame Bovary* just for fun.

She hopes to enter Harvard. Lorelai is deeply involved in her daughter's life, and also presumably better able to understand her daughter because of their age proximity. Lorelai's major concern in life is that Rory will follow in her footsteps and become a young, unwed mother herself.

BROADCAST HISTORY

WB

October 2000–September 2001	Thursday 8:00–9:00
March 2001–April 2001	Monday 9:00–10:00
October 2001–Present	Tuesday 8:00–9:00

CAST

Lorelai Gilmore	Lauren Graham
Rory Gilmore	Alexis Bledel
Luke Danes	Scott Patterson
Sookie (St. James) Douglas	Melissa McCarthy
Michele	Yanic Truesdale
Lane Kim	Keiko Agena
Jess Mariano	Milo Ventimiglia
Richard Gilmore	Edward Herrmann
Emily Gilmore	Kelly Bishop
Dean	Jared Padalecki
Trix Gilmore	Marion Ross
Babette Dell	Sally Struthers
Miss Patty	Liz Torres

Malcolm in the Middle

First Broadcast: January 9, 2000

Malcolm in the Middle, created and executive produced by Linwood Boomer of *3rd Rock from the Sun,* is the story of the Wilkersons, a middle-class family of four brawling brothers and their parents, seen through the eyes of middle child, Malcolm, and what he sees isn't always a pretty sight. He feels that unfortunately, his family has a solid track record that negates any possibility of normalcy.

Malcolm was raised as an ordinary child until it was discovered that he had an I.Q. of 165. Suddenly, he's put in a class of gifted children and everyone starts treating him differently. He's in limbo, caught between the high expectations of the adult world and the longing to be a normal teenager. So what's a kid to do?

His favorite ally in the family is his older brother, Francis, who has been banished to military school. His second oldest brother, Reese, is a bully, whose favorite pastime is pummeling. According to Malcolm, youngest brother Dewey is "caught somewhere between a toddler and a hamster," and his parents are no help either. Father Hal is a bit dimwitted and prefers the role of one of the boys to that of father. Disciplinarian mother Lois is like an army drill sergeant, specializing in psychological warfare. She's cagey and assertive because she has to be, and takes no guff from anyone. Not that anyone could blame her, with four (well, maybe five, if you count Hal) spirited boys in the house. Despite the chaos, it's clear to all the boys that they are loved.

The three boys living at home experience the usual sibling rivalries but act out to the extreme, as when they completely destroy all the Christmas decorations.

The extended family includes Grandma Ida and Hal's father, Walter. Ida is nasty and spiteful. When she tumbles down the front steps of the Wilkerson home and breaks her collarbone, she sues her daughter and son-in-law for pain and suffering. Walter is quirky, cranky, self centered and very wealthy. Hal's side of the family have never really been close because Hal can't stand them, and they all hate Lois.

In season 4, another little Wilkerson is added to the cast when Lois finds herself pregnant. Malcolm thinks that having a new baby around the house is the worst thing that's ever happened. This baby cries nonstop and needs diaper changing all the time, and Malcolm thinks the newborn has two terrible parents. No day care center will take the new baby, Jamie. Apparently it has something to do with the collective juvenile records of the other kids. Finally, out of desperation, the non-religious Lois and Hal decide to join a church, simply because they offer free day care.

Broadcast History

FOX

January 2000–June 2002	Sunday 8:30–9:00
December 2003–present	Sunday 9:00–9:30

Cast

Malcolm	Frankie Muniz
Lois	Jane Kaczmarek
Hal	Bryan Cranston
Francis	Christopher Kennedy Masterson
Reese	Justin Berfield
Dewey	Erik Per Sullivan
Caroline	Catherine Lloyd Burns

Stevie Kenarban	Craig Lamar Traylor
Stanley	Karim Prince
Craig	David Higgins
Ed	Paul Willson
Julie	Landry Allbright
Victor	Robert Loggia
Ida	Cloris Leachman
Walter	Christopher Lloyd

Yes, Dear

First Broadcast: October 2, 2000

If it had been up to the critics, *Yes, Dear* might have been called *No Thank You*. The show was seriously panned early on. *TV Guide* suggested it would be canceled after two episodes. Miraculously, after the fourth show aired, CBS picked up the series for a full 22-episode season, so the sleeper comedy survived.

The show follows the lives of two young couples who have opposing views on parenting. Greg and Kim Warner are the overprotective, yuppie parents of a one year old. Kim is a stay-at-home mom, and is obsessed with being the perfect mother, perfect wife and having the perfect son. Greg is a successful businessman who finds it difficult to deal with her neuroses and keep his wife on an even keel.

Kim's sister, Christine Hughes, is just the opposite. She's a very down-to-earth mother of two, who constantly feels the need to remind Kim that life will never be perfect. Christine's unemployed, blowhard husband, Jimmy, feels that it's his duty to step up and share his philosophy about being a husband and a parent with Greg.

The show deals with the usual bringing up baby situations, but seen from two totally different points of view. Jimmy and Christine's unorthodox method of potty training son Logan, by stripping him naked and letting him run around in the Warners' backyard until he figures it out himself, shocks Greg and Kim. Their solution to the problem is to take Sam out to buy big kid's underwear and the potty training aids that parenting books recommend, which ultimately don't work.

When the Warners have a problem with Sam's developing aggressive behavior with other children, Greg laughs it off and thinks Kim should just let Sam grow out of it, until he sees Sam choking another toddler at the park. He heads off to the library to do some research on how to cure the problem, but Jimmy has a better way to handle it. He tells Greg that when his son Dominic became violent, he found a bigger bully kid to knock some sense into him. Greg agrees to try it Jimmy's way. When Kim and Christine go to a baby shower, Jimmy finds a guy with a trouble making two-year-old who's bigger than Sam, and it looks like the fight is on until Kim and Christine happen to come home early, and Kim blows her top.

In the show's third season, Kim and Greg become parents for the second time. They name their new baby daughter Emily. In a reference to pop culture, Kim and Greg decide to go on TLC's *A Baby Story* to chronicle the birth. The episode used the text, graphics and music from the real show as well as real childhood photos of the lead actors.

The Carol Burnett Show alumni Tim Conway and Vicki Lawrence are frequent guest stars, appearing as Greg's parents, and *Wonder Years* dad Dan portrays Christine and Kim's father.

BROADCAST HISTORY

CBS

October 2000–August 2001	Monday 8:30–9:00
August 2001	Monday 9:30–10:00
September 2001–December 2001	Monday 8:30–9:00
October 2001	Friday 8:00–8:30
December 2001	Monday 9:30–10:00
December 2001	Friday 8:00–8:30
December 2001–March 2002	Monday 8:30–9:00
March 2002	Monday 9:30–10:00
April 2002	Monday 8:00–8:30
December 2002	Sunday 8:30–9:00
April 2002–June 2003	Monday 8:30–9:00
June 2003	Friday 8:30–9:00
June 2003–present	Monday 8:00–8:30

CAST

Greg Warner	Anthony Clark
Kim Warner	Jean Louisa Kelly
Christine Hughes	Liza Snyder
Jimmy Hughes	Mike O'Malley
Sammy Warner	Anthony and Michael Bain

The Bernie Mac Show

First Broadcast: November 14, 2001

According to Bernie Mac, who often refers to himself in the third person, "Bernie Mac don't sugarcoat. Bernie Mac just says what you think but are afraid to say." The angry, hard-edged comic became famous to black audiences as part of the Original Kings of Comedy revue. His stand-up routine is loosely based on his real life, and the sitcom is a kinder, gentler version of the stand-up act. His most famous comedy routine, and the one that serves as the basis for the sitcom, describes Mac's becoming the guardian to his sister's three kids.

The Bernie Mac Show, which won the prestigious 2002 Peabody Award for Broadcast Excellence, was inspired by the real life of family man Bernie Mac. Onstage, Mac focuses on his difficulties caring for his drug-addicted sister's three children after she is incarcerated. In the show, Bernie Mac plays a caricature of himself, a highly successful comedian whose sister's legal troubles lead him and his wife Wanda to adopt her children. While some might have tried to compare this show with *The Cosby Show* early on, the only similarities are that both families are wealthy and black. In truth, with his venomous wit and sharp tongue, Mac seems to be the anti–Cosby.

On the show, neither Bernie nor his wife, Wanda, have a parental bone in their bodies. Having never planned on having children, they have some unique views on parenting. He's busy being a stand-up comic, and she is vice president of a major corporation. The wealthy couple live in a spacious Hollywood Hills house and are loving life. When they are pressed to raise 13-year-old Vanessa, 8-year-old Jordan and 5-year-old Bryanna, it's game on. Bernie believes that kids are "too sassy, too grown and talk back too much." All he asks for is a little respect, and is hard pressed to get it.

There are only two rules in the house. First, it's their *home*, but it's his house. Second, all the stuff in the house is his and no one touches anything without permission. That goes for the TV, the VCR, the DVD and especially his James Brown CD collection. He may not be Cliff Huxtable, especially when he utters such gems as "I'm gonna kill one of them kids," but he tries. Mac's attitude toward his children certainly seems reproachful, but beneath the surface, his tough love attitude is all for show, and they know that he loves them.

Inspired from the intimacy Mac shares with his stand-up audiences, in every episode, Bernie focuses on the television camera and tells his troubles to his unseen audience, "America, you see what these kids put me through?"

Broadcast History

FOX

November 2001–August 2002	Wednesday 9:00–9:30
September 2002–January 2003	Wednesday 8:00–8:30
February 2003–present	Wednesday 9:00–9:30

CAST

Bernie	Bernie Mac
Wanda	Kellita Smith
Vanessa	Camille Winbush
Jordan	Jeremy Suarez
Bryanna	Dee Dee Davis

The Osbournes

First Broadcast: March 5, 2002

Ever since the first dysfunctional television family was introduced some 50 years ago, viewers took comfort in knowing that these improbable, wacky, often troubled folks were just figments of some savvy writer's imagination. Then came reality in the guise of *The Osbournes.*

Rock legend Ozzy Osbourne is probably best known as the man who shocked concert goers years ago by biting the head off a live bat during a performance. But when Osbourne, wife Sharon and their two children decided to open the doors to their home and let an MTV camera crew set up shop round the clock to document their daily lives, those well publicized onstage antics pale by comparison. No writer could have created the characters, dialogue or the scenarios that play out each week at the Osbourne mansion.

Ozzy has mellowed a bit in his old age. While he is still a commanding presence onstage, long-term substance abuse has taken its toll. He shuffles around the house in a seemingly bewildered state of mind and body. Other than the four-letter words that pepper every stuttering sentence he utters, he is fairly unintelligible and rather inept in most day-to-day endeavors. Manager/wife Sharon is the true backbone of the clan and the glue that holds this seemingly dysfunctional family together. Like the proverbial mama bear, Sharon is fiercely protective of her husband, children and the menagerie of animals that share (and soil) their happy home. Son Jack, a budding entrepreneur, and pop star daughter Kelly fight like cats and dogs. Eldest daughter Amy opted out of having her life broadcast to the masses and moved out of the house shortly before production began.

Their day-to-day life is colorful, loud and most of the time chaotic. Sibling rivalry abounds, as do arguments about Sharon's beloved pets, who, in addition to having the run of the place, treat it like a fancy public bathroom. While there is a fair share of comic relief, the Osbournes also share their personal tragedies, as when in the show's second season, Sharon is diagnosed with colon cancer, or when Jack and sister Kelly are admitted to a rehab facility for substance abuse. In early December 2003, while he was taking a day off from promoting a new single he recorded with his daughter, Kelly, Ozzy made headlines when he was seriously injured in an accident while riding an all-terrain vehicle on the grounds of his British estate. He fractured his collarbone, eight ribs and a neck vertebra. Sharon Osbourne said Ozzy had to have an artery transplant because part of his collarbone cut an artery leading to his arm, and he nearly had to have the arm amputated. Sharon told the *Daily Mirror* newspaper that Ozzy's heart stopped beating for nearly two minutes after the accident. She said that a security guard spotted that Ozzy wasn't breathing and quickly used first aid to get him breathing and his heart started again. While Ozzy was back at their Beverly Hills home recuperating, an English tabloid notified Ozzy and Sharon that they had a photo of daughter Kelly in an apparent drug deal. They confronted their daughter, who eventually acknowledged she had a bag full of pills under her bed. Within hours, she was taken to a rehabilitation center in Malibu and entered rehab for an addiction to painkillers.

Despite all the ups and down, fights and hassles, injures and addictions, it's quite clear that this close knit family truly loves each other. As Ozzy so succinctly told the family over dinner one night, "I love you all. I love you more than life itself, but you're all f****** mad."

BROADCAST HISTORY

MTV

March 5, 2002–Present — Tuesday 10:00–10:30

CAST

Ozzy Osbourne
Sharon Osbourne
Jack Osbourne
Kelly Osbourne

American Dreams

First Broadcast: September 29, 2002

President Lyndon Johnson was re-elected in a landslide election over Barry Goldwater, Julie Andrews won Best Actress for her role in *Mary Poppins*, IBM introduced the System 360 computer, the Nobel Peace Prize was awarded to Dr. Martin Luther King Jr., and *American Bandstand* was every teenager's favorite program. Such was America in the mid–1960s, and unbeknownst to the Pryor family of Philadelphia, they were living in an era that was on the verge of major cultural and social changes. At the end of the show's first episode, the family solemnly gathers around the television to watch the coverage of JFK's assassination.

American Dreams follows one family's journey through the joys and pains of America in the '60s and early '70s. While discussing the realities of the 1960s and '70s versus today, executive producer Dick Clark commented, "It's all relatable. We're living in a time when all of the sudden the damn world's changed on us overnight, and we're terrified of what the future brings. Now think of what it was like in 1963: We're not a banana republic, and they've killed our president. It was a hell of a shock. You don't blow up two buildings and make them disappear in a blink of an eyelash. It's unheard of. Yet the times are relatable. You've got the same kinds of people walking around, 'Where am I headed into?' While it appears to be a more innocent time, the truth is it was not."

Father Jack, a good Catholic, owns a television store. Stay-at-home mom Helen soothes her humdrum daily life by watching cooking programs on her local network affiliate, WFIL in Philadelphia. Helen is also embracing the newfound empowerment that the 1960s afforded women, causing a bit of a tear in the Pryor family, mostly affecting Jack. The Pryor children all attend parochial school. Perky teenager Meg is something of a proto-feminist, and loves rock-and-roll. She also wants to embrace the morality of her more experienced teenaged friend, Roxanne. The girls' American dream is to become dancers on Dick Clark's locally produced *American Bandstand.* Teenage son J.J. wants to abandon football, his father's American dream, in favor of pursuing one of his own. Youngest son, Will, and prissy little sister Patty, who can do no wrong, round out the Pryor clan, and are more concerned with simple pursuits, like growing up.

Each episode finds today's current singing stars portraying those of the '60s. American Idol winner Kelly Clarkson appears as Brenda Lee, Alicia Keys as Fontella Bass, and Monica as Mary Wells. Usher, Nick Carter of the Backstreet Boys, Vanessa Carlton, Wayne Brady and Kelly Rowland of Destiny's Child are among the performers who have also guest-starred as singers from the era.

Broadcast History

NBC

September 2002–Present	Sunday 8:00–9:00

Cast

Jack Pryor	Tom Verica
Helen Pryor	Gail O'Grady

J.J. Pryor	Will Estes
Meg Pryor	Brittany Snow
Patty Pryor	Sarah Ramos
Will Pryor	Ethan Dampf
Roxanne Bojarski	Vanessa Lengies
Michael Brooks	Joey Lawrence
Henry Walker	Jonathan Adams
Sam Walker	Arlen Escarpeta
Rebecca Sandstrom	Virginia Madsen

Life with Bonnie

First Broadcast: September 17, 2002
Last Broadcast: April 9, 2004

Second City alumni Bonnie Hunt's improvisational skills shine bright in her portrayal of Bonnie Molloy, a wife, mother, and the gaffe-prone hostess of a morning television show, *Morning Chicago*. The talk show segments of the show are semi-improvised, with lots of Hunt wisecracks and beautifully timed double takes.

Hunt developed "Bonnie" with fellow *Second City* alum Don Lake after passing on an offer to take over Rosie O'Donnell's talk show. "I didn't want to do that because I love being a storyteller," says Hunt. "And I thought, gee, I can be a host on a sitcom, and have real guests who aren't scripted, along with a fictional family life. It was the ultimate combo platter."

Husband Mark is a hardworking family practice doctor, and he and Bonnie are the parents of three young children, Samantha, Charlie and infant Connor. Bonnie's life is trying to effectively balance her job, her husband and their kids. For Bonnie, life at home is chaotic at best. When Bonnie complains about her overwhelming workload, which Mark doesn't fully appreciate, he comments that her job is hardly busy. He thinks it's just this little show they go and do, sitting around and drinking coffee. In the midst of domestic chaos, this attitude sets Bonnie on her ear. They often debate about who in the house is really in charge. Her hosting job on *Morning Chicago* is an equally rushed, often slapdash affair, overseen by a nervous producer, David. Tony Russo, Bonnie's sidekick piano player, comes straight to her show from his Vegas lounge act.

As every working mother knows, sometimes her working world and motherhood collide. In one episode, Bonnie's housekeeper is feeling under the weather, forcing Bonnie to drag the kids along with her to work.

Simultaneously being on-camera on the live show and watching out for the kids running around the set comes to a head when eldest son Charlie injures himself horsing around during a commercial break. Just as the she's back in front of the camera, she hears Charlie cry out in pain. While in some cases, the live show must go on, Bonnie is a mother first and tears off the set to comfort her child, much to the chagrin of producer David.

Broadcast History

ABC

September 2002–October 2002	Tuesday 8:30–9:00
October 2002–March 2003	Tuesday 9:00–9:30
September 2003–2004	Friday 9:30–10:00

Cast

Bonnie Molloy	Bonnie Hunt
Dr. Mark Molloy	Mark Derwin
David Bellows	David Alan Grier
Charlie Molloy	Charlie Stewart
Samantha Molloy	Samantha Browne-Walters
Gloria	Marianne Muellerleile
Marv	Chris Barnes
Tony Russo	Anthony Russell
Holly	Holly Wortell

8 Simple Rules for Dating My Teenage Daughter

First Broadcast: September 17, 2002

As any parent knows, there are no rules, simple or otherwise, for raising teenage girls, especially from a father's point of view, but from Paul Hennessy's prospective, one major rule will be enforced at all costs: "If you make my daughters cry, I'll make you cry."

Based on W. Bruce Cameron's best-selling book, "8 Simple Rules for Dating My Teenage Daughter," the series follows the paternal tribulations of sports writer Paul Hennessy. Throughout his daughter's formative years, Paul spent a lot of time on the road, leaving the child rearing duties to wife Cate. When Cate decides to return to work as a hospital nurse, Paul takes a job as a columnist and agrees to make the duties of raising the kids a shared experience. But Paul's a bit rusty in his parenting skills. He remembers the days of little girls who were the apple of daddy's eye, but things have changed. The girls have grown and matured, much to Paul's chagrin.

Sixteen-year-old Bridget is a beautiful and popular teenager with a different boyfriend each week. Her taste for skimpy, trendy outfits is a little much for Paul's sensibilities. Fifteen-year-old Kerry is the brainy one. She is lacking in self-confidence, so she covers it up with sarcasm. Thirteen-year-old son Rory remains sane enough for Paul to enjoy the other "man" in the family, but that's not to say Paul isn't a little alarmed when Rory can actually identify an eyelash curler and other of his sisters' make-up products.

Paul tries to pal around with his daughters, to no avail. They are just too old and embarrassed to be hanging around with their Dad. They abhor his constant meddling in their love lives. He tries really hard to be hip, but seems to always be a year or two behind in popular teenage jargon, which embarrasses his daughters even more. When he finally convinces daughter Kerry to go to the movies with him to see a new foreign film, he feels like a sophisticated father enjoying a cultural night out, until an explicit sex scene in the film embarrasses him so bad, he's traumatized.

Four shows into the filming of the fall 2003 season, series star John Ritter collapsed on the set. He was taken to a nearby hospital where he was pronounced dead of a previously undetected heart ailment.

Given the fact that everyone involved in the show felt that Ritter would have wanted it to go on without him, the series continues. Ritter's death was written into the series, in the guise of Paul getting up early one morning and going to the store, only to be felled by a fatal heart attack. For the next few episodes, viewers went through the same angst the fictional family and the cast were feeling at the loss of both the fictional Paul and the real John. Storylines revolved around how a family comes together after suffering such a terrible loss. Actors Suzanne Pleshette and James Garner were brought in to portray Cate's parents, who move into the house with the grieving family to lend moral support.

Broadcast History

ABC

September 2002–June 2004	Tuesday 8:00–8:30
July 2004–August 2004	Friday 8:30–9:00
September 2004–Present	Friday 8:00–8:30

Cast

Paul Hennessy	John Ritter
Cate Hennessy	Katey Sagal

Bridget Hennessy	Kaley Cuoco
Kerry Hennessy	Amy Davidson
Rory Hennessy	Martin Spanjers
CJ Barnes	David Spade
Gandpa Jim Egan	James Garner

According to Jim

First Broadcast: September 26, 2001

Known for his starring roles in such movies as *Joe Somebody, Curly Sue, Taking Care of Business, Once Upon a Crime, Mr. Destiny,* and *Jumpin' Jack Flash,* Jim Belushi, a dedicated husband and father of three in real life, takes on the fictional role of husband and father on television along with Courtney Thorne-Smith, who gained international attention on the prime-time soap opera *Melrose Place* and as Georgia on the Emmy Award–winning series *Ally McBeal.*

Jim is a suburban father of three, married to beautiful wife Cheryl, in this traditional family comedy. He's a contractor in a design firm with his younger, more-educated, neurotic brother-in-law, Andy. Andy is Norton to Jim's Ralph Kramden. When not at work, Jim loves bowling, football and hanging out with his six-man garage blues band. Cheryl is his polar opposite. She is smart and sophisticated and willingly gave up dating corporate guys for a life with a simpler man who makes her laugh and adores her. They seem to be the perfect middle-class couple, are very much in love and devoted to each other, but they disagree quite a bit. The problem is, Jim is a stubborn midwesterner, full of himself and just a big kid at heart. He puts up a tough, macho front when his friends are around, but everyone knows that's just "for show." There's a teddy bear lurking under that macho facade. In his mind, the key to a successful marriage is agreeing with everything your wife says, and the best way to raise children is to remain a big kid yourself.

Jim gets himself into predicaments that could have easily been avoided, but he just can't seem to stay out of trouble, as when he agrees to take the girls for the day while Cheryl and her sister go to a doctor's appointment. At the park, Jim leaves the girls with another mom and then flits off to the movies, not remembering who he left them with. Or, when Cheryl has a revealing photo of herself taken as a very private and personal Valentine gift to Jim, he proudly shows it to all his friends.

When he's not getting himself out of trouble with the love of his life, Jim feeds his other passion, music, by playing the blues with his six-man garage band. His passion for music happened one day when Dan Aykroyd asked him to join the Blues Brothers Band as Brother Zee—a possibly daunting proposition. Jim takes a beat, looks at Aykroyd and says the same thing he's been saying all his life. "Yeah, what the hell ... why not? Sounds like a whole lotta fun!" To get ready to play with the Blues Brothers, Belushi crashes rehearsals of the House of Blues' own band, The Sacred Hearts. He sits in with the band and finds it "a whole lotta fun." For the past seven years the band has been called Jim Belushi and the Sacred Hearts. Jim and the boys wrote and recorded the music for *According to Jim*, and band members John and Tony are regular members of the cast.

BROADCAST HISTORY

ABC

October 2001–July 2002	Wednesday 8:30–9:00
September 2002–March 2003	Tuesday 8:30–9:00
May 2003–Present	Tuesdays 9:00–9:30

CAST

Jim	James Belushi
Cheryl	Courtney Thorne-Smith
Dana	Kimberly Williams
Andy	Larry Joe Campbell
Gracie	Billi Bruno
Ruby	Taylor Atelian

The George Lopez Show

First Broadcast: March 27, 2002
Last Broadcast:

The current *George Lopez Show* started out as a four episode midseason replacement that became an instant hit. A stand-up comic in real life, Lopez thinks his show is unlike other comedians' vehicles because it deals more with his life than his act. The series was put together with Bruce Helford, Deborah Oppenheimer and Robert Borden, all from the long-running hit comedy series *The Drew Carey Show*, actress/producer Sandra Bullock, and George himself who serves as the co-creator, writer, producer and star. The original concept of the show was a Latino *Beverly Hillbillies*. "Fortunately," says Lopez, "that concept went out the window."

In the series, George is gainfully employed at a Los Angeles airplane parts factory. When he becomes the first assembly line worker to be promoted to plant manager after 15 years on the job, he takes the responsibility quite seriously. His friends and co-workers rib him mercilessly about becoming "Mr. Clipboard," but still like him anyway. Handling the guys at work is nothing compared to handling his mother, Benny, a co-worker and frequent guest in the house he shares with wife Angie, precocious 9-year-old son Max, and a budding 15-year-old daughter, Carmen. Benny, who raised George by herself, is stubborn, insensitive and constantly lies to George about his childhood, which confuses George in his search for his long-lost dad. To make matters worse, wife Angie has very limited patience in dealing with her overbearing mother-in-law. Also in the mix is nerdy best pal Ernie who works at the plant and still lives with his parents, when he's not being used by girlfriends.

The show focuses mainly on family situations, involving the kids, Angie and mother. Angie and George have been married 16 years. She works as a cosmetics salesperson and her passion for lost causes tries George's patience sometimes, but in the end, her devotion to causes and her patience of a saint in putting up with both George and his mother makes him love and rely upon her that much more. Angie breaks the cliché of constantly finding fault with her husband and doesn't berate him.

Broadcast History

ABC

March 2002–Present	Wednesday 8:30–9:00

Cast

George Lopez	George Lopez
Angie Lopez	Constance Marie
Benita "Benny" Lopez	Belita Moreno
Carmen Lopez	Masiela Lusha
Max Lopez	Luis Armand Garcia
Ernesto "Ernie" Cardenas	Valente Rodriguez

My Wife and Kids

First Broadcast: March 28, 2001

In 1999, Damon Wayans failed with his show *Damon*, which was canceled after only 13 episodes on the FOX network. He decided to take one more chance with TV by developing his own family-oriented sitcom, loosely based on his own life, and with that, *My Wife and Kids* was born.

The first episode was a smash in the ratings with over 10 million viewers in the U.S. alone. Actress Tisha Campbell, who stars as wife Jay, credits Wayan's real-life fatherhood for helping the show with realism. In a 2001 interview, she told Rosie O'Donnell, "He is the best! He really is a dad and it comes through. You can see that." The show received the 2002 People's Choice Award for Favorite New Television Comedy Series.

Michael Kyle thought he had it all together as a husband and father in Stamford, Connecticut. He's a not-so-modern man living in a very modern world, a man on a quest for a "traditional" family. But suddenly, his life changed. He and his wife, high school sweetheart Janet, had three beautiful kids, Claire, Junior and Kady. While Janet stayed at home with the children, he went out and made a living as owner of a fleet of delivery trucks and his successful business kept the family comfortable. But somewhere along the line, things spun out of control. All he wants to know is: What happened to his life?

His stay-at-home wife Janet wants to use her hard-earned college degree, and he has trouble accepting the fact that she has become a stock market whiz. His only son idolizes gangster rappers instead of him and is as dumb as dirt. At his father's request, Junior keeps a pocket notebook in which his father tells him to write down all the stupid things he says. He does a few stupid things as well, like getting his girlfriend pregnant. He lives at home, has no job to support his newly forming family, but still mistakenly thinks that it will all work out anyway. Michael's moody, adolescent daughter's two favorite hobbies are asking him for money and giving him grief. And his youngest daughter rarely lets her Daddy have the last word.

As he teaches his three children some of life's lessons, he does so with his own brand of wisdom, discipline and humor. Unfortunately, in his fervent quest to live the American dream, he is totally overlooking the fact that he's actually living it.

Broadcast History

ABC

March 2001–May 2001	Wednesday 8:00–8:30
June 2001	Tuesday 9:30–10:00
July 2001	Wednesday 8:00–8:30
March 2002	Monday 8:00–8:30
July 2002–September 2002	Wednesday 8:30–9:00
September 2003–2004	Wednesday 8:00–8:30
September 2004–Present	Tuesday 8:00–8:30

Cast

Michael Kyle	Damon Wayans
Janet Kyle	Tisha Campbell-Martin

Junior Kyle	George O. Gore II
Claire Kyle	Jennifer Freeman
Kady Kyle	Parker McKenna Posey
Rosa Lopez	Marlene Forte
Dr. Boucher	Wendell Pierce

All of Us

First Broadcast: September 16, 2003

Wanting to do a sitcom that really reflects a piece of life rarely seen on television, Will Smith and Jada Pinkett Smith put their lives on the line as the inspirations for and executive producers of *All of Us.* The show offers viewers a timely look at many young parents' new, compassionate attitude toward how divorced parents raise their children together. In a recent interview, Will Smith explained why the show is aptly named, "It's really a show about the modern face of family. The divorce rate in America is 51 percent, so it is really a show about all of us."

In yet another "life imitates art" moment, the show's star, Duane Martin, is also a longtime friend of Will and Jada. In fact, it was Martin who introduced the two, and according to Will Smith, "that's why he got the lead." According to Martin, "Baby-mama drama is real in America and we are just trying to bring it to the forefront, because there's a lot of comedy that comes with it and you have to laugh about it."

The series follows the life of Robert James, an entertainment reporter for a Los Angeles television station, awaiting the finalization of his divorce. His girlfriend, kindergarten teacher Tia, is anxiously awaiting the divorce as well. She's very much in love with Robert and wants to marry him as soon as possible. But it seems Tia is not just marrying Robert, because his soon-to-be-ex, Neesee, and their young son, Robert, Jr., will always be a part of their lives.

Dealing with such subjects as post-divorce relationships and children from previous marriages, Smith stresses that the show is really just loosely based on his life with current wife, Pinkett, and their blended clan. Mrs. Smith believes the show is universal. In an interview given prior to the show's debut, she said, "It's really something I'm sure all of us have experienced in some form or fashion." While the popular couple intend to make guest appearances on the show, they prefer to stay behind the scenes, but Will did confirm that the couple's three children will appear in some episodes, since youngsters are needed for classroom scenes.

BROADCAST HISTORY

UPN

September 2003–Present — Tuesday 8:00–8:30

CAST

Robert	Duane Martin
Tia	Elise Neal
Neesee	LisaRaye
Robert Jr.	Khamani Griffin
Dirk	Tony Rock

Happy Family

First Broadcast: September 9, 2003
Last Broadcast: April 20, 2004

They tried to be good, loving parents, but now that the kids are grown, Peter and Annie Brennan are having second thoughts about their parenting skills. Eldest son Todd, who is the apple of his father's eye, is engaged to be married to a beautiful and successful dentist who works in his father's dental practice. But he's having an affair on the side. Middle child Tim is a dork, and although his parents would never admit this to anyone else but each other, they truly believe he's an idiot. He went to junior college, but on graduation day, admits to his family that he won't be graduating after all. Angry, his parents kick him out of the house. He's supposed to move in with friends, but instead decides to shack up with the next door neighbor, a 35-year-old woman he used to call "the spooky old lady next door." Daughter Sara lives on her own, but has no life. Playing Scrabble with her parents on a Friday night is about as good as it gets. "I'm beginning to think we didn't do a very good job," says Annie. "What the hell happened?" she asks.

To make matters worse, the kids are always hanging around. Peter and Annie would love to know what the empty nest syndrome feels like, but the kids don't give them the chance. "They're never really out of the house, are they?" asks Peter.

The kids' lives are in such disorder that friends of the family begin taking pity on Peter and Annie, even comparing their situation to the lives of their friends the Michaelsons, whose son just was released from prison and whose daughter is very promiscuous. The situation escalates when Annie has an event at her home and decides to stretch the truth about the kids. She lies and tells anyone who will listen that son Tim is now a record executive, daughter Sara is now dating a rich attorney named Lars, and poor Todd is the one who was cheated on by his fiancee, not the other way around.

BROADCAST HISTORY

NBC

September 2003–2004	Tuesday 8:00–8:30

CAST

Peter Brennan	John Larroquette
Annie Brennan	Christine Baranski
Todd Brennan	Jeff Bryan Davis
Tim Brennan	Tyler Andrews
Sara Brennan	Melanie Deanne Moore
Maggie Harris	Susan Gibney

Joan of Arcadia

First Broadcast: September 26, 2003

Early in the 15th century, Joan of Arc heard voices in her head that told her she needed to take up arms to save France. In CBS's modern day version of St. Joan, sixteen-year-old Joan Girardi is not hearing voices, per se. She's seeing God. And to make her life even more complicated, God assumes a new identity every time he visits. In the show's premiere episode alone, he changes from old man pervert to cute teenage boy, to an African American cafeteria lady.

Joan and the rest of the Girardis are still trying to find their comfort zone. They are a normal family suffering the aftereffects of a tragic automobile accident that left Joan's brother, Kevin, a wheelchair bound paraplegic at 19. Her parents, Will, Arcadia's Chief of Police, and Helen, who works at the high school that Joan attends, cannot agree on how hard to push their son into resuming something like a normal life. Their younger son, 15-year-old Luke, is a science geek, although he prefers to be referred to as a man of science.

As if the teenage years and a family turned upside down weren't quite enough, in the series opener, Joan catches an old man peering up into her bedroom window while she is getting dressed for school. "There's a pervert outside my window!" she yells to her family. Everyone runs outside to find nobody there. Dad's the only one who believes that she actually saw someone in the yard. He's a bit jumpy about intruders because there is a serial killer loose in the town whose victims are about Joan's age. Everyone else thinks Joan's imagination is getting the best of her.

On the way to school, a cute guy smiles at her on the bus, gets off at her stop and proceeds to strike up a conversation. When he tells her that he was the guy outside her window that morning, she doesn't believe him because of the distinct age difference and appearance of the two men. When he introduces himself to her as God and explains that he can change his appearance at will, she's sure he's a nut. She tells him to go away and never bother her again because her dad is a cop. He admits that he knows exactly who her dad is, then proceeds to rattle off dad's whole life story, as well as her mom's and the rest of the family history to boot, concluding with the fact that he's known her since before she was born, and he will overlook the broken promise she made to him in prayer right after her brother's car accident if she'll just believe that he is God.

After a bit more convincing on his part, Joan pretty much believes him, but at the same time isn't totally sure that she's not just cracking up from the strain. She also can't figure out why he's chosen her. His simple reply is, "I need you to do some errands for me."

Each week, Joan finds out the answer to the show's theme song's opening line, "What if God were one of us?" as she has a divine visitation and does God's bidding.

BROADCAST HISTORY

CBS

September 2003–Present	Friday 8:00–9:00

CAST

Joan Girardi	Amber Tamblyn
Helen Girardi	Mary Steenburgen
Will Girardi	Joe Mantegna
Kevin Girardi	Jason Ritter
Luke Girardi	Michael Welch

Married to the Kellys

First Broadcast: October 3, 2003
Last Broadcast: April 24, 2004

In an interview conducted shortly before its debut, executive producer Tom Hertz explained that the premise of the show was semi-autobiographical. "*Married to the Kellys* is about a guy, an only child, who never had the warmth and camaraderie of a big family. It's based loosely on my real life. After marrying [my wife] Susan, I literally had to learn how to be part of a family that was very different from my own. It's about getting to know each other and family relationships."

As the fictional version goes, when New York writer Tom married Susan from the Midwest, he promised her they would be able to move anywhere she wanted when he sold his first novel. Of course, he was thinking that they'd just move to a nicer apartment in a better part of the Big Apple. Instead, she decided that she wanted to move back to her home town of Kansas City to be closer to her family. Since a promise is a promise, and Tom kept his promises, Kansas City it was.

Living in a peaceful, quiet community is only the tip of the iceberg for Tom. The close-knit and provincial Kelley clan are another matter entirely. It's hard for Tom, a bit of a loner due to his own upbringing, to suddenly find himself in the midst of his large, overbearing and gregarious in-laws. These are people who swoon over pork steaks on the grill, shuck their own corn for dinner, and gleefully sing grace before dinner. Loving his wife very much, Tom vows to do his best to fit in with her side of the family, but he has his doubts.

Susan's mom, Sandy, is warm, charming, but quietly controlling. She keeps tabs on everyone in the family with her "doghouse system" of public humiliation for anyone who breaks the house rules. Dad Bill is the rock of the family and, like Tom, was an only child himself. He gently explains to Tom that being a part of a large, happy family is a wonderful thing, and that it should only take him about ten years to assimilate.

Brother-in-law Chris is married to Susan's sister, Mary. He regards Tom as a threat to his own "favorite son-in-law" status. Mary is chronically competitive and working on her master's degree. She feels compelled to prove her intellectual superiority to Tom at every turn. Then there's Lewis, the youngest in the family, who's shy and socially awkward as a result of growing up surrounded by strong women. While Susan pushes Tom to bond with Lewis, Tom feels the only thing the two men have in common is an awkward silence.

Each episode tests Tom's mettle, as he adjusts to a huge new family, and corn as high as an elephant's eye.

Broadcast History

ABC

October 2003–2004	Friday 8:30–9:00

Cast

Tom	Breckin Meyer
Susan	Kiele Sanchez
Sandy	Nancy Lenehan
Mary	Emily Rutherfurd
Chris	Josh Braaten

Lewis	Derek Waters
Bill	Sam Anderson
Uncle Dave	Richard Riehle

It's All Relative

First Broadcast: October 1, 2003
Last Broadcast: April 6, 2004

Recently engaged Bobby O'Neil works in the Boston pub that his father, "Mace," owns and operates. His Mom, Audrey, helps out, as does his outspoken sister, Maddy. They are a traditional, hardworking, close-knit Irish Catholic Republican family. Bobby's fiancee Liz attends Harvard, is Protestant and knows a lot about art and culture. She was raised by art gallery owner Philip and his life partner, Simon, a school teacher, who happen to be a couple of snobby, upscale, liberal gay dads. The moment Bobby pops the question to Liz, they fear the worst because they know their polar opposite families will have to meet.

In the premiere episode, Bobby and Liz break the news of their secret engagement to their families and each gets a less than warm response. In fact, Bobby's conversation with his folks ends with him moving into Liz's parents' guest house. Naturally, this doesn't thrill Philip and Simon, but at the risk of losing Liz completely, they agree to the situation temporarily until Bobby can work things out with his parents.

Mace is a stubborn, bigoted meat-and-potatoes Archie Bunker type, and the thought of having gay in-laws is abhorrent to him. Philip is aghast at the prospect of his future in-laws as well. Audrey and Simon do what they can to keep their spouses focused on the real issue—that their kids have chosen to marry each other. And at the risk of alienating this young couple, they'd better find a way to blend these two completely opposite families. How Mace will find anything in common with the well-heeled and equally obstinate Philip is anybody's guess.

This new age Romeo and Juliet story with a Hatfield-McCoy twist was first suggested by the chairman of ABC. The show's creators, Anne Flett-Giordano (*Frasier, Baby Talk*) and Chuck Ranberg (*Kate & Allie, Becker*) said they hoped the show would not be compared to *Will & Grace*, as they were looking for something completely new.

Broadcast History

ABC

October 2003–2004 Wednesday 8:30–9:00

CAST

Mace O'Neil	Lenny Clarke
Audrey O'Neil	Harriet Sansom Harris
Bobby O'Neil	Reid Scott
Liz	Maggie Lawson
Simon	Christopher Sieber
Maddy O'Neil	Paige Moss
Philip	John Benjamin Hickey

Hope and Faith

First Broadcast: September 26, 2003

Hope and Faith are sisters who have been living in two very different worlds. Stay-at-home mom Hope is busy with her family-centered suburban life in the Midwest. She's married to Charley and the couple have three very lively children. Her famous soap opera diva sister, Faith, was living in Hollywood until her character, Ashley Storm, of *The Sacred and the Sinful*, was suddenly killed off by her evil twin. Out of work Faith, who never saved a penny, flees Hollywood and seeks refuge in the suburbs with her sister. There is palpable friction between Faith and Hope's husband Charley, who clearly doesn't want his sister-in-law living there, and down-to-earth Hope quickly finds her world turned upside down by her sister's arrival.

She already had her hands full at home dealing with a busy household that includes a precocious preteen, a rebellious teen daughter, and a quirky young son. Hope begins to lose control upon Faith's arrival because even though you can kill the diva off on a daytime drama, you can't take the drama out of the diva. Faith's outrageous antics have a way of engulfing the people around her as when Hope and Faith reluctantly attend the funeral of a distant relative, Aunt Dodi. According to family legend, Dodi stole their mom's heirloom opal ring years ago. But when the women see Dodi wearing the ring in the casket, all hell breaks loose. Faith decides to reclaim the ring, which is lodged on the deceased's finger. In order to get it off, she actually has to lick the finger to loosen the ring. Grotesque as that might be, she feels vindicated by her actions until the sisters realize they're at the wrong funeral, and have unnecessarily pilfered someone else's opal.

The dynamics between the two sisters are similar to those of Lucy and Ethel. Faith is always getting into trouble, and Hope has to step in and try to calm things down. She's usually sucked into the mayhem in the process.

Kelly Ripa, who plays the part of Faith, knows her character quite well. In 1990, she created the role of rebellious teenager Hayley Vaughan on *All My Children,* and throughout the years flourished into one of the soap opera's most beloved divas.

BROADCAST HISTORY

ABC

September 2003–Present	Friday 9:00–9:30

CAST

Faith	Kelly Ripa
Hope	Faith Ford
Charley	Ted McGinley
Sydney	Nicole Paggi
Hayley	Macey Cruthird
Justin	Paulie Litt

Two and a Half Men

First Broadcast: September 22, 2003

Critics called *Two and a Half Men* a "lazy remix of *The Odd Couple, Full House* and *Bachelor Father.*" It is the story of Charlie Harper, a wealthy, swinging single bachelor who drives a Jaguar and lives in a Malibu beach house. He has a lucrative job as the writer of popular jingles. A bit self indulgent, Charlie enjoys everything about his status in life, and the fact that women pop in and out of his bachelor pad at will; but that carefree life gets turned upside down when his soon-to-be divorced younger brother, Alan, and Alan's ten-year-old son, Jake, move into his beachfront home. Alan is Charlie's polar opposite. He's an uptight chiropractor, having difficulty coming to terms with being dumped by his wife, Judith. Alan is the neat and tidy one, while Charlie is a slob.

Complicating matters are the brothers' self-obsessed, controlling mother, Evelyn, and Alan's possibly gay, estranged wife, Judith. Not to mention Rose, a one night stand and current neighbor of Charlie's, who wants to be a part of his life and is willing to do anything to be around.

While Alan gets little sympathy from his hedonistic big brother, the two quickly learn that the one thing in common they share is a love for Jake. They agree to try and create a home for Jake at Charlie's, despite the realization that they'll likely drive each other crazy in the process. Together, these two and a half men confront the challenges of growing up. The growing process isn't always easy, and Charlie makes his share of mistakes, as when he uses his nephew as a "chick magnet" at the grocery store or lets Jake play cards with his seedy poker buddies.

Broadcast History

CBS

September 22, 2003–Present	Monday 9:30–10:00

Cast

Charlie Harper	Charlie Sheen
Alan Harper	Jon Cryer
Jake Harper	Angus T. Jones
Evelyn Harper	Holland Taylor
Judith	Marin Hinkle
Rose	Melanie Lynskey
Laura	Kristin Bauer

Appendix: Honorable Mentions

All families have their black sheep, and television families are no exception. This group is comprised of shows that just weren't as popular as others for a variety of reasons. They never made the top 20 in the ratings and usually vanished from memory in the blink of an eye. Not all were terrible shows. Some were just misunderstood, placed in a bad time slot, poorly thought out sequels, poorly cast or ahead of (or behind?) the times. While some managed to eke out a full season, others only stuck around for a handful of episodes. Despite poor ratings, this downtrodden group deserves recognition—for sheer *chutzpah*, if nothing else.

a.k.a. Pablo

March 6, 1984–April 17, 1984

In this short-lived comedy, comedian Paul Rodriguez starred as a Mexican-American stand-up comic, Paul (still called Pablo by his family), living at home in East L.A. with his large and colorful family. His family were happy for his burgeoning success, but were sometimes offended by the ethnic jokes he told on stage as part of his act.

Aaron's Way

March 9, 1988–May 25, 1988

Aaron's Way was a family drama that told the story of an Amish family who moved to the wine country of California following the death of their son. Despite a decent cast headed by ex-football great Merlin Olsen as Aaron Miller, the show only ran 12 episodes.

Accidental Family

September 15, 1967–January 5, 1968

Jerry Van Dyke starred as a Las Vegas comic and widower who owned a farm in California. Lois Nettleton costarred as a divorcee who lived on the farm with her young daughter and agreed to care for Van Dyke's young son while he was on the road.

The Aldrich Family

October 2, 1949–May 29, 1953

This radio favorite which began in the 1930s was the story of the life of Henry Aldrich, a typical American teenager of the day. During the show's short run, five actors played the role of Henry Aldrich, three actresses played the daughter, and there were three Mrs. Aldriches as well. Having done a great deal better on radio, the show is most famous for its opening lines, which soon became a national catch phrase: "Henry! Henry Aldrich!"

All American Girl

September 14, 1994–March 22, 1995

Comedian Margaret Cho starred as a westernized Korean American woman trying to hold down a job while going to college and living at home with her very traditional Korean family. This was one of the few shows that featured a mostly Asian cast.

The Baileys of Balboa

September 24, 1964–April 1, 1965

Living on a small island in the middle of Balboa, California, cantankerous Sam Bailey ran a small charter fishing boat called *The Island Princess*. He was as unpretentious as his neighbor, Commodore Wyntoon, was snooty. It would have been best for both families to stay away from each other, but Sam's son fell in love with the commodore's daughter.

Bless This House

September 11, 1995–January 17, 1996

Inspired by *The Honeymooners* and starring the foul-mouthed stand-up comic Andrew Dice Clay, the series followed the adventures of a working class couple with a 12 year old daughter and a young son, trying to keep up with the Joneses.

Bonino

September 12, 1953–December 26, 1953

Another early ethnic situation comedy, this time following the life of Babbo Bonino, an Italian American opera singer and a widower with several kids, who decides to spend more time with his children. The series starred Italian American opera singer Ezio Pinza.

Bridget Loves Bernie

September 16, 1972–September 8, 1973

In this "culture clash" family comedy, Meredith Baxter starred as Bridget Theresa Mary Coleen Fitzgerald, a young Catholic schoolteacher from a wealthy family, who falls in love and marries an aspiring writer and part-time cabbie, Bernie Steinberg, who hails from a middle-class Jewish family that owns a delicatessen. Loosely based on the hit Broadway play *Abie's Irish Rose*, the series is said to have been canceled due to the furor of religious groups who protested the show's condoning mixed marriages.

The Byrds of Paradise

March 3, 1994–May 5, 1994

This hour drama starring Timothy Busfield, Jennifer Love Hewitt and *Hill Street Blues* alum Bruce Weitz was the story of a Yale professor who left New Haven with his three children after his wife's death and took a job as headmaster of a private school in Hawaii. Despite a recognizable cast and beautiful location (the show was filmed on Oahu in the Hawaiian Islands), viewers said "Aloha" to the series from the get-go.

The Campbells

January 4, 1986–December 31, 1989

Even though this drama series about a Scottish family that emigrated to their Canadian frontier in the 1930s was on the air for two and a half years, few people have any recollection of watching it.

The Cavanaughs

December 1, 1986–July 27, 1989

The very Irish Barnard Hughes played feisty old "Pop" Cavanaugh, the patriarch of a very large, very Irish Catholic family living in Boston. This multigenerational family were often at odds. Daughter Kit, who left the nest some 20 years before, was now back, and helping to raise her widowed brother Chuck's family. Pop was often caught in the crossfire. A frequent guest star was Art Carney, who played the role of Pop's brother, James "The Weasel" Cavanaugh.

The Charmings

March 20, 1987–April 24, 1987

Simply put, the fairy tale characters of Snow White and Prince Charming, along with their two young sons, Cory and Thomas, fell asleep in the Enchanted Forest one night and woke up in twentieth-century suburbia. In order to fit in, Snow becomes a dress designer, and Prince Charming writes children's stories. Unfortunately, this very short-lived sitcom did not live happily ever after.

The Chisholms

March 29, 1979–March 15, 1980

The show started out as a four-part miniseries, and viewers watched as the Chisholm family began their journey west from Virginia to Wyoming by wagon train in the 1840s. Viewers loved it, and the series was brought back in early 1980 to resume their journey. Unfortunately, Robert Preston, who starred as patriarch Hadley Chisholm, died shortly thereafter. The series quickly followed suit.

The Jeff Foxworthy Show

September 16, 1995–May 26, 1997

Redneck humor was the order of the day in this series adapted from Foxworthy's beloved stand-up comedy act, which made it hip to be a hick. If you liked this show ... *you might be a redneck.* Foxworthy, a Georgia Tech grad who worked as an engineer for IBM before entering comedy, portrayed a fictionalized version of himself. In the series, he owned an Indiana heating and air conditioning company. Wife Karen was a nurse, and the Foxworthys had a seven-year-old son, Matt. The series moved to NBC for its second season, because Foxworthy "wanted to be back around my kind of people," and several things changed with the move. Except for Foxworthy himself and son, Matt, the entire cast, the show's locale and his family members changed. Now living in suburban Atlanta, Foxworthy's character managed the loading dock of a shipping company, there was a new actress playing his wife, Karen, and they added another son.

Daddy Dearest

September 5, 1993–December 12, 1993

Neurotic Richard Lewis joined up with caustic Don Rickles to play father and son in this comedy about a divorced, neurotic psychologist whose recently separated father, an obnoxious used car salesman, moves in with him and his young son.

Daddy's Girls

September 21, 1994–October 12, 1994

Dudley Moore starred as a father of two whose ex-wife has run off with his partner in their women's clothing business, leaving him with three daughters to look after. The show was Dudley Moore's second flop on CBS in 18 months.

Davis Rules

January 27, 1991–July 15, 1992

Despite a stellar cast, the show, starring Randy Quaid, Jonathan Winters, and Bonnie Hunt, tanked early on. Supposedly a '90s version of *My Three Sons*, the show featured Quaid as a widowed grammar school principal trying to raise his three sons with the assistance of his offbeat father.

Everything's Relative

October 3, 1987–November 7, 1987

Before his award-winning role as George Costanza in *Seinfeld*, Jason Alexander starred in this short-lived comedy about two grown brothers sharing a SoHo loft with their meddlesome mother. Alexander's character, Julian, is a sensible, unassuming, divorced small business owner. Younger brother Scott is a hunky construction worker whose values and carefree lifestyle could not be more different from his sibling's. Stories focused on their opposite personalities and lifestyles.

Family Dog

June 23, 1993–July 28, 1993

CBS had high hopes for this animated prime time series that looked at family life from a dog's point of view. If the show had been about the family cat, it might have had nine lives. But even with the likes of Steven Spielberg and Tim Burton as the executive producers, this show didn't stand a dog of a chance in the ratings.

The Family Holvak

September 7, 1975–October 27, 1975

Patterned after *The Waltons*, this show starred Glenn Ford as the Rev. Tom Holvak, a poverty-stricken Southern clergyman living in the South in the 1930s with his wife and two children. Apparently viewers felt that this Depression-era show was just too depressing.

The Family Man

September 11, 1990–July 17, 1991

In yet another series about single parent households, Gregory Harrison portrayed the recently widowed Jack Taylor, a firefighter trying to raise his four kids with the assistance of his live-in father-in-law, played by *Happy Days* alum Al Molinaro.

Family Tree

January 22, 1983–August 10, 1983

The producer of the popular series *Family* brought this hour long dramatic series to television in the hopes it would do as well. The series focused on the altered relationships caused by divorce and remarriage.

The Fanelli Boys

September 8, 1990–February 16, 1991

Four Italian brothers, all of whose lives have gone wrong, move back into their widowed mother's house in Brooklyn to try and straighten themselves out, just as she is about to sell the family home and move to Florida. Ann Moran Guilbert, who portrayed Millie on *The Dick Van Dyke Show* and Grandma Yetta on *The Nanny*, portrayed the matriarch of the family. Christopher Meloni, of *CSI* and *Oz* fame, and *The Sopranos*' Joe Pantoliano portrayed two of the brothers. When the family's funeral parlor business started dying out, so did the show.

The Fitzpatricks

September 5, 1977–January 10, 1978

Classified as a warm family drama, this hour long series told the tale of a middle-class Catholic family trying to make ends meet in Flint, Michigan. Father Mike was a steelworker and mother Maggie worked part time in a diner to help supplement the family income. The emphasis was placed on life lessons and morality, and most episodes focused on the couple's four children.

Gloria

September 26, 1982–September 21, 1983

Four years after *All in the Family* left the air, Archie Bunker's now divorced daughter Gloria was starting a new life as a veterinarian's assistant in the upstate New York town of Foxridge with her 8-year-old son, Joey. Despite Burgess Meredith co-starring as Gloria's crusty boss, people just didn't seem to want to see Gloria unless Archie and The Meathead were around.

The Growing Paynes

October 20, 1948–August 3, 1949

Not to be confused with the latter day *Growing Pains*, this sitcom starring Elaine Stritch was an early live domestic comedy about the lives of an insurance salesman, his screwball wife, their young kids and Birdie, their maid, who, not unlike *Hazel*, usually saved the day.

Happy

June 8, 1960–September 28, 1960
January 13, 1961–September 8, 1961

In 1960, the notion of a talking baby was unheard of until audiences were introduced to the Day family. Father Chris managed a Palm Springs motel. He and his wife were the proud parents of twin boys, David and Steven, and the gifted Happy, whose given name was Christopher Hapwood Day. The notion of a talking baby didn't go over too well with audiences and didn't reappear until the 1998 film *Look Who's Talking.*

Harts of the West

September 23, 1993–June 18, 1994

Beau Bridges starred as Dave Hart in this comedy/drama about an underwear salesman who, after having a mild heart attack, reads a 1957 brochure and packs up his less than enthusiastic family and moves them to the decaying Flying Tumbleweed Ranch in Sholo, Nevada, in the hopes of starting a new, less stressful life. It is a dream come true for Dave, but a nightmare for the rest of his family. Veteran actor Lloyd Bridges costarred in the series with son Beau, as the cantankerous ranch foreman.

The Hathaways

October 6, 1961–August 31, 1962

Elinore and Walter Hathaway were a typical American couple, but most folks thought their "kids," Charlie, Enoch and Cindy, although bright, spent way too much time monkeying around. Maybe that's because they were chimps! Elinore was the booking agent for their show business act, and loved the fuzzy monkeys so much that Walter was often left wondering if he was being made a monkey of.

Hello, Larry

January 26, 1979–April 30, 1980

Trying to make a fresh start after the breakup of his marriage, radio talk show host Larry Adler moves from L.A. to Portland, Oregon, with his two teenage daughters. *M*A*S*H** veteran McLean Stevenson starred as the harassed father, who was much more in control of his radio audience than his two growing girls.

I'm a Big Girl Now

October 31, 1980–July 24, 1981

Danny Thomas returned to the small screen in this father-daughter comedy. Thomas portrayed a dentist, who, when his wife ran off with his business partner, decided to move in with his divorced daughter and seven-year-old granddaughter.

It Takes Two

October 14, 1982–September 1, 1983

Richard Crenna as chief of surgery at a Chicago hospital, Patty Duke as his assistant DA wife, Helen Hunt and Anthony Edwards as their children, and still, this stellar cast couldn't keep this show, about dual careers getting in the way of family life, afloat. Go figure.

The Jimmy Stewart Show

September 19, 1971–August 27, 1972

Three generations living together in an overcrowded household was the premise of this short-lived sitcom which starred screen icon Jimmy Stewart. Stewart played good natured anthropology professor Jim Howard, who let his 29-year-old son and his family move in when their house was destroyed in a fire.

Life with Lucy

September 20, 1986–November 15, 1986

At the age of 75, veteran funny lady Lucille Ball had waited 12 years to return to series television. ABC promised her a huge salary and a lot of perks, including a 22 episode commitment. In the series, Ball played the recently widowed Lucy Barker, who moves in with her daughter's family. Too bad the perks offered by the network didn't include good scripts. Despite Ball's reputation and the addition of co-star Gale Gordon, the show was only on the air for eight weeks.

The Marriage

July 8, 1954–August 19, 1954

Real-life married couple Hume Cronyn and Jessica Tandy starred as New York married couple Ben and Liz Marriott. He was a successful lawyer, she was a former buyer for a department store who became a stay at home mom for their two young children. Cronyn and Tandy starred in the NBC radio version of this show which left the air in the spring of 1954.

Meet Corliss Archer

July 12, 1951–March 29, 1952

Meet Corliss Archer was one of the few long running radio shows of the 1940s that didn't survive on television. The live show was the story of Corliss Archer, a typical teen, her boyfriend, Dexter, and her parents. A short-lived film version ran for the 1954–1955 television season. The series starred Lugene Sanders, who played the part on radio, and later played Babs in *The Life of Riley*.

Mickey

September 16, 1964–January 13, 1965

Mickey Rooney and his real life son Tim starred in this series about a Coast Guard recruiter from Omaha who moved his family to Newport Harbor, California, when he inherited a luxury hotel that was deeply in debt. Sammee Tong, of *Bachelor Father* fame, co-starred as Sammy Ling, the hotel's manager, who caused the hotel's failure by allowing too many of his relatives in on trying to save the place. Ling's crooked cousin was their lawyer, and the mortgage was held by The Ling Savings and Loan with a hefty 17 percent mortgage rate. Mickey and family tried hard to set things straight, to no avail. The show was foreclosed on rather quickly.

The Monroes

September 7, 1966–August 30, 1967

Set in the Wyoming Territory in 1876, *The Monroes* is the story of five orphaned children, aged 6 to 18, fighting to establish a homestead on the land their parents marked out years before, after their parents drowned in the show's first episode.

Mulligan's Stew

October 25, 1977–December 13, 1977

Elinor Donahue, who played Betty on *Father Knows Best,* was all grown up and the mother of three children in this family drama. The Mulligans and their extended family of four orphaned nieces and nephews tried to make a go of being one big, happy family in an overcrowded house. Adding to the problems were the fact that the Mulligan children and their cousins had very different lifestyles and had a lot of trouble adjusting to each other.

My So-Called Life

August 25, 1994–January 26, 1995

From the creators of *thirtysomething*, this hour-long drama series set in Pittsburgh depicted life from a tormented tenth grader's point of view. Said to be one of the best new series of the season, the show didn't attract a large audience, and was said to be a little too melodramatic for anyone but teenagers. As if to prove the point, MTV picked up the reruns shortly after the show was canceled.

The New Andy Griffith Show

January 8, 1971–May 21, 1971

The adage "You can take the sheriff out of Mayberry, but you can't take Mayberry out of the sheriff" proved itself right in this short-lived series. Griffith returned to television in the 1970 dramatic offering *Headmaster* in the guise of Andy Thompson, the headmaster of a coeducational prep school in California. Mid-season, *Headmaster* changed formats and names. Griffith became Andy Sawyer, a husband and father who was mayor of a small town in North Carolina, a character very similar to Sheriff Taylor on the original *Andy Griffith Show*.

New Kind of Family

September 16, 1979–January 15, 1980

A recently divorced widow with three children moves from New York to a rented house in Los Angeles. Upon their arrival, they find a divorced mother and her daughter living there. Since neither family can afford the rent on their own, they decide to share the house despite having very different lifestyles.

Normal Life

March 21, 1990–July 18, 1990

In this forerunner of the highly popular *The Osbournes*, CBS thought it was being innovative when they opted to produce a sitcom based on the unconventional lives of rock icon Frank Zappa and family. After the pilot was made, the network balked. They were uncomfortable with how abnormal the family's life really was, and opted to tone it down a bit. This resulted in a boring, hardly radical offering starring two of the Zappa children, Dweezil and Moon Unit, that put viewers to sleep.

On Our Own

September 13, 1994–April 14, 1995

Based on the real life Smollett family of St. Louis, this sitcom told the story of seven orphaned African American children who fought hard to remain together by trying to outwit the Department of Children's Services.

One Big Family

Syndicated 1986–1987

Danny Thomas was back again, this time as a semiretired nightclub comedian who moved to Seattle to help raise his five grandchildren when his son and daughter-in-law were killed in an automobile accident.

One Happy Family

January 13, 1961–September 15, 1961

Dick Sargent, later of *Bewitched* fame, starred as newlywed meteorologist Dick Cooper, who, with his wife Penny, moved in with Penny's family for one night and never left. Also living in the house were Penny's grandparents, making it three generations living under one roof.

Oregon Trail

September 21, 1977–October 26, 1977

Will the networks ever learn? In this failed western set in 1842, Rod Taylor starred as widower Evan Thorpe, who decided to pack up his three children and leave their native Illinois in search of a new life in the Oregon Territory. Joining a wagon train and becoming its captain in the first episode, the family fought the good fight against Indians, the rough terrain and the weather on their way West, but didn't make it past the critics or the viewers.

The Paul Lynde Show

September 13, 1972–September 8, 1973

Paul Lynde crawled out of his comfortable center square on *Hollywood Squares* long enough to star as Paul Simms, a respectable but high-strung attorney living the quiet life with his wife and two daughters until one of his daughters falls in love with and marries Howie Dickerson, an obnoxious and eccentric long haired, unemployed university student with a very high I.Q. Much to Paul's chagrin, the newlyweds move into the Simms household, causing his tranquil life to take a turn. Real life duo Jerry Stiller and Anne Meara were often seen as Howie's parents, the Dickersons.

The Pruitts of Southampton

September 6, 1966–September 1, 1967

Phyllis Diller tried her luck in a weekly series as Phyllis Pruitt, a wealthy socialite who was found to owe $10 million to the government in back taxes. The IRS allowed the family to stay in their sixty room Southampton mansion and not blow their cover rather than risk a stock market fiasco if the news came out about the family's bankruptcy. The series costarred veteran actors John Astin, Reginald Gardiner, Richard Deacon, Charles Sutton, Richard Deacon and Gypsy Rose Lee. In 1967, the mansion was turned into a boarding house to help stave off the government, and the program's title was changed to *The Phyllis Diller Show.*

The Royal Family

September 18, 1991–May 13, 1992

In his last sitcom, comedian Redd Foxx starred as Al Royal, a letter carrier in Atlanta who was looking forward to a nice, quiet retirement when his soon-to-be divorced daughter and her three children moved in with Al and his wife, Victoria, played by Della Reese. A month into the series, Foxx collapsed and died of a heart attack during rehearsals. His death was written into the show, which continued without him until it went off the air several months later.

The Ruggles

November 3, 1949–June 19, 1952

Veteran Hollywood actor Charlie Ruggles portrayed fictional Charlie Ruggles, the put-upon head of household and insurance salesman in this early family comedy. Produced live at ABC's Hollywood station KECA-TV on kinescope, Ruggles' character was a husband and father to two teenagers, Sharon and Chuck, and a pair of young twins, Donna and Donald. Stories revolved around simple topics such as the care and feeding of rambunctious teenagers, a family of six living with only one bathroom, and the other usual household dilemmas.

704 Hauser

April 11, 1994–May 9, 1994

Fans of *All In the Family* didn't like the idea of anyone else living in Archie Bunker's old house, and loudly rebelled when the Cumberbatch family moved in. John Amos starred as Ernest Cumberbatch, an auto mechanic who, with his wife and business school student son, moved into the famous digs. Even though the show's creator Norman Lear took out ads in the newspaper asking viewers to watch the show and write to CBS to keep it on the air, five weeks into the series, the Cumberbatches were foreclosed upon.

South Central

April 5, 1994–August 30, 1994

Critics loved this show about a financially strapped divorced black single mother, Joan Mosley, trying to raise her family in a very tough inner city Los Angeles neighborhood. Her eldest son had been killed by gang members, and she struggled to raise her two living children in an unsavory and unsafe neighborhood. Most likely, the series was canceled after its initial 13-week run because it was too "real" for prime-time audiences.

Sunshine

March 6, 1975–June 19, 1975

Based on a TV movie of the same name, *Sunshine* was the story of Sam Hayden, a recently widowed musician trying to be both mother and father to his 5-year-old step-daughter while trying to make ends meet.

Swiss Family Robinson

September 14, 1975–April 11, 1976

This classic children's story was a highly acclaimed book and Disney movie, but the shipwrecked Robinson family of the 1800s didn't fare as well as a '70s television program produced by disaster maven Irwin Allen. There were plenty of calamities facing the brave Robinson clan, who somehow fearlessly managed to come out on top when dealing with typhoons, volcanic eruptions, wild animals and other natural disasters. Too bad they never learned how to survive the critics.

Thea

September 8, 1993–February 23, 1994

A widow with four children, Thea Turrell was one tough cookie. She worked in a market by day and ran a beauty shop from her house at night to make ends meet. She was a fiercely protective mother who ruled the roost with an iron fist to keep her kids on the right path. There was plenty of tough love to go around. Nothing ever got past Thea, whose credo was, "Thea knows all, Thea sees all."

The Thorns

January 15, 1988–March 11, 1988

There was no way to dull the pain of this unfunny sitcom an obnoxious, social climbing, self-absorbed, snobbish Manhattan family who lived in an elegant New York City townhouse. Father Sloan Thorn was an insensitive public relations executive, while spoiled wife Ginger was a social climber. Their three children were insufferable brats, whose most frequent form of parental discipline was to buy the kids off. Mike Nichols, who had a stellar record of producing quality shows such as *Family*, must have had a thorny dilemma trying to explain away this one.

Three for the Road

September 14, 1975–November 30, 1975

Alex Rocco starred as Pete Korras, a widowed free-lance photographer with two teenage sons who traveled together around the country in a mobile home on various assignments. The various locales they visited and the interesting people they met along the way provided the stories. Even with teen heartthrobs Leif Garrett and Vincent Van Patten on board as sons John and Endy (short for Endicott), the series had a very short run.

Together We Stand

September 22, 1986–April 24, 1967

Killing off the star of the show to help keep it afloat might work for some, but not even a tragic accident could keep this series from an early demise. Elliott Gould starred as David Randall, a former pro basketball coach who now ran a sporting goods store. He and wife Lori were the parents of four children, three of which were adopted and of diverse ethnic backgrounds. The cultural differences were fodder for the scripts, but apparently not interesting enough to sustain the show. It was pulled from the schedule two months into the series' run, and reappeared the following February, having a new title, *Nothing Is Easy*, and without Elliot Gould, whose character had died in a car accident, leaving poor Lori to fend for herself.

Tom

March 2, 1994–June 13, 1994

It wasn't long after *The Jackie Thomas Show* went off the air that comedian Tom Arnold tried his luck on network television again. This time around, he played a welder, Tom Graham, with a wife and five kids who all lived in a trailer while planning to fulfill his lifelong ambition of building his dream house on land next to a dump, on the family farm. Enough said?

The Tortellis

January 22, 1987–May 12, 1987

In the case of this *Cheers* spinoff, the apple did far fall from the tree. On *Cheers*, barmaid Carla was always complaining about her sleazy ex-husband, Nick. She finally got rid of him when he married a ditzy ex-showgirl, Loretta. Their marriage was soon on the rocks as well, and Loretta moved to Las Vegas to pursue her career. Claiming that he had reformed his bad boy ways, Nick and his eldest son Anthony followed her to Las Vegas to make things right.

Two of a Kind

September 25, 1998–July 16, 1999

The very rich Olsen twins, Mary-Kate and Ashley, starred in this sitcom about a set of twins who lived in an apartment across the street from Chicago's Wrigley Field with their widowed father, a science professor. Add to the mix their young nanny, who happened to be one of Dad's students, and you have the makings of yet another short-lived television family.

Uncle Buck

September 10, 1990–March 9, 1991

This story of an unlikely bachelor who became the guardian to his recently deceased brother and sister-in-law's kids after their untimely death was adapted from the critically acclaimed 1989 movie of the same name, with comedian John Candy in the title role. The show tanked with both viewers and critics early on and never found its niche.

Under One Roof

March 14, 1995–April 18, 1995

This hour-long dramatic series starred James Earl Jones as Neb Langston, a widowed Seattle police officer who shared a two-family home. He lived with his adult daughter and foster son upstairs, while his son and his family lived downstairs. It was the story of a multigenerational black family all living under one roof and trying to get along.

The Van Dyke Show

October 26, 1988–December 7, 1988

Dick Van Dyke and his real-life son Barry teamed up as fictional father and son in this unsuccessful offering. Dick Burgess was a veteran Broadway star who gave up the bright lights to move in with his son, Matt, and his family in rural Pennsylvania. Matt owned a small regional theater, and Dick stepped in to help make a go of it.

Walter and Emily

November 16, 1991–February 22, 1992

Brian Keith and Cloris Leachman teamed up as a pair of bickering grandparents who had the chance to step in and raise their eleven-year-old grandson when their divorced son, who had custody of the youngster, was off on the road on assignments as a San Francisco sportswriter.

Wesley

May 8, 1949–August 30, 1949

This early live sitcom followed the life of Wesley Eggleston, a precocious 12 year old, living in a rural community with his parents and teenage sister, Elizabeth. Real life husband and wife, actors Frank and Mona Thomas took on the roles of Mr. and Mrs. Eggleston, while during the show's short run, two young actors were cast to play the part of Wesley.

A Year in the Life

August 24, 1987–April 20, 1988

This series followed the highly acclaimed three part NBC 1986 miniseries about the lives and interactions of three generations of a wealthy Seattle family, the Gardners. Coming from the fertile minds of Joshua Brand and John Falsey, who created *St. Elsewhere*, and starring Richard Kiley, Adam Arkin and Sarah Jessica Parker, this weekly series never got its momentum going well enough to keep television audiences interested.

You Again?

February 27, 1986–March 30, 1987

Odd Couple alum Jack Klugman this time starred as Henry Willows, a divorced supermarket manager, who led a quiet peaceful life until his 17 year old son, played by heartthrob John Stamos, decided to leave his mom and stepfather to move in with Dad. The show was adapted from the British series *Home to Roost*, which was running at the same time in the United Kingdom. Actress Elizabeth Bennett played the role of Enid the housekeeper in both series simultaneously by commuting between the U.S. and the U.K. She should have received an award for sheer guts.

You Take the Kids

December 15, 1990–January 12, 1991

Gimme a Break's Nell Carter and *Magnum PI's* Roger Mosely teamed up in this short lived domestic sitcom about a blue collar family living in Pittsburgh's inner city. Bus driver Michael Kirkland and his opinionated piano teacher wife, Nell, struggled to raise their four children with the help of Nell's outspoken mother, Helen, who lived in the family basement.

Zorro and Son

April 6, 1983–June 1, 1983

Someone at Walt Disney Productions, which produced the original, successful *Zorro* series in the late 1950s, decided to bring back the legendary masked defender two decades later, in an inane comedy format. When an aging Don Diego, aka Zorro, is injured in his do-gooder quest, he reveals his true identity to his son, Don Carlos, and enlists his help in protecting the citizens from the military government. This results in many clashes between the old fashioned, traditionalist father and his modern son.

Bibliography

Books

Arnaz, Desi. *A Book.* New York: Buccaneer Books, 1976.

Brooks, Tim, and Marsh, Earle. *The Complete Directory to Prime Time Network and Cable TV Shows 1946–Present.* Eighth Edition. New York: Ballantine, 2003.

Duke, Patty. *Call Me Anna: the Autobiography of Patty Duke.* New York: Bantam, 1987.

Essoe, Gabe. *The Book of TV Lists.* New Rochelle, New York: Arlington House, 1981.

Godin, Seth. *The Encyclopedia of Fictional People.* New York: Boulevard Books, 1996.

Hill, Tom. *TVLAND To Go: The Big Book of TV Lists, TV Lore, and TV Bests* Simon & Schuster New York: 2001.

Kleinfelder, Rita. *When We Were Young: A Baby Boomer Yearbook.* New Jersey: Prentice Hall, 1993.

McNeil, Alex. *Total Television.* New York: Penguin, 1996.

Moore, Mary Tyler. *After All.* New York: Dell, 1995.

Phillips, Louis and Holmes, Burnham. *The TV Almanac.* New York: Macmillan, 1994.

Sanders, Coyne Steve and Gilbert, Tom. *Desilu: The Story of Lucille Ball and Desi Arnaz.* Newyon: William Morrow and Co., Inc., 1993

Thomas, Danny. *Make Room For Danny.* New York: G.D. Putnam's Sons, 1991.

Williams, Barry. *Growing Up Brady: I Was a Teenage Greg.* New York: Harper, 1992.

Magazines

TV-Radio Life. March 26, 1954. *The Nelsons Have It.*

Websites

abc.abcnews.go.com/primetime/schedule/

abc.go.com/primetime/marriedtothekellys/show.html

animatedtv.about.com/gi/dynamic/offsite.htm?site=http%3A%2F%2Fwww.tvguide.com%2Ftv%2Fshows%2FshowPage.asp%3FiProgramID%3D7906
classictv.about.com/cs/comedies1/
classictv.about.com/cs/starinterviews/
classictv.about.com/gi/dynamic/offsite.htm?site=http%3A%2F%2Fbonanza1.com%2F
classictv.about.com/gi/dynamic/offsite.htm?site=http%3A%2F%2Flucilleball.com%2Fclassictv.about.com/cs/ilovelucy/
classictv.about.com/gi/dynamic/offsite.htm?site=http%3A%2F%2Ftimvp.com%2Fmy3sons.html
classictv.about.com/gi/dynamic/offsite.htm?site=http%3A%2F%2Fwww.addamsfamily.com%2Fpetticoat.topcities.com/page1.htm
classictv.about.com/gi/dynamic/offsite.htm?site=http%3A%2F%2Fwww.geocities.com%2FHeartland%2FFalls%2F1577%2Fmayberry.html
classictv.miningco.com/
community-2.webtv.net/joanfan/rev/
eightiesclub.tripod.com/id380.htm
8simplerules.tvheaven.com/presskit.html
epguides.com/parenthood/guide.shtml
home.earthlink.net/~joesarno/tvcomics/blondie.htm
mamasmemories.bravepages.com/
members.aol.com/dejavo0/char.html
members.aol.com/dejavo0/intro.htm
members.fortunecity.com/americandreams2002/adpremise.html
members.tripod.com/welcometoprovidence/pro/background.htm
partyoffive.tktv.net/
primetimetv.about.com/gi/dynamic/offsite.htm?site=http%3A%2F%2Fwww.sirlinksalot.net%2Fsopranos.html
providence_uk.tripod.com/welcometoprovidenceuk/id1.html
stianp.freeservers.com/cbios.html
thecosbyshow.sitemonkey.net/photo3.html
thehughleys.com/
tigerx.com/people/obituary.htm
timstvshowcase.com/
timstvshowcase.com/8enough.html
timstvshowcase.com/familytv.html
timstvshowcase.com/rhoda.html
tv.zap2it.com/tveditorial/tve_main/1,1002,273|2590|1|,00.html
tvofyourlife.com/bachelorfather.htm
tvplex.go.com/Touchstone/HomeImprovement/
upn44tv.com/upn44shows/local_story_326061715_htm
us.imdb.com/Title?0070967
worldwideguide.net/guides/index.cfm/GuideID/1/fuseaction/ShowPageType/TypeID/2
xroads.virginia.edu/~1930s2/Radio/day/12pm.html
www.acc.umu.se/~magnus2/movies/growing_pains/
www.andremeadows.com/urkelnet/synopsis.html

www.angelfire.com/comics/osbournes/
www.angelfire.com/hi2/GoldieLoxsWorld/torkelsons.html
www.angelfire.com/mb/hillmans/penny.html
www.angelfire.com/oh/alfclub/
www.angelfire.com/tv2/wifeandkids/aboutshow.html
www.bundyology.com/
www.bundyology.com/production.html
www.canoe.ca/TelevisionShowsF/foxworthy.html
www.carseywerner.net/grace_eng.htm
www.cartoonnetwork.com/watch/tv_shows/flintstones/
www.cbs.com/primetime/fall_preview_2003/
www.classicthemes.com/50sTVThemes/seriesListT-V.html
www.classic-tv.com/shows/ilovelucy.asphttp:
www.classic-tv.com/themesongs/listen/a.asp
www.classictvhits.com/shows/bradybunch/
www.cmongethappy.com/
www.columbia.edu/~asr41/Goldbergs.html
www.cosmik.com/aa-september00/dj63.html
www.ctv.ca/servlet/HTMLTemplate/!ctvShows/Shows/Evening/pent_mywife.html
www.degrassi.ca/dl/NON-DEGRASSI/Torkelsons/
www.edrobertson.com/tvlinks.htm
www.everybodylovesray.com/
www.falcon-crest-tv.de/e/menu.html
www.fatherknowsbest.us/Mainx.html
www.fattyboombatty.com/famousfacesonthweb.htm
www.fox.com/kingofthehill/
www.frasieronline.co.uk/background.htm
www.freehomepages.com/munsters/munsters.html
www.freewebs.com/earthlight/spiritguides.htm
www.geocities.com/EnchantedForest/Palace/6486/KatsGPfanpage.html
www.geocities.com/EnchantedForest/Palace/6486/story.html
www.geocities.com/hollandst/characters.html
www.geocities.com/Hollywood/8163/soap.htm
www.geocities.com/Hollywood/9176/history.htm
www.geocities.com/Hollywood/Location/4127/quotes.html
www.geocities.com/Hollywood/Set/8441/
www.geocities.com/TelevisionCity/9348/diffrent_strokes.htm
www.geocities.com/TelevisionCity/9348/too_close_comfort.htm
www.geocities.com/TelevisionCity/Stage/2950/SitCom/MothersInLaw.htm
classictv.about.com/gi/dynamic/offsite.htm?site=http%3A%2F%2Fmembers.tripod.com%2F%7Emaryanne2%2Findex.html
www.geocities.com/TelevisionCity/Stage/4318/
www.geocities.com/TelevisionCity/Stage/4318/history.html
www.geocities.com/TvPilotGuy/fatherknowsbest.html
www.gilmore-girls.net/cast/index.html
www.gilmoregirls.org/
www.infoplease.com/ipea/A0761113.html

www.infoplease.com/spot/realitytv1.html
www.infoplease.com/spot/tvmoms1.html
www.jerrymathers.tv/index.htm
www.kellie.de/familymatters.htm#About%20Family%20Matters
www.kfcplainfield.com/tv/oneday.html
www.kfcplainfield.com/tv/partridge.html
www.kingfeatures.com/features/comics/dennis/about.htm
www.kingfeatures.com/features/comics/hazel/about.htm
www.lifetimetv.com/shows/golden/retro/index.html
www.madblast.com/view.cfm?type=Feature&display=1543
www.memorabletv.com/showsaz.htm
www.meredy.com/cosmiccow/
www.mortystv.com/cgi-bin/frameit/directframe.cgi?4=
www.mousestars.com/steve/paulpet/ppdrs.htm
www.mtv.com/onair/osbournes/
www.munsters.com/home.html
www.museum.tv/archives/etv/a/htmla/andygriffith/andygriffith.htm
www.museum.tv/archives/etv/B/htmlB/beverlyhillb/beverlyhillb.htm
www.museum.tv/archives/etv/B/htmlB/bradybunch/bradybunch.htm
www.museum.tv/archives/etv/C/htmlC/cosbyshowt/cosbyshowt.htm
www.museum.tv/archives/etv/D/htmlD/dickvandyke/dickvandyke.htm
www.museum.tv/archives/etv/F/htmlF/familyontel/familyontel.htm
www.museum.tv/archives/etv/F/htmlF/familyties/familyties.htm
www.museum.tv/archives/etv/F/htmlF/fatherknows/fatherknows.htm
www.museum.tv/archives/etv/F/htmlF/flintstones/flintstones.htm
www.museum.tv/archives/etv/G/htmlG/goldbergsth/goldbergsth.htm
www.museum.tv/archives/etv/G/htmlG/goodtimes/goodtimes.htm
www.museum.tv/archives/etv/H/htmlH/hazel/hazel.htm
www.museum.tv/archives/etv/index.html
www.museum.tv/archives/etv/K/htmlK/kateandalli/kateandalli.htm
www.museum.tv/archives/etv/L/htmlL/leaveittob/leaveittob.htm
www.museum.tv/archives/etv/L/htmlL/lifeofriley/lifeofriley.htm
www.museum.tv/archives/etv/M/htmlM/mama/mama.htm
www.museum.tv/archives/etv/M/htmlM/mythreesons/mythreesons.htm
www.museum.tv/archives/etv/O/htmlO/onedayata/onedayata.htm
www.museum.tv/archives/etv/T/htmlT/227/227.htm
www.museum.tv/archives/etv/T/htmlT/thirtysomethi/thirtysomethi.htm
www.museum.tv/ETV/J/htmlJ/jeffersonst/jeffersonst.htm
www.mymotherthecar.com/TV/My-Mother-01.html
www.myshelf.com/biography/02/lifewithfather.htm
www.nbc.com/American_Dreams/about/index.html
www.nbc.com/Frasier/about/index.html
www.nbc.com/nbc/Primetime_Preview/
www.oldtvseries.com/
www.outofthenight.com/lost1.htmlgdtvd.tripod.com/my_mother_the_car.html
www.paramount.com/television/7th-heaven/characterbios.htm
www.pcperspectives.com/hillbillies/hillbill.html

www.poobala.com/almostandtork.html
www.poobala.com/maryandphyllis.html
www.popmatters.com/tv/reviews/b/bernie-mac-show.html
www.questia.com/Index.jsp?CRID=television_history&OFFID=se1
www.ravensrealm.com/heaven/show.php
www.rottentomatoes.com/m/JamesDeansLostTelevisionAppearanceTroubleWithFather-1119497/about.php
www.sitcomsonline.com/eddiesfather.html
www.sitcomsonline.com/happydays.html
www.sitcomsonline.com/silverspoons.html
www.sitcomsonline.com/theadventuresofozzieandharriet.html
www.stararchive.com/classictv.about.com/library/blepa.htm
www.super70s.com/Super70s/TV/Comedy/That's_My_Mama.asp
www.televisionheaven.co.uk/kate.htm
www.televisionheaven.co.uk/mccoys.htm
www.televisionheaven.co.uk/soap.htm
www.thecurtisfiles.com/mymocar.htm
www.thesimpsons.com/
www.the-sopranos.com/
www.thewb.com/Shows/Show/0,7353,||152,00.html
www.thirdstory.com/thirtysomething/players.htm
www.timvp.com/dennis.html
www.timvp.com/edsdad.html
www.timvp.com/elr.html
www.timvp.com/familyaf.html
www.timvp.com/goldberg.html
www.timvp.com/goldgirl.html
www.timvp.com/hazel.html
www.timvp.com/munsters.html
www.topthat.net/webrock/faq.htm
www.trouble.co.uk/trouble_tv/diffrentstrokes.shtml
www.tvacres.com/catch_i.htm
www.tvacres.com/catch_o.htm
www.tvacres.com/geographic_settings_general.htm
www.tvacres.com/homepage_tv_acres.htm
www.tvacres.com/tv_resources_coverpage.htm
www.tvclassics.com/
www.tvcrazy.net/tvclassics/americantv/golden.htm
www.tvdads.com/
www.tvguide.com/showguide/showPage.asp?iProgramID=11191
www.tvguide.com/showguide/ShowPage.asp?iprogramID=43451
www.tvland.com/nickatnite/cosby_show/
www.tvland.com/shows/happydays/
www.tvland.com/shows/happydays/character1.jhtml
www.tvland.com/shows/jeffersons/
www.tvland.com/shows/mary/character2.jhtml
www.tvparty.com/50sitcom3.html

www.tvparty.com/recbev.html
www.tvparty.com/recmothercar.html
www.tvtome.com/aolsearch.aol.com/aol/image_home.jsp
www.tvtome.com/Frasier/
www.tvtome.com/HoganFamily/
www.tvtome.com/tvtome/servlet/EpisodeGuideSummary/showid-18/season-1
www.tvtome.com/tvtome/servlet/EpisodeGuideSummary/showid-3449/season-1
www.tvtome.com/tvtome/servlet/EpisodeGuideSummary/showid-463/
www.tvtome.com/tvtome/servlet/EpisodeGuideSummary/showid-613/season-1
www.tvtome.com/tvtome/servlet/ShowMainServlet/showid-10784/
www.tvtome.com/tvtome/servlet/ShowMainServlet/showid-1218/
www.tvtome.com/tvtome/servlet/ShowMainServlet/showid-1349/
www.tvtome.com/tvtome/servlet/ShowMainServlet/showid-139/
www.tvtome.com/tvtome/servlet/ShowMainServlet/showid-1743/
www.tvtome.com/tvtome/servlet/ShowMainServlet/showid-18/
www.tvtome.com/tvtome/servlet/ShowMainServlet/showid-181
www.tvtome.com/tvtome/servlet/ShowMainServlet/showid-251/
www.tvtome.com/tvtome/servlet/ShowMainServlet/showid-3723/
www.tvtome.com/tvtome/servlet/ShowMainServlet/showid-4698/
www.tvtome.com/tvtome/servlet/ShowMainServlet/showid-471/
www.tvtome.com/tvtome/servlet/ShowMainServlet/showid-495/
www.tvtome.com/tvtome/servlet/ShowMainServlet/showid-528/
www.tvtome.com/tvtome/servlet/ShowMainServlet/showid-54/
www.tvtome.com/tvtome/servlet/ShowMainServlet/showid-601/
www.tvtome.com/tvtome/servlet/ShowMainServlet/showid-605/
www.tvtome.com/tvtome/servlet/ShowMainServlet/showid-606/
www.tvtome.com/tvtome/servlet/ShowMainServlet/showid-648/
www.tvtome.com/tvtome/servlet/ShowMainServlet/showid-708/
www.tvtome.com/tvtome/servlet/ShowMainServlet/showid-732/
www.tvtome.com/tvtome/servlet/ShowMainServlet/showid-9461/
www.ultimatedynasty.net/
www.valdefierro.com/times02.html
www.valerieharper.com/rhoda.htm
www.warnerbros.co.uk/television/freshprince/index2.html
www.wchstv.com/abc/accordingtojim/
www.wchstv.com/abc/mywifeandkids/
www.webspawner.com/users/mamafamilyquotes/index.html
www.yesterdayland.com/popopedia/shows/primetime/pt1034.php

Index